WITNESSING THE AMERICAN CENTURY

Allen C Brady

Witnessing the American Century

Via Berlin, Pearl Harbor, Vietnam, and the Straits of Florida

Capt. Allen Colby Brady, USN

with Dawn Quarles

The Kent State University Press

KENT, OHIO

Library of Congress Cataloging-in-Publication Data

Names: Brady, Allen Colby, Capt., 1929- | Quarles, Dawn, author.

Title: Witnessing the American century : via Berlin, Pearl Harbor, Vietnam, and the
      Straits of Florida / Capt. Allen Colby Brady, USN with Dawn Quarles.

Description: Kent, Ohio : Kent State University Press, [2019] | Includes index.

Identifiers: LCCN 2018052116 | ISBN 9781606353622 (cloth)

Subjects: LCSH: Vietnam War, 1961-1975--Prisoners and prisons, North Vietnamese.
      | Fighter pilots--United States--Biography. | Prisoners of war--United
      States--Biography | Prisoners of war--Vietnam--Biography | United States.
      Navy--Officers--Biography. | United States. Navy--Aviation--Anecdotes. |
      Veterans--Florida--Biography. | Sailors--Florida--Biography. | Pearl Harbor
      (Hawaii), Attack on, 1941--Personal narratives, American. | Vietnam War,
      1961-1975--Personal narratives, American.

Classification: LCC DS559.4 .B74 2019 | DDC 959.704/37 [B] --dc23

LC record available at https://lccn.loc.gov/2018052116

23 22 21 20 19   5 4 3 2 1

Let every nation know,
whether it wishes us well or ill,
that we shall pay any price,
bear any burden,
meet any hardship,
support any friend,
oppose any foe
to assure the survival and the success of liberty.
This much we pledge—and more.

—President John F. Kennedy
  First Inaugural Address
  Washington, DC
  January 20, 1961

Contents

Foreword by Jeff Miller   ix

Acknowledgments   xi

Prologue   xiii

Part 1

1   A Flash of Orange Light   3

2   Heartbreak Hotel   6

3   The Code   15

4   Little Vegas   23

5   My Friend Fred and Our Pet Spider   27

Part 2

6   To China in the Springtime   33

7   An Exotic World   42

8   War   48

9   Academy Man   56

Part 3

10   Boring Holes in the Sky   71

11   Operation Hardtack   78

12   Old, Bold Pilots   91

13   Bahia de Cochinos   97

14   Greek Games   105

15   Brinkmanship   109

16   Good Morning, Vietnam   115

Part 4

17	The Third Geneva Convention	125
18	Uncle Ho	132
19	The Cuban Program	138
20	Your Blue Suit	142
21	Escape	147
22	The Bob and Ed Show	152
23	I Will Give You Independence and Happiness but Not Freedom	157
24	Living with Prosperity	162
25	Son Tay Raid	168
26	Release	171
27	Homecoming	177

Part 5

28	Matwing One	195
29	A New Life, a New Navy	198
30	Retirement	205
31	The Mariel Boatlift	211
32	When Retirement Fails	221
33	Reunion	223
34	Where Do We Get Such Men?	230
	Epilogue	234
	Suggested Reading	236
	Index	237

Foreword

Jeff Miller

US House of Representatives, 2001–2017
Chairman, House Committee on Veterans' Affairs, 2011–2017

No one can accuse retired Navy captain Allen C. Brady of not living life to its fullest.

At various points, he has been a pilot, prisoner of war, sailor, ski instructor—and even a stockbroker.

In *Witnessing the American Century: Via Berlin, Pearl Harbor, Vietnam, and the Straits of Florida,* he recounts his life and times with a vivid attention to detail that prompts a profound appreciation of his service, sacrifice, and successes.

And while the more than six years Brady spent as a prisoner of war in Vietnam factor heavily throughout the book, they are just one part of a larger story that takes the reader on an intriguing and inspirational journey defined by one man's courage, patriotism, and resilience.

The son of a Navy submariner whose work sent him around the globe, Brady had seen more of the world before age ten than many people do their entire lives. His childhood memories of life and travels across America and abroad in the pre–World War II era provide a captivating look at events both surreal (a walk through 1938 Berlin on Hitler's birthday) and sublime (a future pilot's first flight as a young boy), setting the stage for the front-row seat he would have for many pivotal events that have shaped our history.

Brady got his first taste of the horrors of war when he was just a boy living in Hawaii, where his father was stationed. He recounts how on December 7, 1941, he could see Japanese fighter planes roaring over his neighborhood on their way to Pearl Harbor, just five miles away. Meanwhile, his dad raced to work in the family car, dodging Japanese bombs along the way.

It was a prelude to Brady's own Navy career, one in which he would fight his own battles: in the North Pacific helping test nuclear weapons; off the coast of

Cuba providing support for the Bay of Pigs Invasion and during the Cuban Missile Crisis; and in Vietnam—first as a fighter pilot and later as a prisoner of war.

Brady's account of his time in captivity is a harrowing warts-and-all portrait of the conditions faced by the more than seven hundred Americans who were held captive by the Vietnamese. The extraordinary discipline, strength, and ingenuity American POWs in Vietnam are known for is on full display.

But less familiar, yet also fascinating elements of the POW experience are also included, such as the contempt Brady and other prisoners had for the "Outer Seven"—POWs who became willing participants in Vietnamese propaganda in exchange for better treatment.

Brady is honest about the toll his captivity took on his life. Although he successfully resumed his Navy career after his March 4, 1973, release, he came home a changed man, with the six years, one month, and thirteen days he spent in Vietnamese custody affecting him as a parent and husband and eventually contributing to the dissolution of his first marriage.

Witnessing the American Century goes on to detail the twilight of Brady's Navy career and his remarkable "retirement," which included stints as a ski instructor, stockbroker, and sailor making rounds up and down the East and Gulf coasts and into Cuba.

Now happily remarried, Allen C. Brady will turn ninety in August 2019. His extraordinary life and accomplishments exemplify the best of his generation and send a powerful message of triumph in the face of unthinkable adversity.

Brady has hosted two reunions with those he calls his "cellmates and brothers" from Vietnam. A get-together in 2000 attracted fifteen former POWs. Nine years later, a similar event brought together just four people, as many in the group had passed away.

He is, indeed, among the last of a dying breed, which is why his story—and this book—are so important.

Acknowledgments

Capt. Brady would like to thank:

The countless friends and acquaintances who have indulged my stories over the years and encouraged me to finally write them down. Beth and Cory DeKraai, for their willingness to read and edit our manuscripts many times over, as well as for the procurement of another fine aviator's jacket. Our neighbors Jean Cotner and Barry Ferraro, for their support and friendship during an arduous summer of hospitalizations and recuperations. Gene and Carol Sharratt, for their loyal friendship and for helping me realize I had an amazing story to tell. Louise (Brady) Smith, for her help and assistance in providing me with those old letters from prison, which I was delighted to learn that she kept, as well as for her superb mothering of our children during the years when she had to do that job all by herself. Archie and Maggie Stokes, for having the persistence and fortitude to make me finally put pen to paper. My cellmates and friends from the Hanoi, who I relied on to make it through those tough years. Fred Crow, for being the best friend and the most crafty accomplice a guy could ever ask for. My children, Richard and Lisa, for growing up to be such outstanding human beings in spite of not having me around for many of the important years. You both make me very proud, and I love you very much. My grandchildren, Drew, Claire, Ben, Grace, Layla, and Coral, I hope you will enjoy reading about my life. Dawn Quarles, who took my stories and made a book of them. Finally, to my beautiful wife Dianne, for making the later decades of my life even more exciting, more beautiful, and more joyous than the beginning and middle ones combined.

Dawn Quarles would like to thank:

Pops, for allowing me to be the one who got to help you tell these incredible stories. I am so lucky to have landed this gig. To the countless students who passed through my classroom over the decades, for always making me feel like a really good American History teacher. This book got me just a little closer to believing it myself. Will Underwood and KSU Press for being terrific to work with. Doug Jolly and Red Iron Designs for the parts of your nights and weekends you sacrificed to make all of our priceless images a huge part of this story. Erin Greb Cartography for her craftsmanship on our superb map of Vietnam. And finally, to my son Ben for being exactly the kind of child I was designed to raise. You are the one who gives me all the really good stories.

Prologue

The rise of Adolf Hitler, the bombing of Pearl Harbor, World War II, the Korean War, America's development of atomic weapons, the Bay of Pigs Invasion, the Cuban Missile Crisis, the Vietnam War, the Mariel boatlift. I observed all of these events firsthand or participated in them. So many sensational occurrences like these, so many people and circumstances shaped America and changed the fabric of the whole world; many of the younger generations are not even aware of these pivotal moments. I want this book to bridge this gap.

I was born into a Navy family: I've traveled around the world twice; I observed Hitler's birthday in Berlin in 1938; I attended the Naval Academy in Annapolis, Maryland, graduating in 1951; then I went on to flight training in Pensacola, Florida, where I received my Navy wings in 1953. I was shot down over North Vietnam in 1967 and spent over six years in the Hanoi Hilton during the Vietnam War. Today, I sit here writing this book at the age of eighty-eight.

I've had an incredible life; even I can see that. It was undoubtedly somewhat stressful at times, but still one I wouldn't trade. As my DD-214, or Certificate of Release from the Navy, shows, I was away from home thirteen years out of a twenty-eight-year career. Of course, the six years in a Hanoi prison greatly distort this number. A number of POWs have written their own accounts of their amazing lives and of what they endured in Vietnam as well and have shared the stories of their experiences in prison. I would certainly never want to inadvertently write something contradictory to their accounts, and I extend apologies to each of them for any instance where that might happen.

My Navy career included shipboard duty, carrier flying, project test flying, post-graduate engineering school, and a significant command. Retirement has its rewards also; this time in my life has involved even more unbelievable adventures, including work in stock brokerage, ski instruction, and a rather exciting life of sailing. I retired from the US Navy after twenty-eight years and

243993

THIS IS AN IMPORTANT RECORD
SAFEGUARD IT.

OFF. REC. 834 PG 699

1. LAST NAME-FIRST NAME-MIDDLE NAME	2. SEX	3. SOCIAL SECURITY NUMBER	4. DATE OF BIRTH	YEAR 29	MONTH 08	DAY 15
BRADY, ALLEN COLBY	M	▓▓▓▓▓				

5. DEPARTMENT, COMPONENT AND BRANCH OR CLASS	6a. GRADE, RATE OR RANK	6b. PAY GRADE	7. DATE OF RANK	YEAR 72	MONTH 02	DAY 01
NAVY - USN	CAPT	0-6				

8a. SELECTIVE SERVICE NUMBER	b. SELECTIVE SERVICE LOCAL BOARD NUMBER, CITY, STATE AND ZIP CODE	c. HOME OF RECORD AT TIME OF ENTRY INTO ACTIVE SERVICE (Street, RFD, City, State and ZIP Code)
		BOSTON, MA

9a. TYPE OF SEPARATION	b. STATION OR INSTALLATION AT WHICH EFFECTED
RETIREMENT	PERSUPPDET CORRY STATION, PENSACOLA, FL

c. AUTHORITY AND REASON	d. EFFECTIVE DATE	YEAR 79	MONTH 09	DAY 30

e. CHARACTER OF SERVICE	f. TYPE OF CERTIFICATE ISSUED	10. REENLISTMENT CODE
HONORABLE	DD FORM 363N	

11. LAST DUTY ASSIGNMENT AND MAJOR COMMAND	12. COMMAND TO WHICH TRANSFERRED
CHIEF OF NAVAL EDUCATION AND TRAINING SUPPORT, PENSACOLA, FL 32509	NAVAL RESERVE PERSONNEL CENTER NEW ORLEANS, LA 70159

13. TERMINAL DATE OF RESERVE / MSS OBLIGATION	14. PLACE OF ENTRY INTO CURRENT ACTIVE SERVICE (City, State and ZIP Code)	15. DATE ENTERED ACTIVE DUTY THIS PERIOD
YEAR --- MONTH --- DAY ---	BOSTON, MA	YEAR 51 MONTH 06 DAY 01

16. a. PRIMARY SPECIALTY NUMBER AND TITLE	b. RELATED CIVILIAN OCCUPATION AND D.O.T. NUMBER	19. RECORD OF SERVICE	YEARS	MONTHS	DAYS
3227-EDUCATIONAL FACILITIES OFFICER	N/A	(a) NET ACTIVE SERVICE THIS PERIOD	28	04	00
		(b) PRIOR ACTIVE SERVICE	00	00	00
17. a. SECONDARY SPECIALTY NUMBER AND TITLE	b. RELATED CIVILIAN OCCUPATION AND D.O.T. NUMBER	(c) TOTAL ACTIVE SERVICE (a+b)	28	04	00
		(d) PRIOR INACTIVE SERVICE	00	00	00
9016-CHIEF STAFF OFFICER	N/A	(e) TOTAL SERVICE FOR PAY (c+d)	28	04	00
		(f) FOREIGN AND/OR SEA SERVICE THIS PERIOD	13	00	00

19. INDOCHINA OR KOREA SERVICE SINCE AUGUST 5, 1964	20. HIGHEST EDUCATION LEVEL SUCCESSFULLY COMPLETED (In Years)
☒ YES ☐ NO	SECONDARY/HIGH SCHOOL 12 YRS (1-12 grades) COLLEGE 6 YRS

21. TIME LOST (Preceding Two Yrs.)	22. DAYS ACCRUED LEAVE PAID	23. SERVICEMEN'S GROUP LIFE INSURANCE COVERAGE	24. DISABILITY SEVERANCE PAY	25. PERSONNEL SECURITY INVESTIGATION
TL: NONE	-60.0-	☐ $15,000 ☐ $5,000 ☒ $20,000 ☐ $10,000 ☐ NONE	☒ NO ☐ YES AMOUNT	a. TYPE BI — b. DATE COMPLETED 15 AUG 58

26. DECORATIONS, MEDALS, BADGES, COMMENDATIONS, CITATIONS AND CAMPAIGN RIBBONS AWARDED OR AUTHORIZED

1. SILVER STAR
2. LEGION OF MERIT {WITH COMBAT "V"}
3. DISTINGUISHED FLYING CROSS
4. BRONZE STAR {2} {WITH COMBAT "V"}
5. AIR MEDAL
6. NAVY COMMENDATION MEDAL {2} {WITH COMBAT "V"}

27. REMARKS

EFFECTIVE DATE OF PERMANENT RETIREMENT: 01 OCT 79.
MEMBER REQUESTS COPY OF DD FORM 214N: ACB

BLOCK 26 CONT'D:
7. PURPLE HEART {2}
8. NAVY EXPEDITIONARY MEDAL
9. ARMED FORCES EXPEDITIONARY MEDAL
10. NATIONAL DEFENSE SERVICE MEDAL
11. NAVY OCCUPATION SERVICE MEDAL
12. CHINA SERVICE MEDAL
13. KOREAN SERVICE MEDAL
14. VIETNAM SERVICE MEDAL
15. UNITED NATIONS SERVICE MEDAL
16. COMBAT ACTION RIBBON
17. NAVY UNIT COMMENDATION
18. REPUBLIC OF VIETNAM CAMPAIGN RIBBON
19. REPUBLIC OF VIETNAM GALLANTRY CROSS UNIT CITATION

AND NO OTHERS ————————————

RECORDED IN OFFICIAL RECORD BOOK
MONROE COUNTY, FLORIDA
RALPH W. WHITE
CLERK OF CIRCUIT COURT
RECORD VERIFIED

28. MAILING ADDRESS AFTER SEPARATION (Street, RFD, City, County, State and ZIP Code)	29. SIGNATURE OF PERSON BEING SEPARATED
P.O. BOX 4105, PENSACOLA {ESCAMBIA}, FL 32507	Allen C. Brady

30. TYPED NAME, GRADE AND TITLE OF AUTHORIZING OFFICER	31. SIGNATURE OF OFFICER AUTHORIZED TO SIGN
J.L. LANDRY, YNC, USN, ADMIN AST PSD CORSTA	Landry

DD FORM 214N
1 NOV 72
PREVIOUS EDITIONS OF THIS FORM ARE OBSOLETE
S/N 0102-LF-002-0202

THIS IS AN IMPORTANT RECORD
SAFEGUARD IT.

REPORT OF SEPARATION FROM ACTIVE DUTY

1

Allen Brady's Certificate of Release, Form DD-214. (US Department of the Navy) four months and found that life still presented a lot of incredible opportunities and a host of misadventures.

People tell me my story is an incredible one. I suppose. It is just my life, and I have always felt thankful to be around to live it. Now I want to share it with the many people who think it deserves to be shared. I hope you enjoy it. Anchors Aweigh!

Part 1

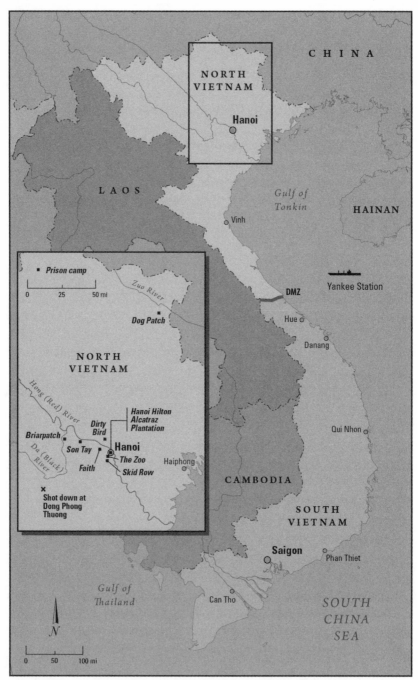

Vietnam prison camps and other important locations during the Vietnam War. (Commissioned for the author, Erin Greb Cartography, 2017)

Chapter 1

A Flash of Orange Light

**Aboard Aircraft Carrier *Kitty Hawk* at Yankee Station,
off the Coast of North Vietnam, January 1967**

Fighter pilots at war don't have time to miss their families. Three weeks after Christmas in 1967, my wife and two small children were halfway around the world, and I was pretty busy myself, intently focused on the task before me: bomb and destroy a series of bridges in the rural northeastern region of North Vietnam. President Richard Nixon had temporarily stopped our US assault because of the holidays, but US jets still continued to attack areas of South Vietnam, which remained occupied by the Viet Cong. We bombed a few obscure targets, being directed by air controllers flying their small observation planes, but when the weather was bad, we were often kept airborne in our trusty A6s.

Just past the middle of January, the weather started to improve, so a large air strike was planned for the nineteenth. Two carriers would participate, each launching three strikes, for a total of six. Normally, strike assignments would come from headquarters in Saigon. Our air wing staff would assign the squadrons that would participate. Then, a strike leader was tasked with briefing the participants on overall tactics, and the A6 contingent would generally serve as the navigation lead to the target area because of our inertial navigation systems. On the first strike of that day, I led the whole strike force to the target area. The strike leader commanding the F4s (fighter group) initiated the attack phase. I was in the lead section of four A6s (attack group). There were F4s and A4s as well, for a total of about twenty aircraft. As we approached the target, I could see the telltale smoke puffs of antiaircraft artillery. We descended to about three thousand feet and went to full power. The F4s on our tail hit burners and passed us. Some A4s were attacking antiaircraft artillery sites with 20 mm guns

3

and rockets. A4s had launched Shrike antiradiation missiles, which home in on the enemy radar signals, launching them high in the air where they would leave contrails. Of course, the enemy could see the missiles, but they would have had to either shut down their radars or have a Shrike missile down their chimneys, so to speak. Unexpectedly, our missile warning light came on, indicating that a surface-to-air missile had been launched at us and was receiving guidance information. The F4s came on the radio and ordered our group to hard turn to port. Shortly after I had the target in my sight, I radioed that I was pulling up, and then all the A6s pulled up as well to gain sufficient altitude to roll into a divebombing maneuver. I acquired the target in my crosshairs and pushed the release button at three thousand feet, then I pulled out and immediately jinked to the left, doing more than four hundred knots. Suddenly, I heard an explosion and saw a flash of orange light. With a jarring thump, the control stick was ripped out of my hand, and although I tried to grab it and continue maneuvers, it gave no response. The aircraft started rolling violently, and I knew it was time to get out.

The A6 *Intruder* has a large canopy that slides rearward on release. When you start an ejection sequence, the canopy slides back and keeps going, eventually leaving the aircraft completely. To initiate the ejection sequence, you are supposed to reach for a yellow handle on the instrument panel in front of you to get rid of the canopy and then pull one of the two available ejection handles, either the one over your head or the one between your legs. After I was hit, the g-forces were so great that I couldn't reach the canopy handle, so I reached for the handle over the back of my head. It was difficult, but I knew that if I didn't find it, that would be it for me! I managed to grab onto it and then pulled as hard as I could. There was a vacuous noise and then a wonderful acceleration as I blasted through the canopy. The top of my seat was higher than my head, so it busted through the canopy first. (Actually, if the rails had been damaged, the canopy might have gotten stuck halfway, and I would have crashed up inside of it, *another* way to die.) My bombardier navigator, Lt. Cdr. Bill Yarborough, who was a skilled navigator and also a great friend, ejected as well. He and I never spoke again, as the g-forces made it impossible for us to talk to each other as we spiraled downward. After I ejected from the plane, several things happened, all of them occurring in no more than a few seconds. When my chute finally deployed, I looked down and saw that the ground was only about a hundred feet below me. I prepared to execute a hard parachute fall, but since there was no wind, I was unable to roll when I hit the ground, and I crashed in a sitting position, which was quite painful. I saw the smoking hole in the ground about a hundred yards from where I landed, the remains of my aircraft. I called out for Bill but got no response. He must have died on impact, his chute failing to deploy fully before he hit the ground. I could see Vietnamese people running toward me, but I was in a wide-open country of rice paddies, with no avenue of escape. I knew I would be captured. The report Lt. Ron Waters, the pilot in the plane behind me, submitted to Navy officials after the crash stated that he saw my aircraft when it was hit and watched it break into two burning pieces and then fall to the earth.

Back home, my family members held their collective breath for nineteen months, wondering if I had survived.

Chapter 2

Heartbreak Hotel

New Guy Village, Hỏa Lò Prison

When the Vietnamese arrived at the crash site, they jumped on top of me and brought me into submission on the ground. I landed hard on my back in a rice paddy field, and as they snatched and grabbed at my hands and feet I struggled to keep them from pushing me down into the nearby water. At first, I feared they were going to drown me on the spot, yet *another* way to die. Some of them held me down while the others yanked off my flight boots and ripped the parachute vest from my body. It was a group of five or six men, all of them pretty petite in stature, thankfully. They lifted me to my feet, tied a tattered piece of cloth across my eyes and nose and tied my arms so tightly with old rope that I could feel the chafing almost immediately.

Then they marched me to their village about a half a mile up a nearby hill. Once there, I was made to stand in front of someone I assumed must have been their village chief. I couldn't see him because I was blindfolded. Whoever he was, he clearly believed me to be his enemy. Without saying a word to me or to anyone, and without any warning, he punched me in the jaw with an ire intense enough to take me all the way down. He said nothing to me after either. Then my captors escorted me to a small building in the interior of their village and had me sit down on a low wooden bench. My blindfold was removed, and I found myself in a tiny room about the size of a toolshed. The floor was dirt, and there were three or four other people squeezed in there with me. Several young men from the village came up to take a closer look at me, curious, like I was a circus oddity. When one of them offered me a cigarette, not wanting to offend, even though I was not a smoker, I smoked it.

I knew that wherever we were, it wasn't very far from the bridge I'd bombed. I also knew that the same location would be targeted again later that day. Con-

6

Shootdown and capture, January 19, 1967.
(US Department of the Navy)

sequently, I had to sit quietly and wait for the explosions to come, anticipating, correctly, that I was also going to have to suffer through the next round of terror with the rest of these guys. About a mile from where I was being held, the A6 contingent continued to drop thousand-pound MK83 bombs and rattle the earth around me. When it was finally over, I was marched out of the village and we headed to a new site for the night. My state of mind was pretty good by this point, because I finally felt in my gut that if they were offering me a smoke and moving me to different locations, they probably weren't going to kill me. If I'm honest, I was a little numb, too, and in reflection I think my calm was perhaps a result of exhaustion more than consolation. It was astonishing for me to relive what happened as those hours in captivity finally started to settle in: one minute I was traveling at four hundred knots, heading for home on the carrier, and a moment later, there I was on the ground, a hostage in enemy territory, captured. I was someone's prisoner. I felt tangible relief that I'd survived the crash; *I was alive!* But there was also the ominous dread of the unknown hours ahead and of what was going to happen to me. I felt acutely aware that this was not survival school. This was not part of any military training or prisoner simulation exercise. This was not one of the nightmares of my dark imagination, when my shipmates and I would joke around about getting shot down on a mission and what we'd do if we were captured, hypothetically speaking. I was in the middle of the real thing, and I'm not ashamed to admit that I wished I were elsewhere.

As they led me along that afternoon, we passed through a few small villages scattered about on our way to the next stop. An advance team of theirs had arrived a bit before us and rallied all the locals to come out and line the pathway as I walked by. They shouted things at me in a language I couldn't even begin to understand, and they threw stones at me. Although the Vietnamese are actually a fairly tranquil people by nature, instinctively I could see that when provoked, like they were tonight, they were certainly prepared to fight and defend their country against someone like me. Even though all that hostility and those threats to me felt somewhat staged, my captors believed their anger was still absolutely justified. We walked on. I spent that night in a small, locked building in a village about two miles from where I was captured. Even though the American A6s were covering the countryside day and night looking for moving targets, the chance of being detected was much lower at night than in the daytime. I figured we probably weren't traveling more frequently because someone up the North Vietnamese chain of command didn't even know I was a captive yet, and motorized travel would be necessary if they wanted to find me and take me on to Hanoi.

Another day passed. We traveled by truck until dark, and then we spent the night in what looked like a grain-storage building. The next morning, we traveled briefly before stopping at a bridge surrounded by Vietnamese people who appeared to be public relations staff or maybe members of their local media. Then, in a completely staged propaganda opportunity, I was forced to walk across the bridge with a tiny Vietnamese girl, who was coached to carry a rifle and to keep prodding me with it, acting as though she was the one who captured me. It was designed to be humiliating, and I was forced to look totally submissive. A photographer there was filming the whole event with a movie camera, and I was glad about that cameraman—I was thinking my picture might get out if their film was actually circulated. Sometime later, sure enough, someone in our government received the footage, and it was the proof the Navy needed to confirm that I was captured but still alive.

After this, I was taken to yet another house, where I was made to lie on the dirt floor, still bound with rope at my hands and now also at my feet. All during the day, Vietnamese villagers would come in and out to gawk at me. Some of the more curious ones would even get a few licks in by kicking me in the legs. It wasn't serious kicking, more of an aggravation than anything, and I knew their intentions were not really to hurt me. I was fairly sure, even in the middle of their harassment, that I would live another day, so it was tolerable for that reason only. When our time together in those rooms got quiet, and in the moments when my captors and I were allowed a respite from the burden of my captivity, I often wondered silently, *Why am I being spared?* And then, *How would one of these men fare in my country if the tables were turned?*

Another night was spent in the back of another truck, and it was rather cold, since it *was* January. I was thankful I still had my socks on, and I was also still wearing my flight suit, but they'd taken my boots, and we'd been walking for days and days. The fatigue and that bitter cold started getting to me, and in moments throughout that night I felt sure I might freeze to death. Mentally, the exhaustion was catching up with me, too, but still, on each one of our marches I paid extremely close attention to how the terrain changed, trying constantly to keep my bearings. Of course it was dark each time we traveled, but at one point I ascertained that we'd crossed a river on a fragile, moveable bridge that could be put in place and disassembled quickly on short notice. I made note of things like that over and over, in case I needed that information for later. Every single detail seemed important.

We finally arrived at Hỏa Lò prison (pronounced *wa low*), which was built by the French when they occupied Vietnam from 1887 to 1954. At the time of French occupation, the country was called French Indochina. This prison was decrepit and dingy and looked like the dungeon from an old horror movie, poorly lit and dank. When we arrived, it was early morning and still dark. I could hear a radio blaring Vietnamese music, which sounds eerily like Middle Eastern religious chanting. Creepy as hell. The building was made of masonry, with chilly brick pathways, lit with incandescent lights that made everything

Hỏa Lò prison, aerial view, 1970. (US Department of the Navy)

Hỏa Lò front entrance.

impossible to see. I was forced to sit on the cold, unforgiving floor with my back up against the wall, tied up like an animal for the rest of the day and night, until daylight came seeping through small windows in the wall the next morning.

You're still alive. It was a hushed voice in my head that became an ever-present consolation to me, a hundred times a day, from that moment on. A reminder that I had a future to look forward to. I still had my life.

The following morning, I was given a small bowl of plain rice and some tea in a metal cup. When there was finally enough light to see the things around me, I noticed a large hook hanging from the ceiling in the corner. I wondered what it was and then hoped it was not what I thought it might be. I sat by myself in that cell for a good long while before the Interrogator finally came in. He wore a light-colored jacket and pants and appeared to be an officer of some sort. His dress was more refined than that of anyone else I'd come into contact with thus far, and he carried himself differently than the locals. He spoke fairly decent English, and his demeanor was strictly business. His voice was low and calm, eschewing friendly small talk. He had one of his assistants tie me up around the ankles, with my legs extended straight out in front of me. Then my arms were bound tighter behind my back, with the rope around my elbows now, too, which I knew couldn't be a good sign. Then the assistant cinched it and wound it up and around my neck. Finally, a stick was placed through the knot at my elbows.

The Interrogator asked me which ship I'd come from. Like a good soldier would, or *should,* I answered him with only my name, rank, and serial number. He then called out for someone else, and in walked a Vietnamese soldier wearing a pith helmet adorned with a net and leaves, the kind that would be used as camouflage. He was undoubtedly of a lower military rank, something I assumed by his rumpled uniform and lack of English skills. I would come to know this man as "Flower Hat," and he is someone very well known to all American POWs who ever passed through New Guy Village at Hỏa Lò, which is where I had the misfortune of being at that moment. The Interrogator left the room displeased with me and Flower Hat proceeded to administer his famous rope trick, which had several variations. First, he held the stick that was lodged in the rope behind my back and twisted it clockwise, which tightened the rope around my neck and forced my neck backward and down, and then the circulation in my arms stopped. I began to choke, and I felt my arms disappear into the cold numbness of low blood flow. The pain was intense enough to kill anyone, and I thought, *I am going to die like this in just minutes.* I drooled on myself and groaned in agony for him to stop, and he did. The very next thing that occurred to me was that I might possibly be the only one of us who gave in so quickly, and then a demoralizing realization came: *If that's true, I've let everyone down already.* Thinking on those kinds of things was almost worse than the torture. I later found out, to the relief of my intense guilt, that no one was ever able to resist being in the ropes. Still, I stayed severely depressed trying to figure out how I could endure the torture longer if it ever happened again. Let me assure you, it would.

The Ropes. Drawings by POW Lieutenant Commander Mike McGrath. (Reprinted by permission from John M. McGrath, *Prisoner of War: Six Years in Hanoi.* Annapolis, MD: Naval Institute Press, © 1975)

Having established the pecking order, the Interrogator returned to my cell after the rope trick and started pounding me with questions about my squadron, the names of other pilots, and potential strike targets. Most of this information wasn't even classified; I knew he was just testing me. I told them I was newly arrived in the squadron and I only knew a few people, whose names I invented completely on the fly. I kept it short, as I knew I had to memorize every single lie I told him in anticipation of being asked the same questions again later. *All liars must have great memories*—remember that. The Interrogator showed me pictures of the destruction caused by American bombing raids. He jabbed at pictures of dead bodies and told me, "Look!" just to get me to feel guilty. It goes without saying that I always felt guilty about any civilian casualties that I caused. However, I also knew that the Viet Cong killed and disemboweled thousands of villagers in South Vietnam, not to mention that the kind of collateral damage caused by my airstrikes was a far cry from intentionally bombing civilians, schools, hospitals, rice paddies, dams, and villages. I knew most pilots, like me, would never engage in those kinds of criminal acts. That's not who we are, and that's not who we were back then. Nobody needed reminding that war is hell, not to mention a really stupid way to settle differences.

Anyway, the Interrogator told me that many of our pilots were, in fact, cooperating with the North Vietnamese under the same circumstances I found myself in. I mentioned a few names of some of the pilots I knew who had been captured, and he said, "Yes, they are all cooperating." I asked if I would be able to meet with them at some point, and again the Interrogator said, "Yes, in the future." Of course he was lying to me. I knew this because I was absolutely certain that the other Americans who were there, men who would become my cellmates, would no sooner betray our country than I would.

So there I was, held as a prisoner in a small cell block in what was later known to all as Heartbreak Hotel. Most interrogated prisoners passed through it eventually for varying periods of time. Flower Hat came to visit me again a few days later and pointed at my arm to see if it was still functional after his rope trick. I made it a point to emphasize that no, actually, it wasn't, but he just shrugged his shoulders and moved on.

After I was in the Heartbreak a short week or so, the prison guards came to move me again. I did not realize how many POW camps there were! Hỏa Lò, that hellhole we would forever call the Hanoi Hilton, was an old French prison, a relic from the days of colonial European occupation. Within it were several subdivisions containing smaller imprisonments. New Guy Village, Heartbreak Hotel, and Little Vegas were further broken down into the Stardust, the Desert

Inn, the Riviera, the Nugget, the Mint, and the Thunderbird. I spent *my* entire captivity first in Little Vegas and later in Camp Unity, but there were a good many camps outside of Hỏa Lò as well, prison units such as Plantation, Alcatraz, the Zoo, Briarpatch, Camp Crisis, Power Plant, Faith, Dirty Bird, Son Tay, and Dogpatch on the outskirts of Hanoi. Camp Unity was part of the Hilton, in another part of Hỏa Lò altogether. We were all placed there after the Son Tay Raid compelled the Vietnamese to close all of the outlying camps.

Chapter 3

The Code

GBU

Whenever they told me I was moving, I rolled up my meager possessions in a straw mat without fuss or comment. I sometimes had to bow to the guards who came to get me, per their custom and according to their written rules for prison protocol, a copy of which we received on arrival at Hỏa Lò. We were kept blind-folded for any transports, and sometimes the guards even turned us around in circles a few times, just to disorient us and disrupt our bearings. I always thought that was pretty stupid, since I knew where the damn door was no matter how many circles I took. When it was time to leave Heartbreak Hotel about a month after I arrived at Hỏa Lò, I felt pretty optimistic, and I hoped I would finally get to join the other "air pirates," the other Americans, who I knew were already in the prison somewhere. I was led into and out of several buildings. I tried to pay close attention to every walk I took. When the blindfold came off, I found myself in a musty-smelling but fairly good-sized cell in another section of the prison, called Little Vegas. The cell contained one wooden bunk, and there was no mattress, no pillow, no sheets—nothing but a raised platform built with old, unevenly cut wooden boards.

I settled into my new home by unrolling my prison-issue straw mat and plac-ing my only pair of black rubber-tire sandals next to my bed, where they stayed unless I was wearing them or needed to use them as a pillow. I'd also been given two sets of pink and dark-red striped pajamas and two pairs of skivvies. In the winter, we were each given two thin blankets. In spite of how bad they smelled, we were thankful to have them, because it got downright frigid in those concrete cells during the cold months. Miraculously, I was also able to keep my socks, the same ones I was wearing when I was shot down. If not for those, I would've had nothing at all to put on my feet for the entire time I was in prison. During the warmer months, we struggled in altogether different ways. Those same concrete cells that stayed frigid in the winter heated up to such high temperatures in the summer that we all suffered from painful bouts of blistering heat rash. During those seasons, we spent most of our days wearing nothing but our Vietnamese underwear.

There was no window in my cell, so I when I wasn't keeping myself busy thinking, I perched on the end of my bunk and stared at the whitewashed concrete wall in front of me, or perhaps the blank ceiling above me, for an endless number of hours, every day. I spent that time in total solitude. There was nothing to read, nothing to watch, and nothing to draw or write with. We were told that if we needed assistance, to yell "bao cao," which meant "I need an officer." This was part of the official regulations we were taught to abide by. We yelled this every time we needed a guard to come to our cell for any reason.

As the days crept by, I continued the practice of tweaking my senses for any little sound, the slightest shift in the light, an unfamiliar smell. I noticed any change in my surroundings, things that seemed different in even the slightest way. Then I started to hear noises that would have gone undetected by a normal person who had the slightest distraction. The noises sounded like hushed murmurs. I sensed a subdued whispering, and soon I recognized something familiar about the male voices talking to each other nearby. I heard the unmistakable *American* in their dialect, and I felt the exhale of an aching, welcome relief. It was an undeniable comfort for me to finally realize that fellow prisoners of war were nearby. Friends . . . brothers.

At mealtime on the evening of that very first night in Little Vegas, I heard the prisoner in the cell nearest the entrance moving away from me as he was led out of his cell and into a neighboring building. He was gone for just a few minutes, and then he returned carrying his dinner and was directed back into the darkness of his room. When the door to my cell opened, I obediently rose for my turn and was led out of the building as well. I continued to be very earnest about learning my way around quickly. I made note of how long people were gone and thought hard about where they might have been taken and why. I counted steps around every turn and around every corner, dropping mental pins on the developing map I was creating in my head. My building was known as the Nugget, and I was in the middle of three cells.

When it was time to eat, I was led from my cell down a walkway and then through an entrance and into another, larger building, called the Thunderbird. Inside, there was a small room at the end of the walkway, and a person could turn either right or left to head down toward other long rows of cells. Just inside that walkway foyer, there was a wooden two-shelf rack, and on one of those shelves were two metal bowls. I nonchalantly took one of them, thinking only of the food I was about to eat and not of the covert moves being made all around me nor of the exchange of secrets taking place right under my nose. I assumed the other bowl on the shelf was for the yet-unknown POW rooming on the far side of me, and I didn't think anything of it as I carried my supper back out with me.

I returned to my cell and crouched on the floor to eat. I shoveled plain white rice into my mouth with an aluminum utensil that looked a like a small ladle with a short handle; perhaps you could describe it as a rather stubby-looking spoon. We used the same spoon for broth and for the greens we were sometimes given for dinner. As I was eating my rice, I bit into something small and hard, smaller than the size of a die. I spit it out and held it for inspection between the tips of my fingers. I was intrigued to discover it was a wadded-up piece of paper made from what we were currently using for toilet paper. I flattened it out, and there it was: a note that said, "We know you're here." It included a communication code that would change everything about my time in that prison. The messenger urged me to be careful, because the "FUZZ" also knew our code. The note warned me, "Messages can come at you in many ways." Then, in the tiniest words I'd ever read, it ended with "God Bless You."

I was astounded; it seemed like something straight out of a Hollywood spy thriller or a James Bond movie.

Now, since one can't differentiate between a dot and a dash while tapping on a hard surface, as you would on paper for Morse code, our methods for using dots and dashes had to be modified so that simple taps would be heard as specific letters of the alphabet. The English alphabet was made into a five-by-five matrix. Since there are actually twenty-six letters, we interchanged *K* and *C*, or sometimes we used a special tap for the letter *K*. The letters *A* through *E* were across the first row, *F* through *J* were along the second row, and so on. You tapped out the location of the letter you wanted. For example, *A* was one tap / one tap, for first line / first letter. The letter *H* would be two taps for second line followed by three taps for third letter. *X* would be five taps then three taps. In other words, the first tap would indicate the row and the second tap would indicate the column. Messages such as "God Bless You" were relayed in shorthand, as, for instance, "GBU," in the same way people now text message each other using abbreviated phrases, like "OMW" for "on my way" or "WBU" for "what about you." We had to synthesize our communications for brevity. A common inquiry would go something like this: four taps / one tap, one tap / two taps, four taps / five taps, and two taps / two taps, which translated to

TAP CODE	1	2	3	4	5
1	A	B	C/K	D	E
2	F	G	H	I	J
3	L	M	N	O	P
4	Q	R	S	T	U
5	V	W	X	Y	Z

The tap code matrix.

"QBUG," a question we asked another prisoner who was just returning from an interrogation. The Bug was one of the more infamous guards who worked us over from time to time, a real winner of a human being, if you like torturers.

After memorizing the code, which took me just a few minutes, I practiced awhile by myself and then tapped my first message to my next-door neighbor, a man I learned was an Air Force F4 pilot. I never saw him face-to-face while we were in captivity, which was not at all uncommon, because the prison guards went to extreme lengths to keep us all apart. To my elation, he answered me back in code, and we clumsily communicated with each other for the next couple of days. I only recall tiny bits about him, but I remember vividly when he tapped to me about the explosion that took his plane down. He said it was forceful enough to blow off his helmet, a detail that remains quite remarkable to me even now. Anyway, he was the first person I communicated with after my arrival at the Nugget. I wish I could recall who he was, because I will never forget that moment when I was once again interacting with someone whose situation was as dire as mine. It gave me hope.

And then, of course, we got caught.

When the guards busted in, I couldn't imagine in my worst nightmares what a punishment in this place, for that offense, might be. I was put into handcuffs with my arms behind my back for what the guards hinted to me would be a rather extended period of time, in what I was already sure would be some ghastly, horrible place. And it was. I was only freed of the cuffs when I was allowed to eat. When I needed to use the toilet, there was a bucket in the cell just for that purpose, but my hands were never graciously released for that. All of my *maneuvers* were done with my hands in handcuffs. If I needed to urinate, I just urinated. I pushed as hard as I could and tried to maintain a forceful arc of piss into the bucket, but ultimately, as the pressure of the stream diminished, I just peed onto my pants. I won't go into the complications of number two, but I'll mention two important things: it required a certain amount of dexterity and balance, and we *all* suffered from constant diarrhea for the entire time we were in prison, which naturally made this situation all the more difficult. Furthermore, when we were being punished there was never any wiping to speak of.

I stayed bound up for several days. The weather changed and grew colder and wetter as February approached. Luckily, it was the start of the Tet holiday period. This is a time in Vietnam similar to an American New Year's celebration. After I had been in handcuffs round the clock for several days, an older Vietnamese woman suddenly opened the metal flap to the peephole in my cell door and spied me sitting on the floor, probably looking pretty defeated and pitiful. She turned to the guards and yelled something that I couldn't possibly begin to understand. A bit later, one of them came in and reluctantly removed my cuffs. I'll never know who she was or what she said to him, but she must have been the camp commander's wife or someone of great power or respect to have that kind of pull.

Meanwhile, back in Little Vegas, the other POWs in captivity continued undeterred in their efforts to communicate with each other during the guards' nap period after mealtime. Let me be clear: it was the guards who slept. Never us. We had work to do. We grew so skilled at tapping that eventually we developed a form of shorthand. If you didn't understand your messages right away, you were usually able to quickly figure them out using common sense. For example, a guard might come to my cell and tell me to suit up by chopping on his arm, which meant "put on long sleeves," because I was going to an interrogation. After I'd been gone a while, when I returned everyone else in the building who heard me leave wanted details. Once I was back in my cell and the area was clear, soon enough someone would start tapping to me through the wall, "Where ya been?" I replied with "QBUG," which in this case meant I'd been quizzed by the Bug. Then to be funny we would tap, "UNEVERGOHOME"—to make fun of him because that was one of his most famous and constant comments to us. To express understanding or receipt of a message, we did a quick double tap to say, "I got it," and so on. It became somewhat automatic, and we all got very good at it. It became second nature.

One day a guard came in and installed a little blue box on the wall of my cell, which appeared to be a speaker. I thought perhaps I would get to hear some good music, maybe something different to listen to besides just silence all the time, but that would've been too optimistic to even wish for. In fact, that very night the camp commander of the prison came on through that speaker and informed us that he would be reading from a book written by some little-known liberal antiwar author. He droned on in his childish, broken English for at least a half hour, railing about the imperialism of America and the United States' intrusiveness into his peaceful little country's private affairs. He then ended his reading with an abrupt and comical "I stop." We welcomed and then relished the dead silence that immediately followed his ridiculous oration. None of us made a sound, and then one deep, loud voice boomed through the halls, a solitary declaration, "BULLSHIT," in perfect American English. Then I heard some timid laughing break out, picking up a bit after a few seconds and getting louder, followed by the guards yelling into our cells and walking the hallways trying to find out who said it. I also laughed out loud at their frustration with us, and at how good it felt to hear a little bit of real American cussing, and then I realized it was the first time I'd laughed since my plane was shot down.

Time crept on, and one day a guard came in and indicated that I was to be moved again. I was transported into the Thunderbird and put in a fairly large cell, still alone. Again at mealtime, when I went to the foyer I searched for microscopic treasures hidden in the metal bowls of rice waiting for me. During the napping period one day, when all was quiet I heard a soft voice whisper, "Prisoner across the hall, what is your name?" I stood up at the small square porthole in my cell door and peered downward through a sliver of space large enough to allow my voice to carry. I could not see anything, because the metal door to my porthole was closed, but we started whispering our names to each other, and I learned who my neighbors were. Bill Baugh was the man across the hall from me, the one who brought me into the fold that day. Jim Stockdale was diagonal and to the left of me. We hurriedly determined the chain of command among us, and Jim turned out to be the ranking officer. I answered Bill with my name and the name of my ship, and he responded, "Commander, would you mind talking under the door?" So I laid all the way down on my stomach and looked under. I could see a few of the other cells along the hallway in both directions, and to my astonishment, each crack under each door revealed an eyeball looking straight at me. We all whispered with each other for a while about the communication protocol. I was told of the rules for keeping out of trouble, including these: If I ever heard a loud cough, I was to stop talking and quickly get up on my bunk or just walk around the cell aimlessly in case the guards were looking in to see what we were doing. One cough was a warning, two was the all-clear, and three meant "I don't know, but be careful." At one point, someone coughed softly once and we waited quietly. A while later, I heard two coughs and then our talking resumed. And so it went, just like that.

Some days later, the door opened, and in walked Hank Fowler, a first lieutenant in the US Air Force and my new roommate. He was blindfolded, and his hands were tied behind his back, naturally. I played it cool for the guards, but it was hard to hide how great it felt to have someone put into my cell with me, someone to talk to. To actually see another American right in front me was exhilarating in a way I can't accurately describe.

Being in the Air Force, Hank was very familiar with the US military's flight schedules, and each day when the air-raid sirens went off, he knew exactly which flight it was and when the next bombing missions would occur. I was always told when to brace myself. Shortly after Hank's arrival, we received another Air Force pilot, a man named Tom Madison. I don't recall his rank, but I remember noticing instantly that his back and legs were injured significantly. He was another great guy, now in the same shitty boat as Hank and me, but we were happy to be a group of three. I asked Tom how he was shot down and he explained to us that he was a "wild weasel," which meant he was a surface-to-air missile hunter. On the day he was shot down, there were two sites, one on each side of him, which trapped him in the middle, and he couldn't possibly take them both out simultaneously. His aircraft was hit as he was trying to escape the attacks from the missile sites. And now, here he was with us in the Thunderbird. We took care of Tom the best we could while his injuries healed, and over the next few months, he seemed to get much better.

Since the day I'd received that first note, I often wondered how this primitive style of espionage had evolved, and during one of our talk sessions as we all laid down on the floor, I posed that question. It had been going on since before anyone could recall. No one in my group knew the name of the person who created it. It seemed that once those first prisoners had perfected how to drop their written notes in strategic places and simultaneously manage to communicate to the whole building, "Do not take the bowls on the lower shelf to the left," it all caught on rather quickly. When a drop was to take place, a prisoner and his cellmate went to get their food, and the cellmate was directed to distract any guards nearby while the prisoner pushed the little wads of paper into their designated bowls of rice. It had worked to perfection since its inception, and we almost always received our written messages in this way.

Unfortunately, the part of the note that said "information can come at you in many ways" didn't register with me as deeply as it should have. In all of their spare time, the older guys staying in the prison often got very creative with their messaging and managed to come up with some ingenious ways to send information to the rest of us. For example, during the guards' daily nap, a prisoner or two would be selected to sweep the central courtyard. This was a chore designed to keep us submissive. The brooms we were given were not like American brooms; they were bundles of some species of swamp reeds tied near the top where you would hold them, sort of like what tall bundles of tree branches might look like if you tied them together and then swept with them. So, to my chagrin, on a beautiful day in the Nugget, they came by my cell sweeping in code and I missed it. I can't even grasp, in retrospect, how many opportunities like this I may have missed as I learned the ropes of prison communication. I also remember how, several years later, once I was attuned to the cues, a tree in the courtyard blew over and then some prisoners were tasked with chopping it up. They chopped on it completely in code, and I picked up on that one!

Later, Cdr. Jerry Denton developed a much more complicated but very useful vocal tap code. It was slow to learn and difficult to understand, but it was efficient in unique situations like a crackdown, where we couldn't walk or move in any way or use our hands. Since our guards were always hacking and spitting, Jerry integrated those normal human behaviors into a code. You would use one cough plus two coughs to indicate one and two in the old twenty-five-letter matrix code. The third position on the matrix was indicated by a throat clearing, fourth position was a hock (as if you were clearing out your sinuses) and the fifth position was a spit. For example, the letter *O* was a throat clearing and hock to indicate the third line and the fourth column in the matrix. Just like the tap code, the first sound was for the row and the second sound was for the column. It was a method of communicating with each other even when Vietnamese guards were right there in the same room with us. Although the vocal tap code never played an integral part in our larger efforts to send messages, and I never used it myself, it was still impressive. Mass communication without an iota of technology.

Chapter 4

Little Vegas

The War within the War

Whenever the air-raid sirens went off, which happened almost daily, we were required to get under our bunks. We could hear the planes overhead, diving low before the sound of bombs detonating rattled the walls of our cells. The flak was heavy, and we could hear metal shrapnel clanking as it bounced off the tile roof above us. There was so much antiaircraft artillery, it didn't seem possible that any aircraft could penetrate the air space. Each of our cells had a small hole through the outer wall at ground level, to let water out when you washed the floor. The floors slanted to the outside toward the wall, and mopping involved throwing a bucket of cold, dirty water on the floor and then sweeping it out of that hole. In the winter, cold air would creep in through it as well, so we often balled up toilet paper and stuffed it in to retain our inside heat. During a bombing episode, the pressure from the explosions would pop that paper right back into our cells. And at night, giant rats would come in through that same hole looking for scraps of food. Thankfully, when we slept we were under mosquito nets, which the rats would usually steer clear of. They were the largest rats I'd ever seen, some of them as fat as alley cats. They would jump up onto our bunk posts outside of the net and poke around. Although they were terribly scary things to look at, I don't think anyone in my cell block was ever bitten. I heard different stories coming out of the outlying prisons, though.

I moved several times during my captivity, so I can't recall many of the exact dates or locations as I was transferred from place to place, but I do remember my big move into a cell with three other POWs, one of whom was Lt. Col. Fred Crow, US Air Force. Other men came and went, but Fred and I would end up being cellmates for over five and a half years. As Fred and I moved around all throughout those years together, we sampled cells of all different sizes and

23

Lieutenant Colonel Fred Crow, US Air Force. (US Department of the Navy Archives)

shapes. Normally, a cell was about eight feet by eight feet. Some had concrete bunks, and others had the two sets of over-under wooden bunks, the kind that would hold four POWs. Our really tough years were spent in the *half* cells, four feet wide, with just one set of bunks. Those were rather tight spaces for two grown men: I could sit on my bunk with my back to one wall and my feet on the other. If your cellmate needed to walk back and forth, one of you was in the way. Our cells were white, which was a plus, but still, we were together twenty-four hours a day in a space smaller than a walk-in closet. Cozy, wouldn't you agree?

Most of the large buildings in Little Vegas had tile roofs with large overhangs to keep the buildings cooler in the hot summers. Unfortunately, the guards hung large thatched screens from the roof overhangs, and this eliminated any breeze we may have gotten and completely blocked our view of the courtyard. Looking in the opposite direction, the cells across the hall faced only a large concrete wall that stood about fifteen feet high and was littered with broken glass and electrical wires to deter us from escaping. That wall and the prison proper were separated from each other by a walkway about ten feet wide, and there were guard towers at each of the wall's corners. It was pretty much escape-proof. The buildings were originally open bays, but to dissect the larger rooms into smaller cells, the Vietnamese closed them in with walls that went to the pitched overheads. In some cases, they constructed small separate partitions between two cells so that they could not share an adjoining wall. This made tapping with each other somewhat difficult. Moreover, many of the cells had built-in leg irons to use in punishment for infractions precisely such as tapping. All in all, it wasn't homey in the slightest, and each day it seemed as if everything I could lay eyes on served as another obstacle to overcome. But at least the ceiling didn't leak, and I had a human bunkmate.

From my cell in the Nugget, if I looked out the window above the wall and past the screens, on sunny days I could see the color blue or perhaps even a nice patch of sky with tiny corners of clouds. To this day, looking up into any typical sunny day still gives me a momentary jolt, reminding me of those unpleasant years when I didn't see much of anything beautiful when I looked above me.

Fred and I were not allowed to speak to each other above a normal whisper, and we were forbidden to tap to our neighbors, but this is where we reminded ourselves and each other that we were in a war within a war. Our captors tried to deter most forms of normal communication, but all of the POWs felt an iron resolve of defiance toward these rules. We were determined to beat the prison guards at their efforts to break us down and to outsmart them. When they tried to test or even weaken our commitment to each other, it only fortified our goal of communicating in as many different ways as we could, just to frustrate the hell out of them and, of course, to keep our sanity.

In the courtyard, there was a series of covered baths, monitored by guards. In spite of that, this was still a place where we were often able to talk quietly. After just a few months, I'd become one of the old-timers. I whispered over the walls to new arrivals and transmitted the code, offering the usual tips to help keep them safe. In addition to learning the names of their units, the type of aircraft they flew, and other basic information, I always learned their birth names and incorporated them alphabetically into my mental roster of all American prisoners. Every POW did this, and one of the things we spent our days doing was reciting over 350 names again, and again, and again until we could recall instantly who was among us. Once a new guy's ID was determined, his name was disseminated through the underground code, and he was encouraged and welcomed with an enthusiastic "Welcome aboard!"

Now, to call this area we shared a "bath area" is a stretch. The tub was made of concrete, and the tap had only cold water. Under the sink was a partial pipe that extended downward and ended about a foot above the ground, just above a concrete draining trough, which carried the waste water out of the building. When a prisoner was permitted to bathe, prison guards would escort him from his cell to the bath area, coordinating it as best they could so that none of us could see each other. Normally, we washed twice a week. Each of us was given a "towel" about the size of a dish towel, and it had to last for the entire duration of our stay. Since I used my towel for exactly 2,236 days, it could stand up by itself by the end of my captivity. Periodically, we were EACH issued a half block of rock-hard lye soap plus a toothbrush and some toothpaste. Interestingly, the toothpaste tubes had lead in them, and we found we could write with the lower corners of the tubes—so of course, we did.

Each cell was given a metal bucket equipped with a top to use when we needed to go to the bathroom. We filled up our buckets together each day, Fred and I, and we emptied them together as well. Each morning, one of us would take a turn carrying it out of the cell to empty the contents. Being allowed to take the bucket out each day after being locked up with it all night was a treat, and the fresh air on this short trip more than made up for the stench of carrying around pails full of our own shit.

Besides our determined tapping, sporadic washing, regular interrogations, and filling and emptying our shit buckets, we weren't left with a lot of other things to do, and consequently, we idled our time away with a lot of nothing. What I would've given to have a book to read! I believe I could have made a respectable dent in the Library of Congress if I'd had the opportunity. We had no music to listen to, no art supplies with which to draw, no writing pads or reading material to flip through. Small talk took up a lot of time, but sometimes it seemed like we even ran out of things to talk about. When that happened, we simply retold our favorite old stories for a second time, which was good fun, especially when we added some spice and exaggeration.

Chapter 5

My Friend Fred and Our Pet Spider

Idle Time

When times were quiet, Fred and I took to insect-watching. The ants were riveting entertainment and commanded thousands of hours of our attention. You could see them cruising around all hours of the day and night, and if just one ant found *anything* to eat, he would high-step it into gear and head back to his fort to tell everyone else. Soon after, a bunch of his ant buddies would return to assess the situation and come up with a plan. On a particularly slow day in the Hilton, Fred and I noticed a dead grasshopper lying prone on the floor. The ants showed up, ready to get to work. They were all over that carcass, with some standing on top of the body, seeming to give everyone else directions. For lack of anything better to do, Fred and I decided to provide commentary to the project.

Clearly, their plan was to cut one leg off and take it back to home base, so they started carrying it straight up the wall. Fred and I eyed the small opening where the wall met the ceiling, and we determined that they were foolishly headed that way. After some heated study of the situation, we agreed that the leg was way too large to fit into that opening. We discussed the logistics of their options and could see the complications unfolding. Indeed, we were right. When they got to the top, sure enough, they had to turn around and bring it all the way back down and do a little trimming. After several trips up and then several trips down, and with more cutting and more trimming, they finally got it up there. This project took most of the day, during which they paid absolutely no attention to us sitting next to each other in our bunks pulling for them.

There were also an outrageous number of mosquitoes and spiders in Vietnam, critters whose sole function appeared to be to torment us or, in a lucky change of fate, to serve as food to the friendly geckos who also lived in our cell. One day I caught sight of a small jumping spider living in one of the leg irons that stayed in the corner of our cell. He had amassed several fly carcasses in various spots scattered around his abode. It seemed as though the flies' insides had been devoured and only the empty exoskeletons remained. The guy was collecting bodies! Not many would have noticed something so irrelevant, but, of course, Fred and I noticed everything that went on inside our cell. One day that spider was on the wall not far from a mosquito, who was also cruising around. The spider certainly seemed interested in the mosquito, but he flew in and then away right when the spider got too close. I wanted to help the guy out, so I grabbed the mosquito and pinned him against the wall. When the spider approached, that mosquito froze, paralyzed. The spider waited patiently, and therefore so did I, and when the mosquito finally twitched, my spider friend jumped in and took him from me. And just like that, we had a pet.

I need to mention here an important differentiation. There are spiders, like my buddy who collected fly bodies, and then there are SPIDERS. In the prison camps, we encountered some of the largest, gnarliest spiders I've ever seen. Fred and I were living in one of the eight-by-eight cells that had the two over-under wooden bunks on opposite sides of the cell. We were both sitting on our lower bunks, facing each other with our backs to the walls. Suddenly, a huge spider the size of a fully extended male hand came skittering down the wooden bunk post that was flush against the wall. About halfway down, it stopped, just inches from Fred's head. I calmly but sternly told Fred, "Don't move." He cut his eyes at the spider and then slowly raised his rubber-tire sandal about a foot from where it was perched and took a swing. He didn't even come close! That spider launched himself up the post and onto the wall above the bed and finally onto the ceiling. So now, the damn spider was upside-down over Fred's bunk. We threw the few things we had at him, which caused him to fall off the ceiling. As he fell, he spread out and flattened his legs, sort of like a whirlybird, and started rotating as he floated to the ground. When he finally landed on the bunk, he ran right under Fred's only extra shirt. We looked at each other with dread, and, although he hated to do it, Fred gave the shirt a few hard whacks from the sandal. Then all was quiet.

On occasion, the camp's power went out, and when that happened, the guards lit a few lanterns in the hallway, which made the lighting in our cells only somewhat better than pitch black. This happened one insignificant night, and while trying to investigate what was going on, Fred got down on his knees to look under the door. Guess who showed up? The dead spider's equally enormous spouse, who ran from one cell to the other and under our door right next to Fred's head before running on down the corridor. Fred almost had a heart attack, and I almost did too! From then on, thinking about being in a dark cell with those beasts, we always kept an overhead light on. Considering all the different creatures that roamed around near us each night, including the rats, leaving our room lit was a small price to pay to get some decent rest. Speaking of the rats, I have a story about them too.

One evening as the sun went down and the cell grew dark, the prison rats assumed their places at the top of the chain of command. In came a big mama and four babies, the babies weighing in at a respectable one or two pounds each. I'd never seen babies come in before. Mama was easily ten pounds all by herself. They were cruising around, looking for scraps of food, and in our boredom, Fred and I discussed our options and decided to have a little fun with them. As the critters skittered brazenly across the middle of the cell floor, Fred inched his way ever so slyly toward their entry hole in the exterior wall. They still didn't take much notice of us, and so we went undetected as Fred wadded up a handful of our toilet paper and plugged up their entryway. They noticed this *immediately,* and Mama calculated correctly that her girth would not permit escape underneath the door. Their frenzy was alarming, and we enjoyed it for a few brief moments until we began to worry about what her desperation might cause her to do to us. We could see her getting more and more agitated by the second, so we unplugged her hole and out they all went. If only it were that simple for the rest of us.

Then, during our many idle hours when we'd run out of bugs to feed or rats to terrorize, Fred and I talked about our lives. Fred was about three and a half years older than I was, so he rated the right to start the discussions about anything and everything. I learned that Fred was living in Honolulu, Hawaii, when the Japanese attacked Pearl Harbor in 1941; his father was a chief radioman stationed on a small ship there. He told me of a few other similar experiences he had growing up, moving around every couple of years, getting to see the world, but there were some rather big differences in the paths of our lives. Fred had dropped out of high school to enlist in the army. He told me he'd always wanted to be a US Army Air Corps pilot, so at eighteen, he was sent to pilot training in North Carolina. Since it was later on in the war, the pool of applicants signing up to serve was saturated so the Army Air Corps simply stopped training pilots, and Fred was sent to Oklahoma to become a bombardier navigator. After he was there for just a short time, that program also ended, and Fred was sent to yet another location in Oklahoma to train to be gunner for bomber aircraft. You can guess what happened next. The gunnery school also shut down, and Fred was discharged and sent home. He returned, disheartened, to Massachusetts, where he earned his high school diploma on the GI Bill. He enrolled in the 5220 Club, a veteran's assistance program, under which the government gave unemployed veterans $20 a week for fifty-two weeks. That was actually a lot of money back then, and Fred lived comfortably; you'd be surprised what $20 would buy. Anyway, Fred went on to Cornell University and enrolled in the US Air Force ROTC program, under scholarship as an English major. He completed his courses there, became an Air Force recruit and fighter pilot, and ultimately joined me in the Hanoi Hilton.

When it was my turn to share, I mentioned that I also lived in Honolulu in 1941 with my parents and my brother. We agreed, it was indeed a small world. I continued on, telling him that I was born on the West Coast and had been fortunate enough to see many places in my life, and although I'd lived in California multiple times, I admitted that I never considered that state my home. Confused, he asked me where I'd lived, what places I'd seen, and what my family was like, so I began with my birth.

Part 2

Chapter 6

To China in the Springtime

My Birth, a Navy Childhood, World War

My father was born in rural Kentucky in November 1901, just after Teddy Roosevelt ascended to the American presidency following William McKinley's assassination. His name was John Huston Brady, but he went by Jack, or Jim-Joe, or sometimes just Jim. In 1923, he graduated from the US Naval Academy, when that institution was marking its seventy-eighth year. I remember him being rather handsome. He was of average height and stature and nothing stood out about him at all, and yet everything did. He had dark, wavy hair, and his 1923 Naval Academy yearbook, *The Lucky Bag,* asked the question, "Please tell me, does Mr. Brady have his hair marcelled?" He wore it a bit longer on top but slicked it back with hair gel and styled it with a deliberate wave combed into the front. His light-colored eyes punctuated a round face, and he was always clean-shaven, almost like he woke up already showered. His voice was as clear as a dinner bell, and it had soft edges. When he spoke, you weren't at all able to detect his Kentucky upbringing. In fact, the vocabulary he used instead hinted at his prestigious education, and in spite of a very average build, he often made people feel like they were standing next to the biggest man in the room.

In 1925, he finished up submarine school in New London, Connecticut. Prior to that, he had served on a battleship, in a generation when training to be a pilot was a newly emerging career option. He dressed casually when he was at home, preferring pressed button-down shirts tucked into his pants, as one would expect of a distinguished man of some respect. Shorts were strictly reserved for the golf course, and he spent a good deal of time there. I occasionally witnessed his quick temper as he threw around a little mild profanity, often about things happening at work or at bedtime when my brother John and I wouldn't stop talking and go to sleep. He and my mother raised us during some rather stressful times, and as

Midshipman First Class John Huston Brady, featured in *The Lucky Bag*, the Naval Academy yearbook, 1923.

JOHN HUSTON BRADY
LAWRENCEBURG, KENTUCKY
"*Jim-Joe*" "*Jim*"

A TRUE son of the state famed primarily for its beautiful women and fast horses, and essentially for its good whiskey. Jim came to us to prove that all sailors are not born on the ocean.

The first term Plebe year he got the dope on the Academics. From then on his favorite indoor sport was keeping them baffled. Re-exams are his fruit and he can calculate on a 2.5 without wasting anything on useless effort. He kept the Dago Department guessing for three years only to give them the chuckle in the end.

His droll wit and ready comeback make all the femmes fall. Keep them guessing is his motto, and he certainly seems to make it work.

Youngster cruise Old Neptune had him off his feed until we hit Panama, but on Second Class cruise he staged a mighty comeback for he had his sea legs and partook of the supreme joy of beholding less fortunate shipmates trying to "hold everything".

"Please tell me, does Mr. Brady have his hair marcelled?"

a result, he was away from home quite often, but he was an attentive father, and I never remember wishing my dad would've done anything differently than what he did. I respected the hell out of him, and I miss him still.

My mother's name was Elizabeth Burrows Colby, and she was born in October 1903 in Mystic, Connecticut. She was raised in a New England Episcopalian family, but they were not devout churchgoers. She attended school at Williams Memorial Institute, a private girls' high school that first opened in 1891. Then in 1923, at the age of twenty, she graduated from Catherine Gibbs Secretarial School in Boston, where she learned shorthand and transcription. By today's standards, this kind of education probably seems rather sexist, but during the Progressive Era, my mother's desire to attend college at all was very forward-thinking and innovative. With regard to her pursuit of a set of career skills, she would've been seen as quite an assertive young woman. My father met my mother in 1925 in New London, and he affectionately called her Betty. She stood no more than five-foot-two and had a very slight, slender frame. I always thought she had pretty legs, and I knew this because she always wore brightly colored dresses, silk stockings, and high heels. She wore her brown hair pulled back into a loose, low bun, sometimes packed into a thick net called a *snood*, with a stark part down the middle and deep red lipstick. Just to add some pizazz to her style, she wore a braided hairpiece attached around the base of the bun. Her role as a Navy wife fit her personality. She was traditional and old-fashioned in many ways, living comfortably within the confines of being a woman of those times, but it *was* the twenties, and she was assertive, somewhat aggressive at times, and even brave when she needed to be. Her demeanor was dyadic; she could be the doting, soft-tempered stay-at-home wife of a naval officer, hosting bridge parties and raising the children, but she was also stoic and resolved, ferociously protective of us and not *ever* prone to panic or hysteria. With my brother and me, she was the most gentle creature I ever knew, and she was my dearest friend for much of my life.

During my father's generation, the military was a popular career choice, partly as a result of the Selective Service Act of 1917. Service in the armed forces more than paid the bills for most families and carried with it a bit of respect. But to young Jack Brady, there was always more to it than that. My dad was a patriot, in the way one suddenly becomes patriotic after being asked by the local congressman to consider an appointment to a rather unknown military academy in Annapolis. My dad accepted his invitation, and from then on service in the Navy consumed his life. Their personalities, my father's and my mother's, melded into a perfectly balanced temperament, both of them evenly disciplined *and* passionate about the things they loved. In the middle of perhaps the worst time in American history for a young couple to start a family, they began their sixty-year journey together in 1926 in Stonington, Connecticut.

Submarining took them across the country to California not long after they married. My older brother, John, was born in June 1928 in San Diego, and I followed soon after him in August 1929, almost a year into Herbert Hoover's doomed four years in office and just two months before the stock market crashed. This clearly indicated a foreboding future for me, and, of course, events to come would certainly test my resolve, would they not? But I digress. In the late 1920s, America was certainly beginning to struggle quite a bit. The symptoms of our impending economic disaster were definitely showing as my parents were

Commander John Brady, with his wife, Elizabeth, in Mystic, Connecticut, 1943.

starting to build their life together. Still reeling from the casualties of our first World War (President Woodrow Wilson called it "The Great War") even middle-class Americans like my parents were forced to ration their supplies, and I seem to recall my father telling me he took a rather significant pay cut in 1933, when the Great Depression was in full swing. The ration board doled out coupons for gasoline. Meat, coffee, and sugar in particular were also very hard to come by for anyone of any social class, but besides those scarcities, tough times didn't really hit my family as hard as they hit others during that decade. In fact, I would later know a kid named Tommy Blivens whose family owned a soda fountain shop in downtown Mystic, and we could go in for an ice cream with soda water on top (today's Coke float) whenever we wanted to. I guess what I'm trying to say is, in spite of America's total economic freefall, I always felt like a pretty lucky kid with a damn good life.

My dad received orders to return to the East Coast again in late 1934 or early 1935, so the four of us set off in our old car to cross the entire United States. Many years later, he told us hysterical and mesmerizing stories about that trip: crossing the bridge at Needles, California; going on across the Colorado River to Arizona, where we encountered a dirt road and stayed on it for a good, long time after. We didn't hit another paved road until Kansas City, following historic Route 66 for a little over a week through some of America's heartland. He boasted to friends that we covered five or six hundred miles a day with no car seats and no seat belts, our fast clip more attributable to the lack of traffic than to the good quality of the roads. Along the way, we stopped and stayed in *tourist homes* because the word *motel* didn't really exist yet. If you want to know the truth, there were hardly any real towns along the way, much less motels. The lodges we stayed in were recognizable only by the signs hanging in their front windows. Moreover, back then there wasn't much to offer travelers in the way of roadside assistance. In fact, my dad said it was quite common for him to change two flat tires in a single day on a trip like that, and he carried the spares in our car. I wish I could recall the sights I might have seen on that trip, but I can't—I was only five or six years old!

After a little time on the East Coast, in Newport, Rhode Island, where the Navy had a torpedo school, my father was assigned to be the commanding officer of the S-37 (a submarine, very small), which was moored alongside of the sub tender, USS *Canopus*. At that time, the *Canopus* was actually anchored halfway across the world, in Manila Bay, Philippines, so my brother and I soon found ourselves heading out with our parents on our first voyage overseas!

We traveled by passenger ship. At that time, much of America's sea traffic was conducted by the Dollar Line, whose ships had a dollar sign on the smokestack and were sometimes named after American presidents. These passenger liners weren't very big at all, and I remember clearly the small number of people aboard compared to today's cruise ships. The ship had a swimming pool made of steel, and the rivets sealing its seams were clearly visible. The pools were painted light green, and some of the kids aboard swam every day during the voyage over. Since we were just twenty-three years removed from the sinking of the *Titanic,* sea travel was both exciting and perilous. (However, even now in my eighties, I still think it's a preferable way to travel.) Our ship was christened the *President Van Buren.* The voyage was supposed to take three weeks to complete, and regularly scheduled stops at various ports of call for one or two days at a time were quite normal, for that's when the ships picked up and dropped off supplies and passengers. All commerce in those days was by sea, so in addition to providing transportation to people, we were also delivering trade goods and mail to other parts of the world. After eight days of ocean travel, we made a stop at Honolulu, Hawaii, and stayed for a couple of days. Then we cruised on for two more weeks before finally reaching Manila, the capital of the Philippine Islands, in September 1935, just a year before President Franklin D. Roosevelt was to be elected for his second term.

Life was fairly nice in Manila. Today, the small apartment we lived in would be considered low-income property. There was no air-conditioning, no television, and none of the other amenities you might find in today's gadgety world. We had a hand-crank Victrola phonograph record player, whose sound emanated from the head that held the needle. On a typical evening, my mother might take us on a streetcar ride to town to watch a movie while my dad worked. Other times, John and I could be found outside playing baseball and snacking on NABs, four chocolate Oreo-like cookies, also sold by the National Biscuit Company (Nabisco).

On the island of Luzon in Manila there was a very nice Army-Navy Officers' Club, and it had a bar (for men only), a formal dining hall, several tennis courts, and a large community swimming pool. John and I both learned how to swim in that pool, and later an older kid we befriended would make many winning bets on me that I could high-dive from the three-meter board. I recall seeing a swimming and diving exhibition starring Larry "Buster" Crabbe when it passed through town and put on a show at the O-Club pool. Larry Crabbe would later be featured in films such as *Flash Gordon, Tarzan,* and *Buck Rogers.* There was one irritating thing I heard my mother mention about that bar, the one for *men only:* the base wives would often call there looking for their husbands. If a husband was sitting at the bar and the wife was asking for him, the bartender would say with a wink, "Sorry, ma'am, he's not here," while looking straight at the husband. This courtesy was extended to all husbands; the bartender knew every one of them, including my father.

In the 1930s, almost all military officers were either Annapolis or West Point graduates, and all of the American families who lived among us came from both varieties. There was no naval base in Manila at that time, not in the way

Army-Navy Officers' Club, Manila, Philippines, 1936.

we understand them today. Everyone who was deployed there simply incorporated themselves into life in the Philippines, living in local housing and putting their children in local schools. But there was a definitive American presence all over Manila, since the islands were an American protectorate. We felt very welcome there. Naturally, each year in December there would be a huge Army-Navy football party. It was held outside, with many tables and chairs set up and decorated out on the sprawling green lawn that stretched out in front of the Officers' Club. There was a large vertical six-by-six-foot plywood board with a hand-painted football field and a wooden ball that was moved around by an employee of the club, according to the play-by-play of the game coming out of the radio speakers at the bar. Because we were halfway around the world, the game didn't start for us until about 0100 Manila time, so the party didn't crank up until very late and carried over into the wee hours of the morning. Of course, my brother and I did not participate in these activities. Instead, we were sent to bed so the adults could enjoy themselves. Back then, children were not included in adult parties the way they are today. My mother's words still resonate in my memory: she firmly believed children should be seen and not heard.

Submariners like my dad did *not* like being called sub-MAR-in-ers, with attention paid to the connotation that comes along with the syllable "sub," because that indicated a status of *less than*. Instead, they preferred being called sub-ma-RIN-ers, and many of them knew a song they liked to sing whenever they spent time serving in the Asiatic Station.

It went like this:

> We'll all go down to China in the springtime!
> We'll all go down to China in the springtime!
> We'll all go down to China on a submarine or liner,
> We'll all go down to China in the springtime!

These guys would go to Tsingtao (pronounced *sing-tow*, *Qingdao* in Chinese), along the east coast of China, for a number of months for sub training. Their wives and families followed behind a few weeks later, on a commercial liner, after their husbands had enough time to arrive and procure living quarters. Then, a new beginning in a new place would start once more. Such was life in the Navy!

During my kindergarten year, my brother and I were sent to live in a boarding school while my mother accompanied my father on his first temporary deployment to China. We actually lived at our school, Mrs. Howe's Academy, under the care of Mrs. Howe herself. Surprisingly, military children were the minority at Mrs. Howe's, and most of our schoolmates were local kids. We had no air-conditioning and often had to seek shelter from horrendous storms during the monsoon seasons. I still remember how loud and terrifying the thunder was, and John and I stayed there with Mrs. Howe in her home throughout many storms, and without our parents, for over four months.

The second time my dad was sent to China, over a year later, we were fortunate enough to accompany our mother to be with him. We sailed on the *Empress of Canada,* a much larger ship than the Dollar Line vessels. This voyage took us from Manila to Shanghai. From Shanghai, we traveled by train to Tsingtao, where the four of us rented a small house on Eltis Hook Beach. Although my father was only a Navy lieutenant, we had a male housekeeper, named Lou, and lots of other hired help. There were sweet, elderly Chinese ladies known as *amas,* and their job was to take care of the kids, much like American nannies. We also had a *coolie,* an elderly man who took care of the yard. They charged next to nothing to work for American families stationed there, and years later, my mother and the other military wives still reminisced about them and missed the close relationships they had, often wishing they could've taken them all back to the United States. My mother, my brother, my dad, and I stayed on in Tsingtao for four months or so and spent a little over two years overseas before world events started changing dramatically.

As 1937 approached, the impending aggression of Japan toward China was becoming a concern for the foreign nationals living there, and as a result, my family left Asia and started making our way back to Connecticut.

Chapter 7

An Exotic World

Wings

My father's orders sent us back to New London, where he was to be a submarine-school instructor. Once again, we embarked on the Dollar Line, this time heading west on the *President Wilson,* the opposite direction from two years prior. We sailed on west until we crossed the International Date Line at the 180th meridian, at which point we were then heading east and on a different day. Our first stop on our way home to America was the Malay Peninsula port of Penang along the northwestern coast of present-day Malaysia. The Dollar Line's ships often stopped to take on cargo before heading back to the United States. When we arrived in port, I saw on the dock stacks and stacks of gold bullion, which actually turned out to be tin. When I was a kid, tin was considered a cheap metal. (That's why we started calling the old Ford Model-T cars tin lizzies and why small houses often had tin roofs.) Today, tin is actually fairly expensive, three times the cost of copper.

Since we were in town for a couple of days, my family and I slept on the ship each night but disembarked each day to see some of the local sites, including a Tiger Balm Garden and several wild monkey parks. If you've never heard of it, tiger balm is an herbal ointment developed by a Chinese family in 1863. We learned that a man named Aw Chu Kin and his sons became very wealthy selling the product and the tiger balm pain relief topical products became quite popular rather quickly—and even today it's sold all around the world. Some of the gardens are quite elegant, and there are now Tiger Balm Gardens locations in Rangoon, Hong Kong, Singapore, and all throughout southeast Asia.

Then we were back under way, headed for the island of Ceylon, known today as Sri Lanka, at its main port of Colombo, just south of India. We stayed there a few days as well, and my parents took my brother and me to town, where we rode on the back of an elephant. You might be surprised to know that they have very prickly hair on their bodies, and since I had on shorts that day, those hairs really scratched up my legs. John and I also met a hundred-year-old tortoise whose back was as big as a reclining chair. We visited the Galle Face Hotel, which I mention only because I would stop there again twenty years later, in 1956, when I was stationed on the aircraft carrier USS *Hornet*, going the other way back around the world.

Under way again, we headed for a shortcut through the Red Sea and the Suez Canal rather than rounding the tip of Africa. On arrival at Suez, we disembarked and took a rented car to Cairo to visit Giza to see the Sphinx and the Great Pyramid. Still today, I remember it being absolutely amazing! I was shocked, and you might be as well, to know that the body of the Sphinx is mostly below ground level, and only the head is what people see in pictures. Anyway, the blocks of the pyramid were enormous, and trying to climb them is a vivid memory to me even now, eighty years later. I needed help to hoist myself on top of them, and my father and my mother had to help me climb from one level to another. John and I also learned that the pyramids are not actually empty but include a winding and intricate series of passageways and crypts throughout.

We reembarked in Port Said, Egypt, and sailed on across the Mediterranean to Naples, Italy. Mount Vesuvius was active and smoking at the time, and we visited the ancient ruins at Pompeii, which was *much* less excavated back then than it is now. Moving on, we sailed to Genoa, Italy, continuing up through Switzerland by train. After a brief stop there to visit Schwarzwald, or the Black Forest, we continued on to Berlin, Germany.

We were in Berlin on April 20, 1938, which just happened to be Chancellor Adolf Hitler's birthday. Everyone was in extremely high spirits, and the level of nationalism was contagious, electric even. People were cheering, and balloons were being released in celebration. The streets were filled with people, children were skipping along and laughing, speaking in a language I didn't understand at all, but it certainly lightened everyone's mood that their leader was having a big day. The shops and boutiques along the streets were full of customers, and everyone, including yours truly, was smiling, hands cupping mouths, and innocently, naively chanting, "Heil Hitler!" I vividly remember the toy stores in Germany. They were fantastic! Extravagant displays of miniature towns with trees and shops that had little electric lights inside, lengths of track sprawling out endlessly in all directions inside the toy stores. It was incredibly fascinating to an eight-year-old. I remember the military trains being my favorite, elaborately painted designs with the tiniest details and lots of moving parts. They sped in and out through the tunnels and puffed real smoke. John and I each picked out a Lionel train, and then my parents left us alone back at the hotel later that evening to play quietly while they went out on the town.

Then we were off again to Paris to see the Eiffel Tower, the Palace at Versailles, and the Louvre. Seeing the artifacts of ancient civilizations and walking the streets of glorious cities at such a young age is both impressive and nostalgic to me now. I wish I'd been old enough and aware enough back then to appreciate all the things I was fortunate to see and do. There's no life in the world, then or now, like a Navy life.

Leaving Paris, we did something quite daring for the times. We flew—*in an airplane*—from Paris to London on an Imperial Airways airliner. When my family boarded that flight, air travel had only been around for two decades and Orville Wright was still very much alive and well. It was the cusp of futuristic technology, and flying in an airplane changed me completely.

To the best of my memory, it was a bi-wing. The lower wing sat on top of the fuselage, and the upper wing was a lot higher, with fixed landing gear. I was sitting next to a window, where I was able to see the left side landing gear and the rubber tire. As the aircraft rolled down the runway on departure, my eyes stayed glued to the mesmerizing spin of that rolling wheel, and when we lifted off, I watched that wheel leave the ground under engine power and I felt butterflies. I decided in that moment that I wanted to be a pilot and fly too. I also decided to go to the Naval Academy, just like my father. Probably not many eight-year-olds decide so firmly which college and career they intend to pursue, but it happened exactly like that, and I never steered away from the decision I made that day when I went into the air for the first time.

London was beautiful; I remember it being very different in every way from the Far East. We saw the Crown Jewels, the Bloody Tower, the Tower of London, Big Ben, and London Bridge. We departed England on yet another Dollar Line ship, although this one, rather small, was named simply the *American Banker*. This trip across the North Atlantic was in rough seas. For some reason, I was one of the few people on board who did not get seasick, and I counted it as another of my esteemed qualifications for joining the Navy. After arriving in New York in May 1938, we took a train to my mother's hometown of Mystic, Connecticut, and moved in with my maternal grandparents, Alfred and Edna Colby. And just like that, I'd completed my first circumnavigation around the whole world; it was a lot for a kid to digest, and it didn't really sink in back then like it does to me now. It was without a doubt an educational and inspirational gift to have had those experiences, and I shall always be grateful to my parents for them.

The first major event in modern history to take place in the little town of Mystic was the Great Hurricane of September 1938, and I was there when it happened. I would go on to live in Florida for thirty-nine years and would endure a great many hurricanes, but not many other storms compared to that first enormous hurricane I experienced in Connecticut, of all places! Storms weren't given names back then, and satellites didn't even exist. Ships that were actually out at sea reported foreboding and ominous weather to the mainland. Most of the time, people realized a hurricane was coming when they noticed the outside pressure drop and it started to rain rather heavily. John and I were at school, at the Mystic Academy, sitting in class watching the weather worsen. As the winds began to pick up significantly, my mother grew concerned and drove to our school to retrieve us. When the three of us reached West Mystic Avenue, there was already a large tree down, blocking the street to our house. My mother didn't want to risk driving any further, and trees were crashing down all around us. She parked the car right on the main street, right on US 1, and we ran as fast as we could in the rain and took refuge in a house that sat on the corner. We didn't know the man who owned the house very well, but he took us in as the weather intensified. We sat huddled in a large room in the front of the house, my mother, my brother, me, and the man who owned the home. After just a short time, the man broke the news to us that the intensity of the storm would be increasing and not dissipating and perhaps we should all move from the living room and to a den on a totally different side of the house. Shortly after we resettled, we heard a crash, and the big window in the living room we'd just left had shattered under the weight of a large tree, throwing glass shards everywhere and destroying the roof. The telephone lines were all down, so we didn't see or hear anything from my dad until much later that evening.

When the storm finally abated, it became eerily quiet, and there was a strange yellow-green cast in the light of the sky. Around sunset, my father finally came home, saying it took him over four hours to drive the ten miles from the submarine base. He told John and me how worried he was, not being able to get out and get to us, and he was visibly stressed. We all hugged; he was so relieved that no one was hurt. As for John and me, of course we thought the whole thing was rather exciting.

It took months to repair roads, restore power, and clean up the town. The local beach resort, Groton Long Point, had been hit quite hard. My grandparents owned three beach houses out there, and the smallest, the one we called "the small house," was built right on the rocks along one end of the beach. Once it was safe to travel around to see all the damage, we drove out to Groton and looked for the small house amid all the downed trees. At first, my grandparents discussed with each other how difficult it might be to estimate the damage, but once we all arrived we quickly discovered that the house was totally gone. Utility lines were sticking out of the ground, and gas hissed out of pipes where stoves had been ripped from their foundations. Unbelievably, there were still unbroken dishes and glasses sitting untouched among the rubble.

Devastated, my grandparents sold the lot where the small house had once stood, along with the other two beach houses they owned there, both of which also sustained significant damage. Many, many years later, my wife and I visited Mystic and Groton Long Point and discovered with quite a deflated spirit that the beach resort that sits there now has home values in the hundreds of thousands of dollars. (So much for holding on to a growing investment! I wish my grandfather had pondered that sale a little longer.) The Mystic River, the life blood of the entire town, rose to seventeen feet above sea level, so at the crest all the stores were completely flooded. Mystic's downtown area was totally destroyed. When this storm came ashore, it had sustained winds of 115 mph, movement was north at 47 mph, and maximum gusts were at 186 mph. Today it would be a Category 3 hurricane. The peak storm surge was ten and a half feet above normal, and the peak wave height was fifty feet. There were more than seven hundred deaths, eighty-nine hundred homes destroyed, and sixty-three thousand people left homeless. The storm had passed west of Mystic, and thus, we were on the east side of it. Anyone who knows hurricanes would call this the *bad* side if you were living in the northern hemisphere, and it was a night I will never forget.

Another event occurring later in 1938, a sad one indeed, was the death of my grandfather, with whom we were living at the time. Back then, most people simply died at home in their own beds. The adults of that generation usually tried to shield their children from such events, so my brother and I were shipped off to the suburb of Auburn, near Providence, Rhode Island, to visit our great Aunt Phoebe and my Uncle Willie while my grandfather drifted on into death. We returned well after his passing and after the funeral had already taken place. John and I saw none of the end of my grandfather's life, and I remember him exactly as he was when I last saw him, strong and healthy. Only a number of years later did I even learn that he'd died of cancer. Adults just didn't discuss those kinds of things with children. He passed away at home, with family nearby and a doctor seeing him a few times a week simply to administer pain medications. There was no hospice, no nursing home, and no nurses. Things were much simpler then, better, I think too. My grandfather was a wonderful, kind man, and I still miss him even after all these years.

It was early summer in 1939 when my father took his exams for promotion to lieutenant commander. When he opened the folder for his last test, his boss had placed an aspirin inside with a good luck note. With his promotion, my father received orders to Submarine Squadron Nine at Pearl Harbor, Territory of Hawaii, and my mother prepared our family to embark once again on another round-the-world trek to a new home. We left Mystic driving a 1938 Hudson Terraplane, and our first stop was New York City. It was the fall of 1939, and the New York World's Fair was in full swing when we arrived, the Trylon and Perisphere the main attractions. (By today's standards, both exhibits would be quite unimpressive.) The Trylon was a tall spire connected to the Perisphere, a very large spherical building featured by the General Motors Corporation. They were connected by what was at the time the world's longest escalator. On display inside was the World of Tomorrow. Visitors rode in open cars than ran along a track, sort of like a kiddie train at a fair. The cars also swiveled back and forth, which was a great deal of fun for us, and we could position ourselves inward to see a modern city with all of the latest gadgets or we could point straight ahead to proceed onto the next attraction. It was an exhilarating ride for the times. Today, it would remind you of EPCOT Center, but a very low-quality, B-version, to be sure! Even today's It's a Small World ride at Disney is more hair-raising than this ride was. How far we've come! After taking in all the sights of the World's Fair, we proceeded on, across the nation, to San Francisco, where the San Francisco Exposition was being held on Yerba Buena Island, near Treasure Island, halfway across the three-mile-long, two-level Oakland Bay Bridge. There, we witnessed exhibitions dedicated to the 1849 Gold Rush and rode a few assorted rides.

Then, it was back to sea again. I believe on that last trip we were on board the *President Polk,* humorously nicknamed the "Slow Polk," as we headed for Pearl Harbor.

Chapter 8

War

Pearl Harbor

John and I were thrilled to be back abroad. When the ship was docking in Honolulu, my family stood on the outer deck and listened to a local band, Hilo Hattie, singing the "Hilo Hop" and "Aloha Oe." My parents watched in amusement while John and I played on the decks, waiting for the ship to be tied up. It was July 1939, and Hawaii was hot but still pleasant, thanks to the trade winds.

We stayed for just a couple of months at the nearby Edgewater Apartments on Waikiki Beach, which in the 1940s was just a row of single-story concrete cabanas. From where we stayed, we could clearly hear the "disappearing guns" from Fort DeRussy, and their loud cannon fire could be heard for miles around as they conducted their training exercises. Anyway, today close inspection of the bottom level of the Edgewater Reef Hotel reveals a row of garages that were the original Edgewater Apartments, where we stayed on arrival into Hawaii before moving to our house in Nuuanu Valley.

The only resorts that existed right on the beach back in 1941 were the Royal Hawaiian, the Moana, and the Halekulani, with perhaps some smaller apartments scattered about along the main drag. Hawaii was still an American territory, a very remote carryover possession of the Spanish-American War, and it was still almost twenty years away from achieving statehood. Very little existed there besides the locals and a fairly *un*-famous US Navy base that housed a handful of battleships in the Pacific Fleet. It also served as an occasional playground for rich and famous American celebrities, but when we lived there, there was absolutely nothing historic or outstanding about Pearl Harbor.

My parents bought a small three-bedroom house on Nuuanu Avenue (now the Pali Highway) situated near the Oahu Country Club. My brother and I were enrolled at Iolani Episcopal Day School, about a mile down the road from where we lived. We walked to school every day by ourselves, accompanied only by a few of the local kids. Sometime after World War II, the school moved near Waikiki and the Ala Wai Canal, where it remains today.

All kids in Hawaii ran around barefooted, and at Iolani, none of us had to wear shoes until the seventh grade. Most of the roads in the neighborhood were asphalt, and many of them had small, sharp gravel stones in their surface. This made a *haole* (a newcomer, pronounced *howlie*) like me suffer considerably until the feet toughened up.

Hawaii was a magical place to live. On the weekends, John and I took a bus downtown to King Street and then transferred over to a trolley bus to Waikiki Beach, all alone, and there were simply zero safety concerns for kids our age, or any age, who were traveling unaccompanied. We made plenty of new friends in our neighborhood, especially the Waterhouse brothers, who had an inground swimming pool and thick-trunked trees perfectly suited for long afternoons playing tree tag. Unfortunately, Wayne Waterhouse fell from one of the enormous trees and broke his arm on one fateful day, and that eliminated tree tag from our list of outside options from then on. Instead, we ventured over to the grassy foothills of the Pali and tried our hand at ti leaf sliding. Ti leaves were large enough to ride like sleds, and once school was out, we zoomed downhill at great clips on many hot afternoons.

My mother was a stickler for reading. When John and I came home from school each day, she would fix us each a PB&J for a snack and have us read a few pages from novels such as Lawrence Klingman's *His Majesty O'Keefe* before going out to play. We periodically checked books out from the beautiful Andrew Carnegie Public Library, and when we finished them, she would return us immediately to pick out a new one.

We often played touch football with the local kids at the nearby Queen Emma Park. There was always a mix of several different races of kids in our neighborhood, and in Honolulu, just like at Iolani, white kids were actually the minority. We went to school with kids from Japan, China, Hawaii, and all over the United States.

When I was old enough to have a job, and eleven years old seemed old enough, my brother and I caddied at the Oahu Country Club. The course was very hilly, and we received eighty-five cents to caddy for a full eighteen holes. We also carried *two* bags on Wednesday afternoons and Saturday mornings. I think the two golf bags weighed more than I did, but it certainly seemed to my brother and me that life couldn't be better than it was in those years. Still, as 1941 approached, we would often hear our parents talking quietly, whispering things like "Czechoslovakia has fallen" and "occupied France," although we weren't sure what those things meant. At twelve years old, who would?

On Sunday morning, December 7, 1941, at eight o'clock, the telephone rang. My father wasn't scheduled to be on duty until nine o'clock, but I jumped from my bed when I heard him yell into the phone, "Good Lord! I'll be right there!" He looked at us with terror in his eyes and said we were under attack by the Japanese and that they were dropping bombs on Pearl Harbor. With that, he raced outside and jumped into our second car, the "jalopy," and sped away. My brother and I got dressed and then ran through the neighborhood shouting, "We're under attack!!!"

Our neighbor Mr. Richter came out and shouted at us to stop spreading rumors, but then a second man came out of his house and shouted that it was true and that he'd heard it on the radio. As we all stood in the road, everyone somewhat in shock, neighbors slowly trickled out when they started hearing the commotion. We all looked up and could see the planes flying overhead above the Pali, the growl of their engines growing loud on approach and then fading away as they went by, heading past us and straight for Pearl Harbor, five miles away. To get a better view, my brother and I ran back home and climbed up onto our roof to watch, until our mother discovered us up there. She hurried us down and into the house and made us sit inside the doorways. She told us she learned that trick when she and my father lived in California and sometimes experienced earthquakes. "There's nothing to worry about," she said, "because when a house collapses, sometimes the door jambs will remain standing." But I knew she wasn't exactly sure about that, or if there was really anything she could do to protect us from five-hundred-pound bombs being dropped out of the bottoms of the planes above our heads. But what else could she do under the circumstances? I knew she was afraid even though she tried not to show it, and things got very scary for everyone that morning, very quickly.

Around midmorning, we heard a car pull over in front of our house. It was my father's friend Sergeant Franks and his wife and their young daughter. We invited them to stay with us until it was safe to return to Hickam Field, where the Army Air Corps was stationed. It seemed that the three of them were bombed out of their house and Sergeant Franks was trying desperately to find somewhere to place his family until the attack was over. When my mother asked him if he saw any old cars like my father's jalopy destroyed along the way during his evacuation, he replied, "Yes, there are many." It was not what she wanted to hear, but, again, my mother showed no emotion at this news. Sergeant Franks retrieved the military rifle he had lying down in the seat of his car and told us he needed to return to Hickam Field to help. The sight of his rifle really excited my brother and me, showing with certainty that all rational thought and common sense had left us both. But we couldn't possibly grasp what was happening. In the excitement of that morning, we could hardly sit still.

The day wore on at a snail's pace, with no news from my dad. Everything was quiet for most of the afternoon. After the initial plane-spotting in the road in front of our house that morning, we didn't see anything else flying overhead. From where we were, we couldn't smell or see anything coming from the harbor, but when night came, we saw the orange glow of fires burning over the far hills. Occasionally, explosions shook the air, and we heard the far-off pelting of machine-gun fire. We didn't know what was happening in the harbor, and we heard nothing from our father for several days, until my mother finally received word that he was alive but was on indefinite post at the submarine base.

We were told that the base was in total chaos and destruction reigned along Battleship Row. Information wasn't completely reliable, but we listened, stunned, as rumors spread about how many of our ships and aircraft had been destroyed, rumors that turned out to be totally true. Thankfully, our aircraft carriers were out to sea at the time of the attack, but our battleship fleet was severely damaged. We heard that the *Arizona* sank right where it was torpedoed and the *Oklahoma* capsized and completely inverted itself. We learned of the thousands of men who were trapped alive, tapping to be rescued, and of the frenzied rush to get to them. Before they were thought to have perished, rescue workers stayed up for days and days without rest, trying to save them.

On the morning he raced to his post, my father and the other submariners scrambled to get their subs out to sea as fast as possible, to guard the harbor in the event of another attack. The power was out at our house for several days after the attack, so it's unlikely that my mother heard President Roosevelt's radio address, telling us of the "date which will live in infamy." I will never forget feeling confused about having to go back to school when I knew wounded people had just been there, being cared for after the attack that changed the whole world forever.

My father finally came back home the day after Christmas, three weeks after the attack. He told us that his drive to the base on that morning of the seventh was harrowing, with bombs going off on both sides of him as he drove. When he arrived at his post and tried to open his car door, it was jammed, and he had to climb out of the other side. He discovered later that a piece of metal shrapnel from an explosion had hit his door about head high and nailed it shut from the outside. "It was a close call even getting there," he said.

We had our family's Christmas on December 26 that year. My father was so happy for us to be back together and safe, finally. After the attack, the islands were under martial law, which meant there was now a general in charge of all of Hawaii. Because I was a kid, I couldn't tell you precisely what was different about our day-to-day lives afterward, but I do remember my mother reliving for me that life in post-attack Hawaii was much tougher on everyone, and certainly not as safe and pleasant as before. My brother and I settled into the routine at Iolani while my father reported to work a bit earlier each day and stayed longer every night. We boys were told about war in simple terms when we asked questions, and there were certainly a few differences even I could pick up on as time passed. We had a blackout every night, which meant that we had to turn off any lights that could be seen from the outside, and cars could not use their headlights, just in case the Japanese had plans to come back. Everyone had a curfew, and anyone behaving in defiance of the laws risked being arrested. We spent the evenings listening to the president's radio addresses in the dark. I recall radio programs such as *The Green Hornet, Big Town, I Love a Mystery, Batman, Fred Allen,* and *Jack Benny.* My mother hurried with dinner and cleaned the kitchen before nightfall. Then she made sure she kept the house dark while John and I played quietly and my father stayed late at the base picking up the pieces and figuring out what America's role in World War II would ultimately be. Life for a kid like me went right on as usual, but I could certainly tell that my world changed after that fateful day. Everyone's did.

On a whim, John and I decided to start a newspaper for our neighborhood. We called it the *Weekly Raider,* and I was the primary writer/reporter and John the editor in chief. It mostly consisted of harmless rumors and neighborhood gossip. My father purloined paper from his office for us and bought us a used mimeograph machine. We reported on people's vacations, and once, when my brother's cat went missing, the headline read, "Porky the Cat of John Brady Missing." We charged two cents an issue and delivered them by throwing them from our bicycles into people's yards each week. When a delivery was late, my mother would actually get phone calls from neighbors wanting to know when it could be expected. In addition to our gossip column and the missing pets features, we also included stories of heroism and frequent editorials. One of our editorials somehow caught the eye of the general in charge of martial law, whereupon we were both invited to his office, where we got our pictures taken and put in the city newspaper. We also received a letter of commendation for outstanding accomplishments in literature! OK, OK, I'm kidding about that part, but we *did* get a letter of commendation, though I wouldn't exactly call the *Weekly Raider* outstanding literature.

Occasionally, men my father knew would stop by our house for a quick visit, have a bourbon and water, and talk shop. I remember meeting one such visitor, a naval officer in the Civil Engineering Corps, also stationed at Pearl Harbor at the time of the attack. He was one of the engineering duty officers involved in rescue and recovery efforts in the weeks after the bombing. My father also invited our next-door neighbor, a friend of his who also worked at the shipyard. As the three of them sat in our living room enjoying their drinks in the dark, one of our guests said to the other, "I think I recognize your voice." After a few questions back and forth, they realized they'd met before, on the bottom of the capsized USS *Oklahoma* during their long days and nights of rescue operations. Later, my father would quip that his guests had met *twice* and still hadn't clearly seen each other's faces.

Life continued on in a new normal way until November 1942, when we were finally evacuated from Hawaii as the war ramped up and my father went on deployment to be the executive officer of the USS *American Legion*. My mother, John, and I left Hawaii on a Navy transport, the USS *Henderson*, accompanied by a few destroyers, which served as an antisubmarine defense escort in the convoy system. We zig-zagged back and forth all the way to San Francisco, waiting every moment of every day for a Japanese torpedo to take out our ship. When we finally disembarked at San Francisco, we were shocked at how cold the weather was, since we were still in our shorts and aloha shirts. The Red Cross was there to greet us, and, believe it or not, we were treated like refugees!

We soon discovered that we'd actually been much better off back in Hawaii, because nothing back there was being rationed. In the islands, we had all the meat, sugar, coffee, and groceries we wanted, but here in the States, most creature comforts and the basic niceties of a regular household were all sacrificed for the war effort. As an example, to get home from San Francisco, we took a train to Chicago and then to New York, and on the morning after we left, while in the dining car, my mother asked for a refill of her coffee but she was told she was only permitted one cup. Welcome to our new life during wartime!

From New York City, we caught another train that took us to New London, Connecticut. Luckily, on that trip we met someone from Mystic who recognized my mother, and this nice man, Mr. Bendett, gave us a ride to my mother's great aunt's house. His son, Roddy Bendett, had been one of my best friends, and the Bendetts owned a clothing store in Mystic. Our family had known them for decades, and we knew that they were Jewish, but of course that didn't mean anything to me at the time. I reflect now that the unfolding war was very likely one of great sadness to them in a way I wasn't aware of when Mr. Bendett was kindly helping us make our way home.

My brother was shipped off to a military boarding school, called the Billard Academy, in New London to finish his first year of high school. This was right after Christmas in 1942. I finished out the eighth grade at the Mystic Academy, the public grammar school that all three of us, John and me and my mother, had attended. Since my Grandmother Colby was also living with us and since we had but one bathroom, my mother decided to buy us a small house on Library Street. It was a three-bedroom, one-bath, two-story house. In the kitchen, there was a gas stove and an icebox, which held one large block of ice that we replaced once a week when we drove to the ice house and picked another one up. You chipped chunks of ice off of the block with an ice pick when you needed ice for your drinks. (Of course, frozen food had not been invented yet, and ice cream was just a dream to have at home.) For heat, there was a coal furnace that supplied hot air through a floor grate downstairs, and each bedroom upstairs had a floor grate, which was just a hole in the floor, that admitted the warm air from below. You could open and remove the grates in each room and actually look down at the lower floor. Just add a partyline telephone, and that was what we called home.

Sometime around the middle of the next year, 1943, my father finally came home to the States to put a new attack transport into commission. Our whole family traveled to New York City for the ship's commissioning, and a few days later my father again left us and headed out on APA 146 (Attack Transport 146), the USS *Knox*, back to the Pacific via the Panama Canal. To conserve fuel, the ship was required to cruise at ten knots; however, my father was so anxious to get there that he proceeded ahead at maximum sustained speed. Upon arrival, the admiral reprimanded him, chafed by his fuel waste, but said, "Well, since you're here, I can use you in an upcoming mission." He could have been speaking of practically anything—Eniwetok, the Marshall Islands, Iwo Jima—who knows where my father went in those times. We do know that the *Knox* participated in a number of important landings, including the attack on Okinawa when the kamikazes were in full force.

Throughout World War II, the whole country was united. Many people took two jobs, especially in the factories that produced war materials. People who had family members in the service would often hang in a front window a small banner with a blue star in the middle. Should a family member die in combat, a gold star would replace the blue one. There was enhanced rationing for all citizens, and families still received food stamps and gas stamps from the ration board.

Sugar and coffee continued to be extremely scarce, and they definitely required stamps. Homes along the Atlantic coast had to keep their window shades drawn at night, to prevent German subs from having an illuminated background that would allow them to see the silhouettes of any American ships on patrol. Minute-by-minute news was not available to us. At the movie theaters, *Movie Tone News,* presented as previews for the featured films, allowed us to see what was happening on the warfront. Additionally, the daily newspapers had maps showing where the various front lines were. The times were mostly optimistic, and everyone was confident that the Allies would persevere, but my dad was gone from December 1942, when we evacuated Hawaii, until early 1946, after the war was finally over. For four whole years, we saw him only sporadically, something that must have been hard on my mother. I was in Washington, DC, in high school at Columbian Prep, when I heard the news that the United States had dropped the atomic bomb on Hiroshima.

Commander John Brady, with his wife, Elizabeth, and sons, Allen (*left,* age fourteen) and John (age fifteen) in Mystic, Connecticut, 1943.

Chapter 9

Academy Man

Service to Country

On August 15, 1945, the same day World War II ended in the Pacific and while my father was still away at war, I turned sixteen. You may remember it as VJ Day. I had heard an advertisement on the radio that guaranteed I could receive a student pilot's license for $100. My mother gave me the money for my birthday, and I hitchhiked to the airport in Salem, Connecticut, where I soloed in eight and a half hours, completing the first step of my lifelong goal to become a Navy pilot. As a student pilot, I could fly unaccompanied, but I wasn't allowed to carry passengers until I logged between thirty and forty additional hours of flight time and passed a written exam for the private pilot's license. I wanted so badly to show my mom what I was working on, but since she couldn't afford the money for all the additional flying time, we made a secret arrangement. I flew to another airport nearby, she met me there, and, being the sport that she was, she let me take her up for a ride anyway, without my pilot's license.

My next goal was to make it into the Naval Academy. In 1947, a candidate needed to pass an entrance exam and a physical and have a congressional appointment. Military officers like my dad were always moving around, and thus they were often unable to establish relationships with most members of Congress. So instead of receiving an appointment, as the son of a regular officer who was also a 1923 Academy graduate, I was eligible to take the entrance exam and compete with other candidates attempting to gain a *presidential* appointment. This was reserved for seventy-five specially chosen slots, awarded by the president of the United States, who at that time was Harry S. Truman. I was still technically a senior in high school, but in my wish to enter the Academy, and in lieu of a traditional graduation, I had been sent to Washington, DC, to finish up at Columbian Prep, which was unfairly called a "cram school." We went to school Monday through Friday and a half-day on Saturday. We lived at the school full-time, and after a full day of classes and a couple of hours of recreation and dinner, we had a three-hour monitored study period.

School let out after my final exams were over, and I went home to Boston, Massachusetts, where my father had just been stationed. Sometime in May 1947, I received a letter stating that I was ranked thirtieth out of seventy-five on the President's list and needed to report to the Naval Academy by June 5. I was sworn into the US Navy as a midshipman on June 11, 1947. The four years I spent at the Academy were not easy by any means, especially the first year, when I was a plebe. I thought at the time that it was about the lowest position in life that a person would ever want to endure. One day, however, I would discover one even lower.

All midshipmen at the Academy lived in one big building, Bancroft Hall. The hall is five stories high with no elevators. Plebes, or first-year students, were required to climb the stairs at double time and find their rooms using the longest route around, which was the outside perimeter. Naturally, my room was on the very top floor, which enabled me to get in great shape by the end of that year. While I was at the Academy, from 1947 to 1951, all the students took the same courses, the only exception being the foreign language, and I chose French because I had already taken two years of it in high school. Otherwise, it was basically the same for everyone: an engineering curriculum stressing marine and electrical engineering. Today, however, there are a number of different degree options offered, including aeronautical engineering and economics.

At the end of plebe year, my class boarded a cruiser and a battleship and we spent two to three months on a cruise to the Mediterranean. We rotated amongst the various ships' departments and did all the jobs that the seaman and the fireman usually did. We swabbed the decks, polished the brass, and cleaned the heads. The cruiser had teak decks, and under the supervision of a boatswain mate we also had to *holystone* the decks and complete other menial tasks. It seemed that even as second-year students we *still* had no relief from doing plebe work! After being abroad for over a month, we recrossed the Atlantic and proceeded to Guantanamo, Cuba, for gunnery training before returning to the Academy and heading out on our September leave.

After our second academic year, our summer training involved aviation. About two hundred of the midshipmen, about a quarter of my class, were flown out to several air stations. One of these was Lambert Field in St. Louis, where I met a young debutante named Sallie Busch. We met one night at the Officer's Club where her mother was throwing a party for the visiting midshipmen. My boys and I spent a great portion of that evening dancing the Jitterbug and having

In 1951, I was featured in *The Lucky Bag,* the Naval Academy yearbook.

Allen Colby Brady

NORFOLK, VIRGINIA

California claims him but he disclaims California . . . world traveler . . . Navy Junior . . . planes and women or vice-versa . . . Navy Tech from civilian life . . . dislikes Maryland weather . . . distrusts all profs . . . ambitious to be 1/c P.O. and not carry a sword . . . acquiring a southern drawl from Norfolk . . . golf . . . town painter . . . the Checker Club addict . . . Lisboa and Roma . . . ask Ace about his educated toe . . . "I'll set 'em up this time" . . . one for the road . . . "First of the night" . . . partial to blondes, brunettes, and redheads . . . weekends? . . . swell . . . Club Royale . . . anytime, baby . . . women and drink and music, although music isn't necessary . . . twenty years or bust.

a really big time. Sallie and her mother invited me and two of my buddies, Deac Chapman and Rich Fontaine, up to their magnificent mansion at Grant's Farm for dinner the next day, and the Busches again hosted us as we toured the family's world-famous Anheuser-Busch factory. They were great supporters of the Navy and were very hospitable while we were in town as their guests. I remember seeing Sallie's picture many years later on a magazine cover.

Our group left St. Louis for Chicago a couple of days later and attended the Railroad Fair there, then made a few more stops along the way before hitting

Pensacola, Florida, a place I'd never been before. I wish I could say I fell instantly in love with this area of the country, but, to be honest, I'm not sure I ever saw anything outside the gates of Naval Air Station Pensacola for the whole two weeks we were here—aside from the seedy dive bars we visited one night along Mobile Highway. We chuckled over our beers at how far we'd fallen since the evening at the Busch mansion just a few days prior! We didn't do very much flying while we were in Pensacola, either, which was certainly disappointing, and overall it was quite an unremarkable stopover. It's amusing now to think back, considering that I would ultimately return here to retire over thirty years later. Nevertheless, following our time in Northwest Florida, we spent a couple of weeks more out to sea on a carrier, then headed back to Annapolis on another September leave.

Life began to get much better for all midshipmen by the time we were second classmen (third academic year) and there were fewer people harassing us. The Naval Academy had great athletic facilities, which included a terrific golf course, so there were plenty of things to do besides party. That's one of the major differences I see between the service academies and the college campus culture of today. I'm not against having a good time, but I believe it has its time and place and should be a rather small part of your college experience. I certainly took my studies very seriously, and I would never have risked disciplinary action, nor would I have done anything to risk getting kicked out of the one college I'd worked so hard to be accepted into.

During the third summer, on my destroyer cruise we were treated as junior officers, we ate in the Officers' Mess, we stood watches normally assigned to officers, and even the ship's officers doubled up so we could live in their quarters. We were now first classmen, or seniors, and we were finally in charge. Naturally, the last year at the Academy was the best of them all. We went ashore and partied with the ship's officers, and I actually considered a career on a destroyer, but the allure of zooming through the skies was still my obsession. On June 1, 1951, the great day finally arrived when I received my diploma and my ensign bars. It was one of two times in my life when I felt most like a free man.

After graduation leave, I reported to the USS *Palau* (CVE-122), an escort carrier, at Norfolk, Virginia. I was the signal officer and the communications watch officer. Our only cruise after leaving the shipyard was to Guantanamo Bay for underway training and the ubiquitous Operational Readiness Inspection (ORI). When the riders from Guantanamo spread out through the ship, they monitored and graded our performance in the engine room operations, including flight operations day and night, gunnery, and combat damage control. After the ORI, we dropped in at Port-au-Prince, Haiti, for some R & R

1st Class—(4th Year's Work)   Academic Year 1950-51

Dept. / Term	Subject	Grade	References / Textbooks
Executive — First Term	Infantry / Naval Organization; Leadership	3.19	Landing Force Manual. U.S. Navy Regulations. Naval Leadership.
Executive — Second Term	Infantry / Military Justice	3.26	Landing Force Manual. Uniform Code of Military Justice.
Sea. & Nav. Summer Term	Practical Navigation on Cruise		Navigation & Nautical Astronomy, Dutton. Various Hydrographic Office Publication 214. Nautical Almanac. Hydrographic Office Publications.
	Practical Seamanship & Operations on Cruise (Weather)		Tactical Instructions. General Signal Book. Watch Officer's Guide. Fleet Tactical Publications.
	Practical Seamanship & Operations on Cruise (Drills)		Navy Department Bureau Manuals.
	Practical Seamanship on Cruise (Ship Maintenance & Administration)		Knight's Modern Seamanship. Navy Regulations.
	Practical Seamanship Drills		
First Term	NAVIGATION — Air Almanac, Great Circle Sailing, Radar Piloting, Loran, Moon Phases, Tides & Currents, Compass, Exact Azimuth Curve of Magnetic Azimuth, Maneuvering Board, Air Navigation, Polaris Navigation	3.10	Navigation & Nautical Astronomy, Dutton. American Air Almanac. Hydrographic Office Publications 214, 218, & 249. Tide & Current Tables, U.S. Coast & Geodetic Survey.
	Communications		General Communications (NavPers 10806).
	Practical Works in Navigation		
	Practical Instruction in Navigation		
	Seamanship & Operations Drills		
Second Term	SEAMANSHIP — Seamanship & Tactics, Tactics & Operations, Seamanship, Operations, & Combat Information, Combat Info	3.12	Knight's Modern Seamanship. Naval Tactics & Operations.
Ord. & Gun. Summer Term	General Ordnance Lecture / Lectures on Practice Cruise / Ordnance & Gunnery Drills on Cruise		Naval Ordnance & Gunnery (NavPers 16116B)
First Term	Fire Control Practical Instruction	3.35	Naval Ordnance & Gunnery (NavPers 16116B)
Second Term	Fire Control Practical Instruction / Fire Control Lecture	3.36	Naval Ordnance & Gunnery (NavPers 16116B)
Mar. Engr. Summer Term / First Term	Summer Drills on Practice Cruise / Combustion Engines	3.12	Watch Standing, Lectures and Drills. Internal Combustion Engines by Jennings & Obert. Combustion Engines Manual, by Dept. of M.E.
Second Term	Naval Construction & Damage Control	3.15	Fundamentals of Naval Construction & Damage Control by M.E. Dept.
Aviation — First Term	Flight Indoctrination & Supporting Lectures / Tactical Control of Aircraft	3.21	Include 6 hours flight. CNO Publication, classified.
Aviation — Second Term	Radiological Defense / Mission & Role of Naval Aviation / Special Aspects of Naval Aviation	3.02	Fundamentals of Radiological Defense, NavPers. Publication. Departmental Pamphlet.
Elec. Engr. — First Term	Electronics	3.25	Basic Course in Electronics, 2d ed, by E.E. Dept. Electronics Laboratory Manual, 1949 ed, by E.E. Dept. (Textbooks used both terms)
Elec. Engr. — Second Term	Electronics	3.39	
Engl., Hist. & Gov't — First Term	Naval History and Term Paper / Special Lectures	3.17	Stevens & Westcott's A History of Sea Power. American Sea Power Since 1775, Edited by Westcott. Potter's Writing the Term Paper. Russell's Fundamentals of Naval Strategy. Lectures in Field of Foreign Affairs by Outstanding Lecturers.
Engl., Hist. & Gov't — Second Term	European Literature and Term Paper	3.24	Cervantes' Don Quixote. Goethe's Faust. Balzac's Old Goriot. Ibsen's Plays. Tolstoy's Anna Karenina. Potter's Writing the Term Paper.
Phys. Trng. — First Term	Golf, Squash, Badminton, Posture and Calisthenics		
Phys. Trng. — Second Term	Recreational Athletic Administration and Tennis		

All marks appearing in column (3) on this form are term marks. If not reported in column (3) separate marks are not assigned for laboratory and practical work, etc., shown in columns (8) and (10) but the quality of work done is reflected in the term mark assigned for regular class work therein in the same or subsequent terms.

Naval Academy transcript, 1951.

51

Issued to the subject student
at his request for his records.

UNITED STATES NAVAL ACADEMY

Annapolis, Maryland   1 3 SEP 1982

(Date)

TRANSCRIPT OF SCHOLASTIC RECORD OF_____ Alan Colby BRADY

(Name in full)

ADMITTED AS MIDSHIPMAN ON___11 June 1947___

(Date)

Graduated 1 June 1951 and commissioned an Ensign in the

(Date and cause of separation)

U. S. Navy. He was awarded the degree of Bachelor of
Science by the   ENTRANCE RECORD Naval Academy.

Method by which qualified:

(X) (a) Regular entrance examination.
( ) (b) Secondary school certificate and substantiating exams. in Mathematics and English.
( ) (c) Secondary school and college certificates without mental examinations.

SECONDARY SCHOOL CERTIFICATE (Includes mention of only those subjects for which credit was allowed by the U. S. Naval Academy)	Unit Value	REGULAR ENTRANCE EXAMINATION TAKEN
Mathematics (Algebra to Quadratics)	1	SUBJECTS · · · MARKS
Mathematics (Algebra, Quadratics & beyond)	1	U. S. History · 3.4
Mathematics (Plane Geometry)	1½	English · 3.3
English (Grammar & Composition)	1½	Algebra · 3.3
English (Literature)	1	Physics · 3.5
Physics		Pl. Geom. & Pl. Trig. · 3.3
		Chemistry · 3.9

NOTE: PASSING 2.50

COLLEGE CERTIFICATE
(Includes mention of only those subjects for which
entrance credit was allowed by the U. S. Naval
Academy)

Semester Hours

NOTE: For the completed course at the
Naval Academy, Mr. Brady stood
No. 339 in a class of 725 members.

Certifying Secondary School and College:_____

ATHLETIC RECORD AT U. S. NAVAL ACADEMY
Awarded: Received awards in Soccer
(SEAL) and Fencing

Robert W. Clark
Assistant Registrar

†† Marks reported in column (3) are the average of the marks for the one or more subjects comprising the work of the term in the department indicated.
* Actually at class. One period of approximately 50 minutes is considered an hour.
(a) It will be noted that this column represents total credits in semester hours earned not only during the academic years but also for the summer courses at the Naval Academy, as well as the time spent on the practice cruises.

All students at the Naval Academy pursue the same course of instruction which is along engineering lines leading to a Bachelor of Science degree upon graduation, and is intended to qualify the students for service in the U. S. Navy. In the Department of Foreign Languages, however, the students do have the choice of studying one of the five languages indicated.

SCALE OF MARKS

Distinction_____4.00 — 3.40
With Credit_____3.39 — 3.00
Passing_____2.99 — 2.50
Failing_____2.49 — 0

U. S. Naval Academy Press—12-13-49—500

Me as a young aviator at Naval Air Station Pensacola, 1952.

then returned to Norfolk to resume underway training. I was able to qualify as an officer of the deck, a direct representative of the captain, underway *and* in port, which was good for my career.

Finally, I received my orders to return to Pensacola in May 1952, to report for flight training. This would undoubtedly be the best tour I would have in my entire naval career and is certainly a big reason why I came back here to retire. We had five weeks of preflight at Naval Air Station (NAS) Pensacola, three months at Whiting Field in Milton, Florida, leading to soloing, more flying to gain experience, and, finally, acrobatics. The acrobatics final check ride was my third flight on one particularly hot and humid day. I met the assigned instructor, then picked up my parachute and received a plane assignment. Let's say it was plane "number 102." I preflighted the plane and climbed into the front seat. As I was taxiing out, the instructor pilot asked me what aircraft I was assigned to, and I replied "number 102." He paused, then asked me what plane I was in. I looked out at the number on the wing and it was not "102." I almost ran myself off the taxiway. He laughed and said he watched me get into the wrong plane and so he knew I'd screwed up, but thankfully he was a cool guy and had already switched me over to my current plane. To my relief, I passed the check, but it definitely taught me a lesson about paying attention to details.

Then onto Corry Field, now called Corry Station, for instrument training and night flying. Night flying was a new experience. We boarded about twenty pilot trainers (or SNJs, the North American T6 *Texan*) then taxied out in order, with the first group of ten taking off in a line, climbing to about a thousand feet, and circling the air station field. Then, the second group of ten took off, with the first plane in that group going straight ahead and the other nine following behind before turning downwind. They were each instructed to shoot five landings and then transition into the flight pattern. As our group (the second, of which I was supposed to be the second plane) climbed to a thousand feet, one by one the upper group started descending into the pattern. It was a great master plan, and I thought I was crystal clear on the instructions, but I ran into a problem. Like I said, I was supposed to be the second to take off in the second group. Unbeknownst to me, number one didn't show up. Apparently, his aircraft didn't crank and he never even took off. I never knew this. So when I took off, I assumed I was number two, but I wasn't. I was number one, and everyone was following *my* lead! If you are confused, rest assured; so was I.

I kept looking for the plane ahead of me, the one I needed to be following, but of course there wasn't one. I flew straight on ahead, and when I reached the Gulf of Mexico I decided to turn and head back. When I made my turn, I could see the other eight planes following right behind me. I believe they would have followed me all the way to Key West like a row of ducklings. Naturally, the officers in charge back at the field said they'd never seen anything like it, and after my flight departed, all grew quiet as we disappeared over the horizon. The controllers didn't know what to do, so they just waited until they finally saw our little group coming home to roost. Afterward, I thought my career was over. Fortunately, the officer in charge had a sense of humor and thought it was hilarious. He said it would make a great story at a bar one night, some comic relief for everyone when we all needed a break from the normal mundane routine. Then, it was on to Saufley Field, also in Pensacola, for formation flying and air-to-air gunnery.

On to Barron Field in Foley, Alabama, for carrier qualifications, or boat quals. These were broken up into two phases: field carrier landing practice followed by six arrested carrier landings aboard the USS *Monterrey,* our training carrier. All of these training phases were flown in an SNJ trainer known as the *Yellow Peril*. Next, it was all-weather flight school at NAS Corpus Christi, Texas. There, I would ultimately be assigned to fly the AD aircraft (for *Attack Douglas*, known today as an A-1), or what we call the *Douglas Skyraider*. However, in the first five weeks of advanced training, we had two student aviators and one instructor pilot, and we flew the SNB-1 *Kansan* Twin Beechcraft. The SNB came equipped with several fuel tanks, with a pilot-operated fuel selector switch. If one of our tanks were to run dry, the engine would quit and we could receive a poor grade on that skill test, so together the other student there with me, Al Alman, and I came up with a solution that protected both of us. Once the gauge showed less than .2 percent in the tank, the guy in the back, who was keeping an eye on this, tapped the guy up front on the elbow with his foot to let him know, and he would switch the tank over. It was a great plan, and Al and I never came up short. At the conclusion of this phase, we finally had our instrument cards but still did not have our wings. This was unusual, because most pilots typically went to all-weather flight *after* receiving their wings. We were the first class to go through all-weather flight in the Beechcraft *before* we went on to Cabaniss Field.

Finally came the advanced phase of my flight training in my first fleet aircraft at NAS Cabaniss in Corpus Christi. The almighty, all-powerful A-1 *Skyraider* was my first single-piloted, one-cockpit aircraft, and there was no instructor! So after learning how to start the damn thing, which was not easy to do without it back-firing, I simply cranked up the bird and drove it almost at full power around the ramp to learn how to control it before taking to the skies. Now, the *Skyraider* is a big airplane. It has a 3000 hp radial engine, a four-blade propeller with a twelve-foot, six-inch diameter, and an impressive eight-thousand-pound ordnance load, the same as a World War II B-17 bomber. When I became airborne, it was like soaring with angels, but to be honest, in the beginning all I could think about was how in the world I was going to get the thing back on the ground. Actually, as it turns out, the AD was pretty easy to fly and land, although I still admit that it was a little nerve-racking those first few times.

On my last training flight, I had my first in-flight emergency. Our instructor had five of us in five planes to keep up with, so it got little chaotic up there. In this particular instance, we were making overhead dives while firing at a *towed sleeve,* a pennant-shaped cloth target that was towed behind a separate plane and used for machine-gun practice. When I pulled out, my propeller over-sped and I lost control of its speed. I decreased my airspeed by flying with the nose of the aircraft pitched up as high as possible, almost at stall speed, then flew back to the field and landed without further incident. Anyway, after all this training

United States Navy
Naval Air Training Command

Know all men by these presents that

Allen Colby BRADY

has completed the prescribed course of training and having met successfully the requirements of the course has been designated a

Naval Aviator

In Witness Whereof, this certificate has been signed on this 10th *day of* June 1953 *, and the Seal of the Naval Air Training Command hereunto affixed*

_____
Rear Admiral, United States Navy
Chief of Naval Air Advanced Training

Flight School Certificate, 1953.

Rice Hope Plantation, Moncks Corner, South Carolina, 1953.

was done, I was designated as a naval aviator, and I received my wings on June 10, 1953, *without* carrier qualifying in the AD *Skyraider*. This was because the Korean War was ongoing and the Navy was short of necessary carrier-suitable AD aircraft, so Korea was where I thought I was headed next.

After I got my wings in Corpus Christi, I took a couple of weeks' leave to go to South Carolina to visit my parents. My dad was retired by that time, having left the Navy as a rear admiral after thirty years. He and my mother had moved to Rice Hope Plantation near the town of Moncks Corner. They'd purchased Rice Hope the previous year and discovered they'd taken on a humongous job of maintaining a large home and many acres of land on the Santee Cooper River.

Part of my short time at home on leave was spent helping them with the maintenance on this big old house. Wanting me to have at least a little downtime before leaving South Carolina, my parents arranged for me to be invited to Folly Beach as a guest in the beach home of some friends of theirs, sort of like a small vacation before I left for Korea. While staying at Folly Beach, I met a very pretty young lady named Louise Johnson, who lived in the area. Louise was nineteen years old when we met, and she and I spent our brief time together swimming and hanging out at the beach. I was on leave for a little over a week, so I was only able to stay at the beach just a few days before I had to go on to California to get to my new squadron. Fortunately, Louise and I continued to correspond.

Louise Johnson, age nineteen, 1953.   Ensign Allen C. Brady, 1951.

We got to know each other by writing letters, the only thing you could really do with any regularity to stay in touch with someone back then. Our affection for one another grew slowly into something more serious, and I received quite a bit of ribbing from my buddies out in California who saw it unfolding.

Ultimately, I proposed to her, again by letter, and, thankfully, she said yes. When we married in December 1953, we had not seen each other even once since we met at Folly Beach that summer. We exchanged vows in a small church in Pinopolis, South Carolina, and as was the custom there, all the men went into the kitchen during the reception and drank quite a bit of straight whisky, although I tried to measure myself. Then Louise and I headed to Columbia, South Carolina, in a borrowed car before flying to New Orleans for our honeymoon, and soon after, I took her to our new home out in Alameda, California.

A few months before Louise and I married, while she was still on the East Coast and I was on the West Coast, my squadron was returning from Korea, and that war was winding down, ultimately ending in August 1953. Unfortunately, I did not get to participate in liberating South Korea. While in Alameda, California, I was a lieutenant junior grade assigned to Attack Squadron 95 (VA-95). Many of the older pilots in that squadron were combat veterans from World War II. We called them "retreads"; they were recalled to duty to participate in the Korean War. In those days, when a squadron returned from a deployment, some pilots left to go to other assignments and then new pilots, like me, would join the squadron. In general, it took about a year to go through a complete squadron training cycle, which included familiarization flights; navigation, deployments to Fallon, Nevada, for gunnery and bombing; and, finally, carrier qualifications, both day and night. This needed be completed prior to a deployment. So in my case, all this was done rather quickly, and soon I was ready to get back to the fleet.

Part 3

Douglas AD1 *Skyraider*, 1954. (US Navy Archives)

Chapter 10

Boring Holes in the Sky

Jet Puke

When deployment time arrived, our air group was to fly across the country to Naval Air Station (NAS) Norfolk, then board the aircraft carrier USS *Hornet*. While flying off the *Hornet* in the *Skyraider*, I made one of those dumb decisions that makes us wonder to ourselves how we survive over the years. I was scheduled to fly with a group of four or five guys from our squadron as an aggressor aircraft trying to shoot down other friendly planes. I was supposed to dive down, loop around, and have a great big time while the friendlies took a defensive posture, using a World War II tactic called the Thach Weave, named after the naval aviator who developed it. Now for the dumb part. Before I launched from the ship, I realized my radio transmitter was down, yet my receiver was still operational. I should've downed the aircraft right then and missed the flight exercise, but no, I really wanted to go. It was a nice day with just a bit of haze, perfect for flying, so adrenaline prevailed. On one of my passes, as I pulled up the engine just quit. It got very quiet, and, of course, since my transmitter was dead, I was unable to call anyone. I slowly descended toward the ocean about ten thousand feet below and headed back toward the flight, gliding like a paper airplane. When the flight leader didn't hear from me, one of the other planes pulled alongside, and I indicated to him with hand signals that I had no transmitter and was heading ashore. Then, as my plane descended, my engine began to sputter a little, and a hunch told me I had carburetor icing. Sure enough, as we proceeded toward home, the engine continued to gain momentum and by the time we arrived back at NAS Norfolk, I had full power again. The ship radioed for me to go get the aircraft checked and return to the boat the next day. Whew!

After a few weeks of operations in the Norfolk area, the ship got under way for the Philippine Islands via Naples, Italy, the Suez Canal to Columbo, Ceylon (where I again visited the Galle Face Hotel), Singapore, and finally to Manila Bay at Sangley Point. We slept ashore on a floating bunkhouse, which was actually air-conditioned. Heaven!

We flew our aircraft ashore at Sangley so we could do some training flights while the ship was moored. To the best of my recollection, there were three carriers in Manila, only two of which I remember: the *Philippine Sea* and the *Hornet*. On July 23, 1954, two Chinese LA-11 prop fighters from Hainan Island shot down a Cathay Pacific *Skymaster* civilian airliner in international waters. On that day, Clark Air Force Base in Manila received a distress call, and a US Air Force SA-16 seaplane was dispatched to the scene to search for survivors. Britain's Royal Air Force in Hong Kong also launched two *Havilland* fighters plus a *Sunderland* sea plane. On arrival, the *Sunderland* was unable to land due to rough seas, but the SA-16 arrived, landed in the lee behind a small offshore island, then taxied to the scene and picked up all of the survivors and flew them to Hong Kong. In all, ten of the nineteen passengers and crew survived and made it to Hong Kong safely. Meanwhile, the carriers *Philippine Sea* (CV-47) and *Hornet* (CV-12) were emergency sortied to the scene. Navy officials monitoring the situation decided that both carriers would alternate launches, with the *Philippine Sea* going first, followed by the *Hornet,* and I was in this second group. On July 26, the first sortie from the *Philippine Sea* arrived on scene and was suddenly jumped by two more Chinese LA-11s. A dogfight ensued, and the ADs shot both of them down, with no observed survivors. Paybacks are hell, aren't they? The next sortie, of which I was a participant, flew in the area for several days afterward, but we were unable to entice any more LA-11s to reengage us. Early on, the Chinese claimed that they thought the civilian airliner was a military plane and later, when their admission into the United Nations was in jeopardy, apologized for the incident. They also assured everyone that the pilots responsible for downing the *Skymaster* were properly executed for their role in the event. Truth be known, it's unlikely that a pilot of any nation would go rogue and shoot down a passenger airliner without orders to do so, orders certainly coming from someone way up the chain of command. So China's record of events was very likely a big lie. In any case, I think those involved learned their lesson.

During the remainder of that cruise, we visited Hong Kong; the Philippines; and Yokosuka, Japan, before heading home to the States. On one of our stops, we ferried to the island of Macao, then a Portuguese colony, and a handful of us went into a local bar and enjoyed a drink with Clark Gable. A day or two later, a typhoon delayed our departure, so rather than make our scheduled stop in Hawaii, and since we were in such a hurry to get home, we were authorized to

The USS *Hornet* with F9F-6 *Cougar*, 1954.

"go great circle" back to San Francisco to meet our scheduled arrival date. (A "great circle" is the largest circle that can be drawn on a sphere—in this instance, a globe—and includes the equator and all longitudinal lines. The shortest distance between any two places on earth would be the part of the great circle that passes through them.)

Once we were back home in Alameda, half the crew was to go on leave for two weeks and the other half was to stay on duty. This kind of arrangement was normally made after a long deployment, and once all those who went on leave returned, the other half got to go home for a little rest and some time with their families. A few months after arriving back home, my squadron-mate and Naval Academy classmate Dick Stanley and I were interviewed by the prospective commanding officer of Attack Squadron 216 at Moffett Field at the southern end of San Francisco Bay. Cdr. Frank Ault was commissioning a new squadron and needed to staff all of the officers and enlisted men. Dick and I accepted the offer, and both of us moved to Sunnyvale. This new job turned out to be an administrative nightmare. All new squadron orders had to be written, and all the flight and maintenance manuals with all kinds of new and different changes—all shipped separately from one another—had to be integrated and made current. It was mind-numbing paperwork, and as I was the new squadron administration officer, that was *my* task. There was a long list of reports that needed to be sent, some monthly, some quarterly, and others annually. The list of things we had to do was impossibly long, so with Commander Ault's permission, I only filled the few report requests that seemed relevant or urgent and then waited until I received a message requesting others. Sure enough, we only received about half the requests for overdue reports that we would have filled otherwise, and thus, we completely eliminated about half of all the paperwork we were supposed to have sent. Dick and I were ahead of our time with our own early version of the Government Paperwork Reduction Act.

One new aspect of our squadron, the VA-216 Black Diamonds, was that we were to be certified to carry nuclear weapons, which was fascinating for the pilots of that generation, like me. After our administrative inspection, I again changed jobs, per an agreement with Commander Ault, and I became the squadron's ordnance and special weapons officer. I had to attend a school for "nukes" and had to train to deliver weapons in an entirely different manner than what I was used to as a *Skyraider* pilot. These new tactics were to provide safe separation of the bombs from the plane before they detonated. Obviously, the bang from a detonated nuke is so big that you need to be at least one or two miles away, at a minimum.

Commander Ault was a hard-charger, and I flew more hours under his command than any other squadron I'd served with up to that point or since. I requested permission from him to participate in advanced level air-to-ground bomb and rocket training exercises at the now decommissioned Fleet Air Gunnery Unit at NAAS El Centro, the same location where the Blue Angels train. You may have seen the unit's fighter pilot counterpart training unit portrayed in the movie *Top Gun,* and I'll mention here that I was never a fan of that movie, knowing that if a pilot were to pull the kinds of flybys and other stunts that Tom Cruise did, he'd find himself "in hack" (grounded) and most definitely on the commanding officer's shit list. Anyway, after completing my training cycle, I was deployed aboard the carrier USS *Yorktown* to the Far East with a stop in Hawaii for the ubiquitous Operational Readiness Inspection.

Although this cruise appeared relatively calm at the onset, once again trouble loomed on the horizon in Asia. The skirmish I soon found myself in became known as the First Taiwan Strait Crisis, and this faceoff took place between September 1954 and April 1955. It started out as an artillery shelling contest between the People's Republic of China (or Communist China, i.e., *the bad guys*) and Taiwan (Formosa), which was part of the Republic of China, recognized as the rightful government of China (also known as the Republic of China, i.e., *the good guys*). After World War II, Communist China drove the

Aboard the USS *Yorktown:* Ensign Bob Valentine, Lieutenant "Willy" Wilson, uniden-tified Navyman, and Lieutenant Junior Grade Allen Brady.

Republic of China off mainland China so Republic forces evacuated to Taiwan with the assistance of the US Navy. The Republic of China continued to occupy the Quemoy/Kinmen and Matsu Islands off the coast of China as a first line of defense, because it wanted to use the islands as a stepping-stone to recapture the mainland, which was totally unrealistic unless the United States commit-ted to another unwinnable war *without* the use of nuclear weapons. However, during this period, the Republic of China and the United States were concerned that Communist China would try to finish off the Republic by bombing and invading Taiwan, so since we were on station in the Formosa Strait anyway, and since Congress had already authorized President Eisenhower (through the Formosa Resolution, January 29, 1955) to use US forces to defend the Republic of China and its possessions in the Formosa Strait, we spent part of the cruise patrolling the area. Apparently, due to the United States' known possession of nuclear weapons, Communist China, understandably, backed down. Whether it was because of the likelihood of being wiped from the face of the earth or was because *yours truly* was on patrol, the rest of the story is known. Today, Taiwan remains a separate, independent entity, in spite of talks between the Republic of China and Communist China about official reunification. In fact, in late 2016, newly elected President Donald Trump spoke on the phone with Tsai Ing-wen, the President of Taiwan, in a congratulatory phone call following his election, and the American media and Communist China both had a fit about this, stating that Trump was communicating with a country that wasn't even recognized as the *real* China. Furthermore, it doesn't seem that Hong Kong would be in any arrangement of bliss either if the Republic of China's administration decided to reunify. There has been a great deal written about the relationship between Taiwan and the People's Republic of China and many other of the world's countries. The number of countries recognizing the Republic of China is constantly changing and I still keep an eye on the situation, remembering that I was there when it was pretty stirred up.

Although I am proud of my time in the AD *Skyraider,* and that time totals about sixteen hundred flight hours, I must confess that I had a desire to try out those new-fangled jets they were developing. In the 1950s, commanding officers had much more authority and discretion with regard to the use of their squadron's assets. That would later change, of course, and probably for the good, but back then if you had a good relationship with your squadron commander, you had some pretty generous perks. While at Sangley Point, I asked the night fighter operations officer, a very amiable and laid-back individual (thankfully), if it would be possible for me to check out the F2H-3 *Banshee* they were flying. He got an OK from his commanding officer, whereupon I simply had to study the aircraft manual, take a written test, and pass a blindfolded cockpit check. Of course, the commanding officer's discretion only applied to a flight from a runway and not a carrier, but still, the next time we were back at Sangley, I was more than ready to go. They assigned another pilot to fly after me in a chase plane, and we manned the runway.

It was incredibly different flying jets, and my learning curve was tremendous. For example, in the AD you could not go to full power while holding the brakes, because the aircraft would nose up (that is, the nose of the plane is up). Not so with a tricycle landing-gear jet. Moreover, in the AD, to take off you went up to about 50 percent power, then released the brakes to go to full power. In the *Banshee,* I released the brakes, added full power, and then the aircraft began to *creep* down the runway. Jet engines do not spool up—spin fast enough to create boost—very quickly, which is why when you are coming aboard the carrier you want to keep the power way up, generally over 80 percent, especially if you missed your landing. If the power was low and you were late in your approach and needed to add a lot of power quickly, you probably wouldn't make it. There were *so* many major aerodynamic/engine performance differences between props and jets, especially older jets, and looking back it still fascinates

Me with my son, Richard, February 1956.

me. I feel very lucky to get to say I was there during that historic transition and I learned how to fly both.

Off I went in the *Banshee!* When I eventually sped up and got airborne, I raised the gear, brought up the flaps, and wondered what else to do. *Nothing*, apparently, just keep going at 100 percent. In an AD, you had to pull back the throttle, reduce the prop speed, worry about cowl flaps, fuel mixture control, oil cooler doors, et cetera, but in a jet, you just pushed the go knob, pulled up the gear and flaps, and you were done until you reached altitude! I was able to get another flight logged in the *Banshee* while we were temporarily shore-based at Atsugi, Japan, and after returning to Moffett Field six months later, I was also able to squeeze in another three flights as well. While I was there, a classmate of mine was instructing at the jet instrument school, and with his commanding officer's permission, he gave me a short course of five flights in the TV-2 (T-33) *Shooting Star* to cover jet instrument penetrations and approaches. You can be sure that by the end of all this, I considered myself a jet puke.

By November 1956, my tour in VA-216 was over and I moved my family, which included my wife and my new son, Richard, who was born in February that year, to Albuquerque, New Mexico, to begin my tour at the Naval Air Special Weapons Facility on Kirkland Air Force Base.

Chapter 11

Operation Hardtack

Albuquerque to Eniwetok

The Naval Air Special Weapons Facility was later renamed the Naval Weapons Evaluation Facility; it seems the military can't stand to keep the names of commands the same for very long. Anyway, this was a great tour! I was able to fly many different aircraft, such as the AD F2H (small *Banshee*), TV-2 (T-33, *Shooting Star*), F7U-3 (*Cutlass*), A4D (*Skyhawk*), FJ4 (*Fury*), F9F-8T (*Cougar*), and a few others too minor to list. My father and mother visited us in Albuquerque not long after we settled in, and with my commanding officer's permission, I was able to take my dad up in the T-33. He got a real charge out of that flight, and it made me so happy to be able to show him how to fly a jet. I think his favorite part of the experience was when I taught him how to roll the aircraft. Since there were still no jet airliners operating at the time, he'd only flown in a plane just a few times in his whole life. As he was a career submariner, it was certainly a remarkable moment for me to be able to show him the world from the cockpit of a jet at thirty thousand feet as opposed to seeing it from underwater.

As you will recall, and as the whole world will forever remember, the use of nuclear weapons started with the *Manhattan Project* during World War II, and global warfare would never be the same. After the test-firing of the first nuclear detonation at Alamogordo, followed by the back-to-back drops over Hiroshima and Nagasaki, nukes had certainly arrived to the party. Development of and research on nuclear weapons systems involved production facilities at Oak Ridge, Tennessee, for uranium enrichment; Hanford, Washington, for plutonium production; and the Los Alamos Laboratory at Los Alamos, New Mexico, for weapons design. As nuclear-weapon project pilots were on the cusp of marrying nuclear weapons to tactical aircraft, lucky guys like me were asked to assist the Field Command of the Armed Forces Special Weapons Project at

Sandia Base in Albuquerque. Additionally, the Cold War continued to simmer between the United States and the Soviet Union, and both nations were also rapidly developing the technology for nuclear weapons. The arms race was on. As a result of all these factors, the Air Force Special Weapons Project headquarters in Washington, DC, quickly began to grow, like all good US government agencies do. That facility was tasked with developing newer, bigger, and more efficient weapons, and the research gathered from the development of these nukes came as a result of testing cleaner, less radioactive bombs both in Nevada and out in the Pacific Ocean.

In 1957, I was reassigned as a project pilot in the Weapons Effects Department at the Naval Air Special Weapons Facility. When I reported for duty, I assisted the Field Command by dropping inert bombs, including parachute-retarded bombs. I dropped these several times over established bombing ranges for approximately six to eight months, and the information that we collected was used to drive the research and development of future bomb construction, especially with regard to impact and trajectory. At one time, an abandoned airport in Texas was leased so we could make high-speed, low-altitude drops and avoid having the bombs skip down the runway and end up way beyond the target.

Testing real nuclear materials was a bit more complicated, though. Therefore, the US government decided to continue with its test detonations way out in the Western Pacific, in remote locations like the Marshall Islands, places like Bikini Atoll, a crescent-shaped group of coral islands literally out in the middle of nowhere. I was involved in Operation Hardtack, conducted at Eniwetok Atoll, another island group, sitting at a whopping 2,696 miles north-northeast of Australia. It was understood that these test detonations were strictly experimental, and these blasts were repeatedly adjusted to make America's nuclear bombs *cleaner*. Ideally, they would produce less radiation—the damage created by the bombs dropped on Hiroshima and Nagasaki was utterly devastating, and there was nothing left of those places afterward but a smoldering nothingness where big, bustling cities once stood. The casualties numbered in the hundreds of thousands in their aftermath, and, sadly, they were all civilians. My understanding was that, while it was well known that nuclear bombs give off big bangs regardless, one of the primary goals of the testing projects was to create more efficient bombs, causing minimal levels of radiation exposure.

For decades, the US government had been conducting its nuclear testing in places like Bikini and Eniwetok, where bomb yield was not as big of a problem, and the plan was to modify two early models of the *Douglas* A4D *Skyhawk* and two North American FJ-4 B *Furys* to make them capable of collecting and

Me in the cockpit at Eniwetok, 1958.

recording data from the test blasts. That's where I came in. When the project pilots and other staff deployed to the Eniwetok Proving Grounds in February 1958, we had plans to stay for two to three months, depending on the results we achieved.

The shot schedule revealed that in my time on Eniwetok, I would get to participate in approximately six detonations. The pilots in our unit were given an estimated, or expected, yield and a positioning, or precautionary, yield for each detonation. The degree of difference between the two gave us an idea of the degree of uncertainty of the yield, and we then decided whether we wanted to participate in that detonation or not. One particular scheduled shot had quite close expected and positioning yields. The device they were testing was a service weapon whose yield was slightly increased, which certainly gave us a boost in confidence. The officer in charge of the project pilots contacted the Navy Bureau of Aeronautics and requested a waiver of the current thermal and over-pressure limitations, which enabled us to position our aircraft closer to the bomb when it went off. This request was approved, we went with the new limits, and our bomb detonated exactly the way we wanted it to. The bombs detonated at Eniwetok were

Douglas A4
(A4D) *Skyhawk,*
1958.

not strapped to our airplanes and dropped as previously described; they were placed on barges out in the lagoon, and we flew over the top of them, clearing the danger zone just seconds before they were detonated, trying to deliberately sustain a little damage to the airplanes. The barge, positioned between ten and twenty miles from our base, was very large and was made of steel. It was the kind you might see plying up and down a river in the United States. I asked one of the engineers what happened to the barge during the detonation, and he replied, "It completely vaporized."

Douglas Aircraft Corporation, headquartered at LAX in El Segundo, California, modified the A4D. The planes were tested for over-pressure limits by taping shut all of the potential air leaks in the fuselage and then sucking most of the air out, creating a vacuum inside. During the test you could see all of the ribs and stringers outlined on the fuselage. I believe they were tested to 10 psi, and since we were limited to 3 psi, we were not too worried. Strain-gauge thermocouples and heat-absorbing strips were added to the fuselage as well, as were numerous other scientific instruments, things like cameras and microphones for recording the detonations. Also, a three-hundred-gallon modified external fuel tank was carried on the aircraft centerline, which was also crammed with the latest state-of-the-art scientific equipment.

We received our specific project research goals and limitations from the Bureau of Aeronautics, now known as the Naval Air Systems Command. They determined the limits of over-pressure, skin temperature rise, and the amount and type of radiation we could absorb before the levels of radioactivity we were exposed to proved dangerous. Good thing, because we certainly didn't want to come home neutered! Once all of these modifications were complete, the planes were sent to Eniwetok in the hold of a large freighter, and we followed behind via the Military Airlift Command out of Sacramento.

We arrived at Eniwetok in the middle of the night and were issued some army shirts and shorts and film badges to record our accumulated radiation while in the test area. We were also given liquor cards, enabling us to buy some duty- and tax-free libations. We wondered if that might be for our wake, should we not make it back alive! I'm only joking. Our living quarters in Eniwetok were metal Butler buildings, housing two to a room and equipped with hot lockers (wooden lockers with lightbulbs inside, which stayed on constantly to keep the inside of the locker hot and dry) to stow our clothes. Panels in the upper walls of the building opened outward to give ventilation, since there was no air-conditioning. The bunks were over-and-under style. We had communal showers, but alas! no swimming pool. We had a small club for drinking and playing pool and shuffleboard, and we had an outdoor theater that showed movies after dark, even though it was guaranteed to rain on you every single night. There were pet dogs on the island, but all of them were male so that there were never any puppies born. The dogs also wore film badges around their necks to make sure they weren't turning radioactive either. On our days off, we sometimes walked from island to island and looked for shells. We had to be careful, though, because tidal currents around the Marshall Islands were swift and dangerous, and the rapid rise and fall of the tides meant that hiking paths were only accessible at certain times.

There was a B-52 bomber that also participated in the nuke project at Eniwetok. I heard a rumor that when it left Hawaii headed our way, its pilot couldn't raise the nose gear, so the plane flew all the way to Eniwetok with it extended, which would've added a significant amount of drag and would have consumed an insane amount of fuel. It's a testament to the B-52's fuel capacity that it could accomplish such a long trip under those conditions. In any event, it was convenient that this happened, because it saved those on board from having to fly around in circles to burn off enough fuel to land safely. The next morning, however, the crew had to take off well before H-hour, or the time of detonation, so that they could again burn off enough fuel to land safely later that day. Now, the island we were staying on was not much bigger than the runway where this bird took off from, so an early morning flight-mission departure would mean "rise and shine" for the rest of us who were still asleep. I'll never forget being awoken when it took off the next morning less than a quarter of a mile from where we were bunked. The sound of the engines most certainly startled everyone on the island, and it definitely got me straight up out of bed. Then it got louder and more fierce, and I thought, *If it gets any worse it will be coming right through our bunkhouse.* The whole building shook and rattled, and I heard a great many voices screaming "My God!" as it took off.

On shot day, we rose at about 0400, got a steak-and-egg breakfast, and then received a briefing. We proceeded to our assigned aircraft, preflighted, strapped in, and then cranked up our plane. I was feeling both excitement and a little normal nervousness. I taxied out and held short of the runway before switching from tower frequency to controller frequency. The controller asked me to switch my radar beacon on and off several times so he could lock on to me, then we headed back to the tower for takeoff. I was more than ready, and the adrenaline was pumping.

Our test flight plan involved flying directly over and past the bomb site less than a minute before detonation. We borrowed four aircraft from the Naval Air

Preflighting, Airman Page (*left*) and me, 1958.

Test Center at Patuxent River, Maryland; two would be at three thousand and four thousand feet, and two would be at eleven thousand and twelve thousand feet. We also received four Navy and Marine air controllers from an Early Warning Squadron out of Hawaii, assigned to the designated project pilots for the duration of the project. Each aircraft was modified with a radar beacon, and to distinguish the four of us from one another each beacon had a distinct frequency. The last piece of the puzzle was the arrangement for four M-33 Marine radar vans to track our flight patterns, again, one van assigned to each of us.

Inside each van was installed a vertical panel that came equipped with a tracking pen. That pen would trace the path of the aircraft on a large sheet of paper with a flight pattern printed on it. It automatically hit the paper every one second when it received tracking information, and ultimately it produced a series of dots lined up in a row, representing the aircraft's flight path. Each van had its own receiver from the control tower, and the controllers could hear the test shot countdown in real time. To synchronize the dots with the shot countdown, the controllers also could lift the pen manually and drop it down onto the printed flight plan at any time. The printed flight pattern had a racetrack design, consisting of a fourteen-minute flight pattern, with five-minute legs along each side and standard two-minute turns at each end. We flew our aircraft twice around the pattern, then on the third time around (on the final five-minute leg) at two minutes, the pen jumped over to a separate two-minute line and sped up proportionally. Then it again automatically jumped to a thirty-second line, speeding up proportionally as the countdown continued and the detonation time approached. Our abort criterion required that we were to abort if in the overall pattern, with H-minus-two minutes to go, we were even two seconds late. Our group repeated this exercise at least once before each detonation, and after participating in eight shots, the average positioning error for our four aircraft was 0.3 seconds. In other words, we became a well-oiled machine. The controllers were great, the pilots were great, and the equipment was great. What can I say? John Burns, if you're still out there and if you're reading this, I say, "Well done!"

The day before a scheduled shot, our controllers set up the tracking sheets, the ones that marked the precise location of the device to be detonated. Then the station sent a helicopter out to the barge and had it hover over the device. All four vans tracked the chopper, and all four controllers confirmed the device's location. On the afternoon of the day before the test, we all got airborne and gave the controllers a little practice running us around the pattern. When we were directly over the bomb, the controller gave us a verbal mark, which meant the pen knew the exact location of the device. We were able to roll our aircraft on its side so we could look down and see it, and this was a confidence maneuver for us. If time permitted, in the early hours on the morning of the detonation, just to put ourselves at ease, we were again allowed to get a visual on the device, which was lit up in stark contrast against the dark water below.

When I reached my assigned altitude, the controller steered me into the pattern as quickly as he could so he could time our two five-minute legs, trying to determine the effect of wind on our ground speed. It was still dark outside right up to shot time, so the controller gave me a mark, or a warning to stand by, and when I was over the lighted barge where the bomb was positioned and when I rolled the aircraft on its side and looked down, I could see the light on the device right there below me. Hallelujah!

Once I was on the final five-minute leg and reached the two-minute mark, the controller switched the pen to the two-minute line and ultimately to the thirty-second line. At H-minus-two seconds, we were not allowed to transmit until after detonation. Then the bomb was detonated. A few seconds later, the controller said to stand by for shock arrival, and I braced myself. Since I was in a high-altitude pattern when the shock arrived, I got a fairly big jolt from below. *A nuclear bomb has just detonated below me.* How many people can say that? At that point, I pulled back the thermal curtain that hung across the windows inside my aircraft, removed my light-restrictive filter glasses, and looked out. Since I was always flying away from the detonation, the explosions were behind me and I never got to see the telltale mushroom cloud from the air as one might expect, but, thankfully, I did observe the gorgeous sight of the sun rising on the horizon in front of me on another beautiful day on earth.

Another facet of this operation was the necessity to carry two extra 150-gallon fuel tanks so we didn't run out of fuel. It was essential to drop the empty tanks during the final trip around the pattern, because keeping the tanks attached would hinder achieving all the data that was needed. We were flying at four different altitudes; dropping a couple of tanks on someone below you could spoil his whole day. Therefore, from time to time, we had to skew the patterns a certain number of degrees to avoid this. Fortunately, to my knowledge, no one was ever hit by an errant fuel tank, but it still seemed quite expensive to waste all of those tanks.

Returning to the airfield, the weather had us at a low ceiling, which required a ground-controlled radar approach. Once I landed, I had a good feeling that we'd acquired the data we needed and could head back to the States soon. After all, this was supposed to be my shore duty. On inspection, I definitely noticed some damage to my aircraft, just as we had intended. The access door panels under the fuselage on the A4s showed that the screw holes had significantly elongated, from the panel being dragged when the shock wave hit the door. Some of the quartz-dome thermocouples were also broken, and the main door on the underside of the plane had a large dent that looked as though someone whacked it with a sledgehammer. The Radiological Defense Lab in San Francisco had installed several gun-sight-aiming-point cameras, which were heavily filtered, since they were pointed directly at the fireball during detonation. Unfortunately, we didn't get any results from these cameras until all the film was sent home and processed afterward. For the first several shots, there was almost nothing to see on the film except for a small dim light, but on the last shot, the filter burned off when it hit the thermal wave and revealed a beautiful motion picture of a nuclear detonation. The project was a success! In the summer of 2017, the Lawrence Livermore National Laboratory, with permissions from the Departments of Defense and Energy, released video footage (no audio) of several of these 1958 detonations—retrieved from their top-secret vaults—to the public so that the footage can be better preserved and shared. In an ironic twist, I watched the Operation Hardtack detonations first from the inside of the aircraft where that technology was newly emerging and then again this past summer on Twitter.

I ran into an old friend and former Academy classmate of mine, Danny Maringello, on the island one night. He was a submariner like my dad, and we met up at the bar to have a few drinks and talk about the project. Danny was also on the project; one of these test shots was detonated underwater. Danny's sub was suspended underwater by cables, and its role, like the airplanes', was to sustain some intentional damage. He told me he had joined a small crew on board at the time of the detonation and they anxiously hoped the submarine wouldn't leak and sink to the bottom.

When the test blast took place, several of us watched the underwater shot from the beach, and this did not require the filter glasses. I was expecting a huge wave bearing down on us after the explosion, but that's not what happened at all. It was actually quite phenomenal. When the bomb detonated, thousands of tons of water rose up into the sky, creating an enormous hole in the lagoon. All of the surrounding water rushed in to fill the hole, causing the water recede out until we could actually see the bare bottom of the ocean for hundreds of yards in front of us. When the water on the beach suddenly disappeared, something in my gut said to head the other way, fast! Sure enough, when all the water that was shot into the air came tumbling back down into itself, it created a tsunami, and all that water came rushing back toward us, but not as steady lines of small waves. It was just one huge tidal wave that rolled back in rapidly, all at once. It was much like the tsunami in Indonesia in 2004, when an underwater earthquake caused the same phenomenon.

It was time to use our liquor cards! We'd accumulated a fairly decent stockpile by the time we departed. I sought the local customs official and asked him that, if possible, our supply vans be inspected and sealed so that they couldn't be opened again until reentering the United States. He agreed, and they were stamped and sealed, indicating that they contained "scientific instruments." They did contain instruments, of course, but they also had a few cases of bourbon, too, for our homecoming party. The vans and aircraft both returned to the United States safely and in perfect condition. We didn't lose a single bottle.

Before departing the islands, a few of the pilots wanted to have one more little bit of fun before heading home, so we retrieved the used 25 hp outboard motor and an old fifteen-foot boat we'd procured from a government list of excess property before we'd shipped to Eniwetok. The boat and motor came over right along with all our other gear and included two sets of SCUBA gear we'd also purchased. And one more thing; before we left, I quickly read through a book by Jacques Cousteau about the key points of diving, which essentially warned of two things: do not dive very deep and do not stay down for very long—good advice that still applies today. But other than that, I must admit that I had no training whatsoever in scuba diving. In our hangar on the island, we had a 3000 psi air compressor, which was more than enough to fill our tanks. We put the tanks in a fifty-five-gallon drum full of water to keep them from overheating during the filling, a trick I learned from Monsieur Cousteau. We were most definitely breaking every rule of the sport by today's standards, but this was 1958, and there really weren't any regulations back then, lucky for us. And anyway, who would have cared—diving in that lagoon was as spectacular as we dreamed it would be, as magnificent as anything I've ever seen. The depth underwater in those atolls gradually increased to about eighty feet and then dropped off precipitously into an endless dark blue haze. The coral heads beneath us rose about fifty to sixty feet above the seafloor and were teeming with thousands of small, brightly colored anemones, dories, and moray eels. It was a breathtaking scene, the biggest and most beautiful aquarium I'd ever seen, something that quite literally took my breath away! We needed to keep constant watch behind us for the large great white sharks lurking nearby, sharks so numerous, in fact, that the US Navy tested a series of shark repellants in those very same waters. It was difficult not to think about being eaten while you were also so busy taking in the scenery.

On my return home, I was tasked with writing a report aimed mainly at military types, particularly pilots, to help them understand the consequences of being that close to a nuclear detonation. My takeaway advice was certainly to fly straight away from the blast, but as long you put a few miles between you and the bomb, you should survive. I mentioned that in my time on that project, there was a scheduled detonation at Bikini Atoll about thirty minutes prior to ours. Naturally, we were informed and advised to look the other way when it went off. In fact, with that test blast location just 190 miles from us, it could easily blind anyone who looked straight at the explosion for a significant period of time. It would be crucial, should a real nuclear exchange ever take place, that the pilots would be aware of other "friendly deliveries" in the vicinity.

All people hope that an exchange like that never occurs, but in light of the events unfolding around the world at that time, especially in the military, we all knew the importance of planning for any contingency. During my time in the Marshall Islands, wearing special glasses, I observed several nuclear detonations from the ground, and the size and power of those blasts were impressive. Still, just a few short hours after the explosions, you could look over the vast Pacific Ocean and see nothing but an ordinary skyline where once a mushroom cloud loomed, and you got the impression that maybe the whole thing was really no big deal. Believe me—it was. The Eniwetok Proving Grounds tests were momentous and historic, and we were just a small part of it. I summed up my report by saying that even though it took me away from my family for three months, as military operations often do (and during my shore duty, no less), participating in our country's first series of nuclear research tests was an incredibly humbling experience. Hopefully, all pilots get to do something incomprehensible like that at least once in their career. Looking back, it is not lost on me at all that I was part of something that literally changed the world.

Life back in Albuquerque returned to normal, or at least what pilots consider "normal." I was scheduled as the Naval Air Special Weapons Facility duty officer weekly, and that job sometimes required me be at the facility after regular working hours and on many weekends. The duty officer often had to meet any of our aircraft that returned to the facility during these odd times. Once when I assumed the duty, I learned of a project about to take place involving two F-8 *Crusaders* and two pilots, one of whom was John Glenn, the man who would later become the first American astronaut to orbit the earth. Project Bullet involved the two aircraft leaving the West Coast and racing to the East Coast to set a new cross-country speed record. The pilots planned to use their afterburners to climb to high altitudes and then to descend to twenty thousand feet several times just to refuel, then they were to keep repeating the process until reaching the East Coast. The first refueling stop was to take place near Albuquerque, but there was some concern about the weather on the day of their flight. Early that morning, as duty officer I was the one who received the call from the project coordinator, asking for someone to get airborne and climb above twenty thousand feet, note the weather, and suggest a suitable altitude to refuel. It was well before working hours, so I called our executive officer, who told me to jump into one of our aircraft, take off, and gather the requested information. I selected a T-33 *Shooting Star,* since it had two seats, then took off with one of our ground crew members on board and had him record the weather status. Unfortunately, the second racing pilot accompanying Glenn damaged his in-flight refueling probe and had to drop out of the race, but Glenn continued on and sped across the finish line in record time. Project Bullet created a new cross-country speed record, and, of course, Glenn later entered the *Mercury* astronaut program. I claim no credit for the success of his project or his later fame and fortune, and

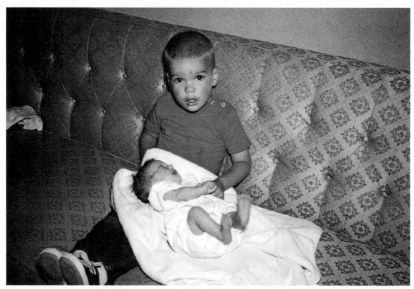

My son, Richard, with my daughter, Lisa, Albuquerque, New Mexico, 1959.

none was ever given either, but just like everything else I've been witness to, it was an honor just to get to say I was there.

In the late summer of 1959, Louise and I welcomed our daughter Lisa, named after my mother, Elizabeth. She completed our family of four just as my tour in Albuquerque was coming to a close. My thoughts, of course, turned to yet another move to live in yet another place in our great country, which would likely involve racing to somewhere all the way across the United States, just like my parents had done with my brother and me. I requested to detach in September so I could get established at my new assignment well before Christmas, and although my early request was approved, when my orders arrived, instead of giving me a new long-term placement, they directed me to proceed straight to the Naval Aviation Safety School at the University of Southern California. I completed safety school there on December 18, 1959, and then found myself *finally* heading back across the country with my family. We moved to Jacksonville, Florida, where I was given orders to report to the A4 Replacement Air Group just as President Eisenhower and the rest of the free world were getting their bellies full of the Soviet Union's favorite Communist darling, Fidel Castro.

Chapter 12

Old, Bold Pilots

Castro's Mortars

I checked into the A4 *Skyhawk* Replacement Air Group (VA-44 *Hornets*) at NAS Jacksonville in January 1960, just a year after Castro seized control of Cuba. Prior to commencing the A4 curriculum, I completed the Instrument Refresher Course in the F9F-8T Dual *Cougar*. Back during my tour at the Naval Air Special Weapons Facility (1956–59), I'd earned a special instrument rating, or a "green card," as it was known then. The green card required two thousand hours of flight time, many more than what is required now, plus a comprehensive in-flight test. It allowed its holder the privilege of signing his own flight clearance as well as a little bit of prestige to boot. We used to joke that we also had a "blue card," which was nothing more than a card with a hole punched in it, and when it was held up to the sky, the sight of blue meant it was a "go." I had an advantage in that I had over two hundred hours in the A4 *Skyhawk* (or the *Tinker Toy*, or *Heinemann's Hotrod*, as it was also known) that I'd accumulated in Albuquerque. In fact, I was told that I was the first pilot to check in with prior A4 time. This was perhaps the simplest aircraft I ever flew. On my first familiarization flight, it was a little breezy, so my instructor/chase pilot thoroughly briefed me on the perils of crosswind landings. I actually knew this already because while flying the A4 in Albuquerque, I had frequently encountered crosswind landings, as there was only one duty (active) runway. I felt comfortable with the conditions, and I knew that we only canceled flights when we observed tumbleweeds blowing across the runway. As luck would have it, I survived that first landing just fine, but, to his chagrin, my instructor blew a tire and had to be towed in.

The program was great, a very efficient unit. After a number of flights encompassing low-level navigation, night flying, and acrobatics, we flew our class to Guantanamo Bay, Cuba. We stayed at Leeward Point Airfield and conducted regular air-to-ground bombing and rocket training. When we took off in our planes, headed west, a short distance just ahead of us there was nothing but a fence separating the United States from Communist Cuba. Castro had gone to some trouble to set up a mortar range near the fence just to intimidate us, and although I never saw any mortar rounds, all US pilots made quick right turns right after takeoff in the hope that we wouldn't see any either.

One day I prepared to take off. I had the engine at about 80 percent, then I let go of the brakes and advanced the throttle to 100 percent. A hunch in my gut immediately told me something wasn't right. The distance I moved the throttle seemed shorter, and the aircraft accelerated more slowly than normal. These were very small variations, but it was troubling nonetheless, considering where I was. On the left side panel, just short of the throttle quadrant, there was a switch labeled "Fuel Control, Auto/Manual." In "Auto," the fuel control metered the fuel going to the engine to prevent the engine from flooding should the throttle be advanced too quickly. So just after takeoff, right as I was about to commence my right turn to avoid Castro's mortars, the engine lost power and started decelerating. My hand went straight to the fuel control switch, and I rolled the aircraft to the left, toward the water. I really don't recall even thinking about it; my hands just went to those knobs and turned those switches almost instinctively. Sure enough, as I flipped the switch to "Manual," the engine surged right back to 100 percent. Still, I declared an emergency and was cleared to land the aircraft. When I taxied back to the flight line, I kept the engine running and told the flight line plane captain to get a power plant mechanic. When he climbed onto the wing and looked in the cockpit, I pointed to the fuel control switch, then placed it in the "Auto" position. We both watched the engine decelerate and shut down. He got the picture alright: something was wrong. Enough said.

I still wasn't out of the woods. At the end of that deployment to Gitmo, in the spring of 1960 while on my way back to Jacksonville, still flying the A4, my aircraft lost pressure so I had to reduce my altitude. The canopy and both the left and right sections of the windscreen in front of me frosted almost completely over, and I couldn't see anything on either side of me. I could barely see where I was going, but, thankfully, enough of the middle section of the windscreen was just clear enough for me to navigate my way back, thanks to an almost invisible fine wire heater inside the glass. I returned to NAS Jacksonville, called in a request to land, and immediately downed the aircraft. As a rule of thumb for pilots, everything goes right or everything goes wrong. There is rarely anything in between.

Fortunately, the rest of this training went smoothly, and I completed it with seven day-carrier landings and six night-carrier landings on the USS *Indepen-*

dence, CVA-62. After I checked out of the Replacement Air Group, I drove to NAS Cecil Field in Jacksonville with my family and checked into Attack Squadron 34 (the VA-34 *Blue Blasters*) flying an A4D2.

Once aboard this squadron, I was assigned the job of training/safety officer. I was able to pass on to the other squadron pilots my experience with the nukes at Eniwetok. Of course, my job was also to schedule numerous briefs for the pilots on safety issues. It was fairly common for a pilot who had been on leave for a while or who'd been sick to receive special refresher briefs to ensure he was kept up to speed, always in an attempt to keep pilots in constant training mode. Even in the bathroom stalls, we had a large photo of the A4 cockpit on the back of the door and on both sides. You couldn't get away from your training! Of course, while we were on deployment, we were frequently in port for anywhere from a week to ten days, which would often require a comprehensive safety brief for *all* of the pilots. My first deployment was to the USS *Saratoga* (CVA-60), home-ported in Mayport, Florida, near Jacksonville Beach. This cruise had us going to the Med for a short spell, then up to Norway to participate in a large NATO exercise. It was sort of hairy flying there, as the terrain was completely unfamiliar and although the weather was warm, the water was bitter cold, which at times resulted in the formation of low cloud banks or thick fog. This could be quite dangerous for flying, because there were absolutely zero suitable landing fields in that area. Still, flying in and out of the Norwegian fjords was spectacular! Since we were north of the Arctic Circle, we had to wear "Poopy Suits," waterproof flight suits that could help you survive the cold water in case of an over-water ejection. We flew there without incident for a few weeks, and then after completing the exercise, we were sent back to the Med to rejoin the Carrier Task Force 60 as part of the US Sixth Fleet.

We also made port calls at Barcelona, Spain; Cannes, France; Naples and Genoa, Italy; and Athens, Greece, some more than once. During a typical deployment, we stayed in port about 50 percent of the time. After each port call, the ship would get back under way, and as soon as we had sea room, we would get right back to flying again. We flew seven days a week from 0800 until 2300, with the exception of Sunday, when we would start flying at noon. To assure the taxpayers we weren't just boring holes in the sky all the time, the United States made arrangements with Spain, France, and Greece, allowing us to conduct low-level training flights over prescribed routes in those countries. Naturally, the patterns were through sparsely inhabited areas, but they gave us great views of these places from the air. The exercises were incredible and provided such invaluable practice, although, unfortunately, we lost one pilot on a low-level flight when he flew too low through a deep canyon in the mountainous regions of Greece, hitting a narrow canyon wall in a tight turn. We were all briefed about these kinds of hazards, especially noting that the aircraft would slide slightly sideways during tight maneuvers and you wouldn't be able to see the canyon wall, because it would be *under* you as you flew through. There's an old aviation saying that goes, "There are old pilots, and there are bold pilots, but there are no old, bold pilots." I recognize that our career choice required us to have a penchant for taking measured risks, but as I grew older and wiser in the cockpits of a great many Navy airplanes, I also recognized more clearly how the young guys always managed to find danger quicker. Arrogance fades with maturity, thankfully, and having one deadly scenario after another playing out right in front of me certainly made me a much better, more careful pilot.

I flew one mission in an A4 from the Med to Belgium and back where I was joined by an A4 tanker with a three-hundred-gallon buddy pack, which was an in-flight refueling pod. We both climbed to thirty thousand feet and headed toward the target at Brussels. We computed a flight profile that would take us to a specific point where I could receive fuel, where even after being topped off, I still had enough fuel to get to the target and back to the ship *and* the tanker had enough fuel to return to the ship as well. Who needed a huge tanker when we had this going for us? Nice!

One of our jobs involved being the duty tanker during all flight operations. We always had an A4 tanker up there, from the first flight of the day until the last. The only function of the A4 tanker was to orbit the carrier at twenty thousand feet and be prepared to give fuel to any incoming pilot who might be having difficulty landing aboard or was low on fuel. This tanker was an essential resource because there were very few emergency landing fields in the Med, and they were only used in extremely dire situations. On each flight schedule cycle (each cycle being an hour and a half), the incoming tanker would receive any extra fuel from the off-going tanker, a measure taken to try to improve fuel efficiency. Or, if necessary, the tanker could dump its fuel to get down to landing weight. Either way, the worst flight to be on was the last cycle of the day. As the last of the planes were coming in each night, the tanker would drop to ten thousand feet and continue circling the ship until every other aircraft was safely recovered. At this point, the air boss transmitted over the radio, "Tanker, your signal is BINGO. Expedite." This meant the tanker pilot needed to start dumping fuel *and* he needed to descend as quickly as possible onto an eighty-thousand-ton carrier steaming on ahead into the wind, one waiting for him and telling him to HURRY to get into the pattern and land. The tanker pilot was sort of busy already, trying to get everyone else on board, and yet he was also rushed to make his landing in the pitch black, at about 2330. Talk about a high-pressure work environment!

Once all aircraft were recovered, the deck crews needed to fuel and arm them (if necessary) and re-spot the aircraft for the 0800 launch the next morning. Humorously, journalists who visited carriers from time to time during regular flight operations commented that they observed several crew members sleeping on the aircraft wings and in other random places, and they reported that it often seemed like everyone was always napping. That couldn't be further from the truth! Those crews, like the tanker pilots and all the other pilots, had to stay up to prep for the next day's flights. You could hear over the ship's PA system, "Secure from flight quarters!" and the time might already be 0200 to 0300. Knowing that at 0600, just two or three hours later, the PA system would again blast, "Flight quarters, man your flight quarters stations!" the crew knew there was not much time to sleep. In the typical A4 squadron, we might have had eighteen plane captains for twelve aircraft, and it was required that one plane captain be with each aircraft while under flight quarters. If you do the math, considering that crew members also needed to eat, sleep, and bathe, as well as do their jobs during flight quarters for seven days a week for the entire time they were at sea, they deserved the sleep any way and anywhere they could get it.

Toward the end of the cruise, while the *Saratoga* was out to sea en route to Athens, there was an engine room fire. Ironically, a fire is one of the worst things that can happen at sea, because even though the ship is surrounded by water, aboard-ship fires are very difficult to control. Unfortunately, in this incident there was a small set of staterooms adjacent to the pilot ready rooms, one deck down from the hangar deck. Because they were trapped down below, several officers in those staterooms perished from smoke inhalation when the emergency alarms sounded and the ship went into general quarters lockdown. Afterward, I was tasked with taking an inventory of their personal property, and although I had all of their clothes laundered, I couldn't get rid of the smoke smell. I felt such tremendous remorse, knowing that the survivors would receive their loved ones' property reeking of how they died.

During another, earlier stint on this cruise, one of the pilots from our sister A4 squadron failed to respond to the landing signal officer's frantic wave-off signal when his approach speed was too slow. His aircraft struck the back end of the flight deck, and his plane crashed into the carrier. From what I can recall, he was under automatic fuel control, which was standard procedure at the time, but it was determined that the fuel control possibly malfunctioned under auto fuel power. Regardless, both the aircraft and the pilot were lost, and this always gets the attention of people up the chain of command. That this particular aircraft engine did not respond to the throttle concerned the Bureau of Aeronautics back in Washington, which in turn required a change of procedure to prevent similar incidents. The details of the accident—including the consideration of pilot error, any potential aircraft malfunctions, and even the type of fuel being used—were all transmitted back to Washington. Until the cause of the accident was ascertained, all pilots were switched to manual fuel control during carrier approach and landing. This was a little hairy, because abrupt, manual movements of the throttle increased the likelihood of a total engine flameout. At any rate, we all finished the cruise using manual fuel control and, thankfully, had no further complications.

Ultimately, the investigation concluded that the Navy's switch from JP-4 jet fuel to JP-5 appeared to be the cause of the problem. It seemed that JP-5 retained more water than JP-4, and when the fuel got cold-soaked at high altitude, the water froze, interfering with the normal operation of the aircraft's fuel control. I was relieved to hear there was no pilot error, no landing error, and no system failure at any level. It was simply a learning curve that often comes along with new technology and changes in equipment. It was still unfortunate, to say the least, and another good pilot lost his life.

I have dozens of stories just like these, and all are heartbreaking. It never got easier to do the tough jobs, or to see the sadness on the faces of the families, or to participate in the harder parts of what was often a rather dangerous career. It was back then and still is the price you pay sometimes when you serve in the military, and carrier operators are more aware of this than perhaps anyone. What a disheartening death it was each time a young man lost his life too soon. I never, in my entire career, completed a deployment without losing someone. Making the ultimate sacrifice was often just part of the daily dangers of military life and that part of my chosen career hasn't changed at all even in the hundreds of years since Americans first began serving. I still think it's the most honorable sacrifice there is: to give up your life serving your country.

Chapter 13

Bahia de Cochinos

Kennedy's Disaster

In our many years as prisoners of the North Vietnamese, Fred and I made a habit of colorfully critiquing the practices of the US government, often about how they ran the armed services in an less-than-efficient manner. Since my tour of sea duty ended in the early summer of 1960, many changes were taking place in Washington, DC, including a presidential election season that would ultimately bring us President John F. Kennedy. Drastic shifts in Washington party politics often made these bureaucratic growing pains especially noticeable in military circles. And in my opinion, in his short time as our commander in chief, Kennedy made a few surprisingly remarkable and important strides regarding military operations. First, he established a new special forces military unit, called the Green Berets; although some army units were already wearing actual green berets by the late 1950s, President Kennedy designated that accessory as part of the official uniform for that newly created, secret special-ops unit in 1961.

Second, he tasked the armed services with maintaining what we called "level readiness." Up to this point, Navy Air Groups (now called Air Wings) that had just returned from one deployment began a long and intense training cycle, which could easily take more than a year, before another deployment could begin for them. Navy squadrons were especially vulnerable to this, because of the requirement that pilots remain carrier-qualified before they could be deployed. President Kennedy's plan required establishing replacement training wings whose carrier qualifications (car-quals) were kept constantly up to date, which provided the fleet with a steady supply of fully trained pilots at all times. These pilots and air crews were able to instantly replenish flight crew losses due to normal military rotations and sudden combat losses. When new pilots completed flight training, they were assigned to a fleet squadron with aircraft the pilots had not normally flown before. The Replacement Air Groups had the same types of aircraft as the new pilots and more senior pilots coming off of shore duty were designated to fly as instructor pilots.

This new training program also involved SERE (survival, evasion, resistance, and escape) training, ground school for the new aircraft, renewal of instrument qualifications, navigation, and weapons systems, culminating in day and night carrier qualifications. The level-readiness program took about five months to complete, and the graduates were then deployment-ready and completely carrier-qualified. Pilots were often sent directly to their fleet squadrons, which could quite possibly already be deployed. In these cases, the pilots were sent off to their units and once aboard ship were sent on training missions as soon as possible. It was a very rigorous program, but it established a truly prepared and level-ready system for Navy carrier pilots. It literally changed everything, making combat naval (or Navy) aviation forces ready to go to sea and conduct combat operations at a moment's notice, something nobody had ever done before. Anyway, when my cruise on the *Saratoga* finally ended, we departed the Med. The outgoing and incoming carriers rendezvoused to brief the incoming commanding officer and the air group on any intelligence for targeting, to turn over the target folders and wish them well. After that was accomplished, all that was left was just our trip back across the pond and back home to join our families, at least until the next deployment, which history would show was going to be a doozy.

During my two weeks' leave after returning to Cecil Field in Jacksonville, I opted to stay close to home in Jacksonville. My parents, who were still living in South Carolina, came to visit us. One day while we were all lounging around the house, I received a phone call from the squadron duty officer telling me that I was to report to night field carrier landing practice that very evening. I told him I didn't understand, since I was on leave, and he said he had no idea what it was all about either.

I soon found out that *all* leave was being canceled and the whole squadron was instructed to report for duty as soon as possible. Once all of the pilots were back, we had a squadron meeting to inform us of the emerging situation. We were told that our A4 squadron (VA-34 *Blue Blasters*) would undergo a short deployment on an antisubmarine-warfare carrier, the USS *Essex*. The carrier would normally carry two S2F aircraft and two antisubmarine-warfare helicopter squadrons, but it was being instructed to leave one of its squadrons behind while our squadron gave the carrier fighter protection. This was very unusual, since we were not configured for air-to-air warfare. We carried no air-to-air missiles, and our two 20 mm cannons were for strafing only and were bore-sighted specifically for that purpose. It just simply did not make sense. Still, it was not our place to ask questions, and, as usual, we did what we were told. Most of our newer pilots had never flown aboard a smaller carrier like the *Essex,* and my job was to do extensive briefings to prepare them. Another part of my job was to act as if everything was totally normal, but if I'm being totally honest, I was used to seeing a supercarrier, and when I instead saw what looked like a postage stamp in comparison, I was pretty disturbed.

All of the squadron gear and our crew were both trucked and flown up to Norfolk, where the *Essex* was berthed. Once the gear and the crew were aboard, the *Essex* got under way, and we prepared to fly out and meet the ship and land our twelve A4s on the carrier somewhere east of Jacksonville. When we arrived at our hangar that morning, there were several Carrier On-board Delivery (COD) aircraft on the ramp. These were twin-engine prop S2Fs configured to carry passengers, cargo, or maybe mail, and they were on loan to us from several fleet carriers whose names were emblazoned on the sides. We were so confused, wondering why COD planes from all these various carriers were there. It was strange, to say the least. We took off from Cecil Field and rendezvoused as a twelve-plane formation and headed out to sea to find the *Essex.*

All twelve aircraft came aboard with no wave-offs or bolters. Carrier landings are pretty fascinating, actually. Aircraft carriers have an angled landing deck about ten degrees left of the axial deck, which is parallel to the ship's centerline. There is an optical landing aid, which at the time was either a mirror system or a Fresnel lens. In either system, as the pilot approaches, he sees a small, round light called the *meatball* and a line of green lights on both sides of the meatball, along two arms that run parallel to the horizon. When the pilot sees the meatball exactly between the green lights (called *datum lights*) he is on *glide path,* exactly where he needs to be. When the meatball is above these, he is too high, and, when it is low, he is also low. The carrier deck has lines painted on it outlining the landing area, which is illuminated at night. As the pilot, you have an angle-of-attack indicator, and when the ball is in the center and the angle-of-attack indicator is at three o'clock and you are descending at the proper rate, you are in great shape! The trick is just to keep it that way. Since you are landing on the angled deck, there is nothing in front of you, so if the tailhook of your aircraft fails to hook a wire on the carrier deck, you just fly off the end and go around for another approach. This is what we call a bolter; for a bolter pass, as soon as the pilot hits the deck, he goes to full power. Engine lag was a constant concern, and the need to keep the power up on a jet engine was critical. This all happened very quickly, and the pilot needed to pull the power back the instant he felt his tailhook grab the wire. Easy enough, right?

Anyway, back to our mission. Once we landed our planes, we dismounted, located the ready rooms, then proceeded directly for a meeting. The ready room looked like a small movie theater, with comfortable leather seats equipped with fold-down desks where we generally hung out and received briefings before our flights. As the *Essex* plowed south, we were told there would be no flight operations until we reached a designated point somewhere south of the western part of Cuba, and it would be several days before we arrived. I thought, *What in the world?* Finally, the day *after* reaching our destination, the captain of the *Essex* came to our ready room to give us the briefing we'd been waiting for. Then, strangely, he asked both the enlisted man who manned the sound-powered phone and our air intelligence officer, our *ensign,* to leave. Ironically, our air intelligence officer was someone we relied upon heavily to keep us informed of enemy activities, and he'd been called back from his own honeymoon to be there; yet he was being thrown out of the room! Thankfully, after our commanding officer intervened on his behalf, he was allowed to return to do his job assisting us in the operation. The captain then explained to everyone assembled, specifically the pilots, that what he was about to tell us could not leave the room. We were warned not to discuss it with anyone or write home about it. Then, he outlined the approaching Bay of Pigs Invasion.

By the time Kennedy was elected president, Fidel Castro had been the president of Cuba for almost two years. In 1961, we can be sure, there was perhaps nothing more terrifying to our brand-new American president than the threat of a staunchly Communist government taking root a minuscule ninety miles from the Florida coast. Kennedy most certainly felt intense pressure to make a bold move to quickly combat this threat and to establish himself as a fearless defender of the United States against any plots Castro might hatch against us. He wanted to lend assistance to the small but growing revolutionary movement to oust Castro, but certainly he believed that any kind of official operation would look like the United States was brazenly invading Cuba.

Three ships left the Yucatan peninsula on April 13, 1961, carrying over fourteen hundred Cuban paramilitaries opposed to the Castro regime. The CIA had trained these counterrevolutionaries all over the United States, in places like Useppa Island in southern Florida. Under Kennedy's direction, once they landed in Cuba their plans were to overthrow the Castro government by rallying the population and ousting him, hoping that once a beachhead was established, most Cubans would rise up voluntarily and join the fight to bring

Lieutenant Allen Brady, 1961.

him down. Little did anyone realize the sheer size of his military and that Castro had built up a twenty-five-thousand-man army, a two-hundred-thousand-man militia, and nine thousand armed police officers who were already there and were waiting for us. Starting on April 15, 1961, eight CIA-supplied B-26 bombers from Guatemala commenced bombing raids on Cuban airfields and then quickly returned to the United States. Our squadron's task was to give air support to the B-26s to protect the ships while they were en route to Cuba. We were specifically told that our task was complete when the ships reached a specific point the night before the landing. We were told that under *no* circumstances were we to participate in the attack itself, nor were we to fire at any Cuban forces, and we didn't.

The landing force, consisting of five infantry battalions and one paratrooper battalion, was known as Brigade 2506. The landing took place at night on April 15, on a beach named Playa Giron, in the Bay of Pigs on the southern coast of Cuba. Initially, the force was successful, but the Cuban army counteroffensive, led by Fidel Castro himself, soon appeared to gain the upper hand. In fact, while flying a combat air patrol, our squadron's executive officer spotted a friendly B-26 flying away from Cuba at full power with his engines smoking, pursued by one of Castro's propeller fighters that was shooting at him over international waters. The executive officer made a high-speed pass at the fighter without firing on him, which caused the fighter to withdraw posthaste. Except for that, we didn't see any further flights by Cuban fighters.

We flew low past the ships for a few days and could see the fighters excitedly waving to us, not knowing what fate awaited them. Of course, being offshore, none of us knew little more than the basics of the course the battle was taking. Apparently, President Kennedy was visibly frustrated when the mission wasn't achieved as quickly as the CIA had assured him it would be, so someone from his administration called our admiral and asked for an on-scene evaluation. I'd just landed my A4, and as I climbed down, several sailors with paintbrushes were painting out all of the markings on my plane, which I could only assume was an attempt to hide our identification. When I entered the ready room, my commanding officer told me and one ensign that the three of us were going right back into the air and into Cuba on a reconnaissance flight to see what was going on. We were told to leave our dog tags and any identification behind with the squadron duty officer, which confirmed my suspicions that the situation was deteriorating. This was unnerving to say the least because no one wants to be shot down over enemy territory without identification, but, being good soldiers, we complied.

The commanding officer briefed us that he would fly at five hundred feet while Ensign Potzo and I positioned ourselves about a thousand feet behind and five hundred feet above him. We approached the coast and flew up into the Bay of Pigs, where we saw a grounded freighter burning. We didn't see anyone around it. As we continued inland, an antiaircraft vehicle suddenly opened fire at the commanding officer. He jinked left and then right, and though the tracer rounds were all around him, he wasn't hit. Then the same gunner began firing at Potzo and me. The little yellow balls came our way, but again, no hits landed, thankfully. The commanding officer accelerated to full power and started a right turn, descending to about fifty feet over the highway leading to the main beach. There, we saw trucks, tanks, armored vehicles, and marching soldiers, bumper to bumper, heading that way, and there was no question by then that all was lost. While still in the area, I flew over and reported in to one of our destroyers I saw nearby. I was slowly cruising along about a mile off the Cuban coast when an artillery round splashed a few hundred feet short of the ship, followed by another splash slightly past the ship. They called me to say they were being attacked, and I replied back that yes, they were bracketed, and to get the hell out of there. Black smoke immediately belched from the ship's stacks, and the destroyer rapidly departed.

. . .

By April 20, the invaders, trained by the United States, surrendered. Many were put into Cuban prisons, and I have a pretty good idea of what happened to them there. Casualties included 176 killed and more than 500 wounded for the Cuban army and 118 killed, 360 wounded, and 1,202 captured for Brigade 2506. Additionally, approximately 4,000 Cuban militia police were killed or wounded or went missing. We received orders to return home and were informed that we couldn't tell our families or anyone else what had transpired. Of course, after we arrived at our homes, there was an article in the newspaper by a well-known journalist, named Drew Pearson, describing the entire operation in detail, even giving the names of the ships that carried Brigade 2506 to Cuba. So much for classified information! Also, we found out that all the letters we wrote home, even though they contained no classified information, never even left the *Essex.* The whole debacle was, of course, a great embarrassment to President Kennedy and the United States. Fidel Castro was the winner of the day, and his victory guaranteed his entrenchment in that country for another fifty years. Many Cubans still haven't forgiven the Democrats for this fiasco, and President Kennedy would count this failed mission as one of his great presidential disappointments. Bad intelligence from the Central Intelligence Agency set Kennedy up to grossly underestimate the number of people who were armed and ready to defend Castro. The CIA misrepresented the passions of the Cuban people in rising up against Castro's military and placed Kennedy in a predicament where he walked into a serious confrontation undermanned and underprepared.

We made it safely back to the ship to give our report, which no doubt increased our president's frustration. Since some of the revolutionaries made it safely to some of the small offshore islands, we stayed on station for more than a week more to try to help evacuate them. We got some help from another carrier operating off Gitmo about five hundred miles to the east. A couple of ADs and a few A4s landed aboard to help search for survivors, who were also rescued by our helicopters.

One of the A4 pilots that came from the carrier off of Gitmo was an old friend of mine, John Yamnicki. He was also a Naval Academy graduate from the Class of 1952, and we spent the evening telling stories. He told me he was once on a Med cruise preflighting his A4 when he leaned over the catwalk to look into the aircraft tailpipe with his flashlight. He lost his footing and fell eighty feet into the Mediterranean Sea. Luckily, he still held onto his flashlight, so when he came to the surface, he waved his light toward the destroyer, which was positioned astern of the carrier as a plane guard, and thankfully they spotted him. His injury turned out to be nothing more than a split lip and a big dose of humiliation. No one saw him fall, so when the flight deck was ready to launch him, control called the ready room to find out where the pilot of 206 was. The duty officer replied that the pilot had manned his aircraft some time ago and his helmet was still hanging on the 20 mm cannon. About that time, the destroyer radioed that it had plucked one of our pilots from the water. If John had not held onto his flashlight or had he been knocked unconscious, he probably would have been another casualty. One might think John was a very lucky man, but, unbelievably, some forty years later, he was a very unlucky passenger on American Airlines Flight 77, the airliner that crashed into the Pentagon on September 11, 2001.

Chapter 14

Greek Games

Some Time on the *Sara*

We returned to Cecil Field in Jacksonville, and after finally taking a little bit of leave, our squadron resumed its normal training cycle. During a sea duty tour, a pilot's time is split between a squadron tour and a shipboard/staff tour. Naturally, the squadron tour was always preferable, but we all put in our time. While still on the USS *Saratoga*, back when I was returning from the Med prior to the Bay of Pigs Invasion, I was dining with an old Academy classmate of mine, Bill Harvey. He was assigned to the embarked staff of Commander of Carrier Division 6, which consisted of two aircraft carriers, usually headed by a rear admiral. Since Bill was soon completing his staff tour at sea and would be looking forward to a squadron tour, he asked me if I would consider replacing him. It certainly seemed more appealing to me than flight deck officer, hangar deck officer, or catapult officer, so I accepted the offer, and Bill introduced me to a man I knew only as Captain English, the staff operations officer, who was happy to get an easy replacement who came highly recommended. Captain English made the call to the Bureau of Navy Personnel and the deal was done. My squadron tour with VA-34 ended in August 1961, and I reported to the Commander of Carrier Division 6 shortly before we deployed back to the Med, again on the *Sara*, for the next six to seven months. One advantage of being on Carrier Division 6 was that VA-34 was back on the *Saratoga*, too, so since the new squadron CO was my old squadron executive officer, he allowed me to log flight time with them. Back then, aviators needed to fly a hundred hours a year to receive flight pay, so while we were deployed, we often had to log our flight time in Navy twin-engine aircraft provided by a command in Naples. Another land-based squadron stationed there would fly the planes out to whichever ports we were in so the ship and staff aviators could squeeze in a little time in the cockpit. The higher-ups finally realized that this practice was not very cost-effective. In fact, in most cases, it would have been a lot cheaper to pay flight pay! So, getting flight time logged in the Mediterranean ports of call came to an end not too many years later. Nevertheless, it was still quite an advantage for me to get to fly with the squadron at sea, and it was a hell of a lot more fun too.

Speaking of great fun, you might be surprised to know that aviators actually have an incredible sense of humor. One of the other A4 squadrons on this cruise was flying the new A4C *Skyhawk,* a modification of the A4 A and B that we were flying, and the new cockpit configuration created a problem for short aviators. When approaching a carrier landing, with the aircraft nose up, short pilots like me had some difficulty seeing over the instrument panel to view the carrier deck. Trying to draft a properly worded message to officials in Washington, DC, regarding this flaw, the writers of the memo were at a loss as to how to describe the distance between the pilot's eyes and the part of the body that sits on the seat. They chose the phrase "interanal-occular distance," and upon hearing it read aloud, we practically fell out of our chairs laughing. The message was submitted and forwarded to Washington, DC, as written, and we received no response from the higher-ups when they received it.

A rather unfortunate event would soon follow, like it always did. This one occurred when one of our aircraft's tailhooks grabbed the cross-deck pendant during landing and the wire broke, then flew across the deck and into the legs of the flight deck officer. Bob Pfeiff was a good friend of mine who went through flight training and safety officer school with me. After the accident, he was flown off the carrier to a military hospital in Germany. He told me that his injuries left one leg repairable but the other one was another story altogether. The doctor gave him a difficult choice. He told him that if he tried to save the one leg and failed, he would have to cut it off above the knee. Or he could remove the leg below the knee immediately. Without hesitation, Bob told the doctor to take it off.

Many months later, he arrived in Jacksonville unexpectedly and called me up on a stormy night and asked if I could pick him up at the airport. I was glad to, and he spent a few days relaxing with me and my family. My son, Richard, who was five years old at the time, was rather intrigued with Bob's detachable leg. Bob pointed out that the leg being wooden was very convenient, because he could hold his socks up with thumbtacks. Richard was fascinated! I asked him where he was headed next, and he replied that he was to be the chief test pilot for Bell Helicopters out of Fort Worth, Texas.

. . .

On the previous cruise, the commander of the Sixth Fleet and the head of the (Greek) Royal Hellenic Air Force established a bombing competition between our respective countries. Since there were two carriers in our task force, we had to first have a fly-off between the A4 squadrons on both American ships. This would determine who would get to shore base in Athens to compete with the Greeks at a target near Thessaloniki, north of Athens. The Greeks won the first year of the competition, but since we'd only sent one observer, there was a good deal of speculation that the competition was lost in the spotting towers. I was tasked with organizing this fly-off; I decided I would play it safe and take an additional spotter with me just to be sure.

For the A4 squadron fly-off, the RAF offered their target at El Adem in Libya, about eighteen miles south of Tobruk. Our carrier's helicopter flew me out there, and on my arrival I was warmly received by a couple of RAF personnel. They were excited about having company, and I spent the night with them eating and drinking to excess. The Brits drank me under the table! They got me extremely drunk that night, and the next morning I had to stagger out, hungover and with no breakfast, so I could start the big competition. There was an exchange of messages between El Adem and both carriers as to the locations of both the target and the bullseye. When I entered the tower, I could hear radio chatter; there seemed a lot of confusion, as the reported hits did not seem to match the hits the pilots were observing. When the bombing was complete, the RAF ultimately realized that the coordinates given to the pilots were incorrect. Since we all agreed there wasn't enough time to refly the whole contest, I collected all the hits on a chart and organized the correct coordinates of the target bullseye and carried everything back to the ship. Then I had representatives from both squadrons assist me in replotting all the hits. After all was said and done, the winners of the fly-off competition were from the *Sara,* beating out the squadron from the USS *Shangri-La.*

About a week later, when the ship moored at Athens, a Navy first class petty officer and I met with our Greek counterparts, then headed out via a Greek helo toward a small town near the target. It was a spectacular trip flying up the inland sea, and the water was spectacular where we landed. We were met by some Greek military types who escorted us over to our quaint little hotel. On the way, we stopped at a small roadside stand, where we purchased a couple of live chickens, which we promptly threw into the backseat with us. That night we all went to dinner, where I presume they cooked those same chickens and served them to us. We also drank quite a bit of ouzo, a licorice-flavored aperitif that is the Greek national drink. I can report with pride that the petty officer and I drank the Greeks under their own table, redeeming some of my self-respect after my bout with the Brits. The next day, with *two* of us in the spotting tower, the Americans from the *Saratoga* won handily.

Chapter 15

Brinkmanship

The Cuban Missile Crisis

At the completion of that cruise, the *Saratoga* returned to Mayport, where we were reunited with our families. Again, we took some much-needed leave before our next evolution commenced and we moved the staff to Norfolk, Virginia. Our orders were to embark on the USS *Independence,* in preparation for a fleet exercise called PORTREX, which stood for "Puerto Rico Exercises." This involved air bombing by squadrons from the *Independence,* shore bombardment by cruisers, and an amphibious landing by the Marines.

For some background, after the failed Bay of Pigs Invasion and once there was a confirmed presence of US Jupiter missiles in both Turkey and Italy aimed at the USSR, Fidel Castro accepted the Russians' request to plant ballistic missiles in Cuba, believing it would protect his country from any invasion the United States might again be plotting. Soviet president Nikita Khrushchev ordered the construction of missile launch facilities in the western region of Cuba, and after an American U2 reconnaissance plane verified the existence of approximately a hundred missiles and the construction sites, President Kennedy must've felt as if he had the world on his shoulders. Should he attack the Russians head-on and risk global nuclear war, or should he sit back, idle, and let them place their missiles in our backyard? It couldn't have been easy to weigh the consequences of any of those scenarios. What he decided to do was pivotal: without actually taking an aggressive offensive stance, he ordered a military blockade to surround the island and to prevent anything else from entering Cuba. And the showdown began.

We got under way on the *Independence,* accompanied by a number of other ships, and headed toward Puerto Rico around the middle of October 1962. En route to Puerto Rico, we received a message from Washington, DC, directing us to proceed to a point out in the Caribbean south of Cuba and be prepared to execute a Department of Defense plan. We crossed a demarcation line out in a remote area of the Atlantic Ocean, at which point we were required to switch over our radio traffic to go through San Juan, Puerto Rico, instead of Washington, DC. This entailed a one-hundred-fold increase in traffic between DC and the tiny San Juan station, which was completely unable to keep up. As such, our staff did not receive most of the information being transmitted to us about what the hell was going on back in Washington or what intel we were supposed to be receiving.

The assigned destroyer division commander who was accompanying us re-quested an audience with the commander of Carrier Division 6 (the admiral) and we helicoptered him over to our ship. He then confessed to the admiral that he had been made aware that we were not getting our messages because he had, in fact, been receiving them instead and had inadvertently read much of the infor-mation. Of course, what he admitted to the admiral was a huge security breach, and he knew he was not cleared to read our communications. Nevertheless, he was relieved that the admiral was appreciative of his haste in recognizing the er-ror and in delivering our intelligence to us. We immediately switched our radio frequencies, and the messages began pouring in. You might guess, I was the lucky soul tasked with going through the new communications as well as the backlog of messages the commander of the destroyer division delivered to us, which, to my horror, numbered in the hundreds. It took me weeks to get through them all.

We had a plan ready that, when directed, commenced an attack directly against Cuba. We called up the air group commander and gave the order to load out the aircraft with suitable conventional munitions, including bombs, rockets, and napalm. As the planes were being loaded, we proceeded rapidly to our designated position. For us to confront Russian ships in international waters caused a great deal of worry not only in the United States but through-out the rest of the world. We sat south of Cuba for two weeks with very little information coming out of Washington, DC. Those of us who were waiting out this standoff knew only that there was some hustling going on diplomatically behind the scenes. It was incredibly intense, to say the least, and we were more than prepared to act if the president ordered us to do so. It really was that close. There is absolutely no question that we were playing brinkmanship, and most Americans were already quite concerned about our deteriorating relationship with the USSR, with good reason. Under international law, the United States' blockade was both diplomatic and military. We waited anxiously to see if the Soviets would call our bluff by running the blockade right on past the American ships in an act of pure defiance. Kennedy made it known beyond a doubt that he would respond militarily if this route were to be taken. As such, slight panic swept across the United States. People began stockpiling rations and prepping their fallout shelters, preparing for the worst.

To everyone's relief, at the very last minute the Soviets blinked first and their missile-carrying ships turned around and headed home. It was as close as we've ever come to exchanging fire with the Russians, an event that could have tremendously altered the history of the world. The Soviets agreed to remove all of their missiles and all IL-28 bombers from Cuba, and in return, the United States agreed to remove our missiles from Turkey and Italy. We also promised not to invade Cuba unless provoked, a pretty broad vow that had lots of interpretations.

Conveniently, our nation had already planned to remove our missiles from Turkey and Italy, so the Russians' resolution was reasonable enough. The deal with regard to invading Cuba was not a problem either, since the failed Bay of Pigs Invasion ensured that the United States would not have the stomach for another Cuban confrontation. Fortunately, we never had to test our resolve *or* our promises. Additionally, a Washington-Moscow hotline was established, inclusive (so I've heard) of an actual red telephone with a direct connection between the two presidents, which somewhat reduced US-Soviet tensions. It's my understanding that the hotline still exists today. In reflection, I can still admit that those were two pretty tense weeks, and I, for one, did not get much sleep while I waited it out on board the ship.

When that crisis was over, the Carrier Division 6 staff was flown from Guantanamo back to Mayport. My tour with the division was almost over, and I received my orders to the US Naval Post-Graduate School in Monterey, California. In June 1963, Louise, the kids, and I headed back across country again.

A few days before I was to detach, the staff received a message from the Bureau of Naval Personnel saying that I'd been selected as one of thirty-four naval aviators asked to volunteer for the *Gemini* astronaut program, the part of the NASA space program that conducted much of the initial research improving the space travel and exploration techniques that would eventually put an American on the moon. Although several senior staff officers counseled me not to volunteer, I certainly couldn't help myself. Adrenaline always prevailed. As I traveled with my family to California, I spent most of my time in the car filling out all the government paperwork for this project. I assumed my chances were slim, and that certainly turned out to be the case. A couple of months later, I received a kind letter from NASA thanking me for volunteering and notifying me that I had not been accepted. I learned later that three other astronauts in this same program perished when a fire broke out in the cockpit of their capsule, and when I heard this news I thought, *That could've been me,* so it brought some perspective to my disappointment.

At post-graduate school, I ran into a former pilot in my air group who told me he'd actually made it past the first cut. Impressive! But then he went on to Houston and was cut in the second round. He said the competition was incredibly intense; as an example, he told me about one candidate who was an Air Force fighter pilot with over four thousand hours of flight time *and* a PhD in astrophysics, and even he didn't make the cut. Imagining the credentials of the men who did serve in that program sure makes me proud to have even been considered.

I checked into the post-graduate school, where I was enrolled in the weapons systems engineering curriculum. This was a two-year program with a mixture of graduate, near-graduate, and undergraduate courses, plus laboratory and classroom recitation periods. They were on a quarter system, and in two years a person accumulated what amounted to 122 classroom hours plus 60 lab hours, with 55 graduate hours. It was, hands down, the toughest school I ever attended. It was almost totally science- and math-based, with studies of subjects that had such fun names as vector algebra, differential equations, theory of a complex variable, electromagnetic fields, non-linear sample data systems, et cetera. Because the bulk of the academics involved electrical engineering, we ultimately received bachelor of science degrees in electrical engineering for our trouble.

I was sitting in class one November afternoon when a messenger delivered the news of an assassination attempt on President Kennedy. When we later heard that the president had passed, all classes were canceled for the next day, and a ceremony was held on campus in his honor. The president's death was certainly a traumatic event for the Kennedy family and the entire nation. Later, in our cell, Fred Crow and I discussed John Kennedy many times and agreed that we'd both been pretty impressed with his treatment of America's servicemen, and we had both liked him a great deal personally. Although he was a Democrat, we could admit that Kennedy proved himself a very sharp and talented young man. His sudden death certainly went down in history as one of our nation's greatest losses.

Like they all did, this tour came to an end. I received orders to the Naval Ordnance Test Station (later changed to the Naval Weapons Evaluation Facility) at China Lake, California. This was a fantastic tour! I was assigned to Michelson Laboratory, where conventional weapons were theorized and tested. The laboratory was named for Dr. Albert Abraham Michelson, who was at one point a professor at the US Naval Academy. Michelson was credited with having been the first scientist to successfully measure the speed of light and the diameter of a star and was the first American recipient of the Nobel Price in Physics in 1907.

Anyway, while I was there I was able to get back in my beloved A4 to do some weapons testing. At this time, the air war in Vietnam was just getting under way.

Shortly after I arrived in China Lake, a couple of A6s flew in for a quick evaluation to determine the cause of an unusual A6 loss over North Vietnam. From what we could ascertain, an American A6 pilot basically shot himself down. The reason for this was twofold. First, a new dive-bombing technique had been developed; it was quite accurate but problematic in execution. Second, we discovered a flaw in the use of a particular variety of electronic fuses that apparently had not been sufficiently tested. This combination of factors made it so that some bombs, when released, became armed prior to achieving a safe separation time (distance) from the aircraft. When several bombs were released simultaneously, they sometimes collided with one another in midair, and, thus, the possibility of premature detonation was much greater than originally thought. This theory was confirmed by theodolite photography and an array of dummy bombs released in a testing series. Needless to say, after our research confirmed our suspicions about the cause of the A6's problem, we sent an urgent message to the fleet warning of the dive technique and prohibition of the fuses until further testing was accomplished.

One day, I was flying an A4 with six bombs equipped with snake-eye tails. If you dropped at high speed and low altitude, say fifty to one hundred feet, a bomb without some form of retardation or drag built into it, the bomb could stay underneath the aircraft until detonation, which wiped out the plane. The snake-eye tail consists of four blades, sort of like a ceiling fan, held against the bomb by a strap until released. On release, the strap comes off and the blades snap open, causing significant drag, which creates a short, safe detonation profile for the bomb and allows for safe separation from the aircraft.

As I roared down the path toward the target, I first crossed a distinguishable object, known as the initial point (IP), at which point I punched a button on the stick, which was supposed to start a timer that would release the bomb at a preset time. On my first run, when I pressed the mic button to report that I was crossing the IP, I felt a little jolt underneath me, and the range tower called me and said I had actually released a bomb. *What?!* Of course, there was no damage done, but the tower crew didn't get the photographic data it initially wanted. I thought I screwed up and figured maybe I'd pushed the wrong button. So I circled around again and commenced a second run. When I reached the IP, I again pressed the mic button, and again a bomb ejected. *What the hell!!* I shut down all the switches on the armament panel and departed the range. I called the airfield tower, reported that I had hung ordnance (bombs that had been released but had not

The kids and me skiing, Dodge Ridge, California, 1964.

left the aircraft) and made an approach, carefully avoiding any populated areas. Thankfully, this was easy to do on a remote station in the middle of the Upper Mojave Desert. Once I was back in the flight line, the remaining four bombs were offloaded from my aircraft, and a technician with an electric checking device started assessing each station (the bomb holding location, or multiple ejector rack) on the plane, beginning with Station Number 6. A green light would show that the station was safe, and a red light would mean the ordnance was hot. The technician went from Number 6 to 3 with all green lights. I began to sweat, as it appeared that I was definitely the problem. But lo and behold, Stations 1 and 2 both showed red lights indicating, to my relief, that they were bad.

This was the time of year when selection boards reported out. I was in the zone to make commander, along with another classmate of mine stationed there. Once we found out we were both promoted, we realized that neither of us had the hats with scrambled eggs on them, so I borrowed a T28 from the air station, flew us both over the Sierras to Naval Air Station Lemoore, and purchased two hats from the exchange. Now suitably adorned, we both flew back to China Lake. About two weeks after the Commander Board reported, the Aviation Command Selection Board met and awarded me an aviation command. I looked forward to receiving orders as executive officer of a squadron. Then, as executive officer for about fifteen months, if a recommendation came from my commanding officer, I would fleet up to commanding officer.

Chapter 16

Good Morning, Vietnam

Yankee Station

My tour at Naval Ordnance Test Station China Lake, California, was scheduled to be two years long. After less than a year, however, I came to work one morning and discovered that I had orders to report to Attack Squadron 85 (VA-85) in Vietnam, detaching immediately. A person being deployed normally received travel time plus four additional days to report to a new duty station. In these orders, however, I had to report to the A6 Replacement Air Group (VA-42) at a date that omitted the extra four days and shortchanged me one travel day. I wondered what the emergency was.

I tore across the country with my family, stopping briefly in Louisville, Kentucky. Preoccupied with a great many tasks and still trying to tie up loose ends, when I tried to check into a hotel, I was surprised that the clerk said they were full and I probably wouldn't be able find a room in all of Louisville. When I asked why he said, "Because of the race." "What race?" I asked, to which he replied, "The Kentucky Derby!" He must've thought I was a complete moron. I had to go about fifty miles further to find a place to stay!

On arrival at Naval Air Station (NAS) Oceana in Virginia Beach, Louise and I rented a small house and settled in. After checking into VA-42, I asked if they knew why I had received early detachment from China Lake. The air war in Vietnam was still in its early stages, so that didn't seem an urgent situation. I was able to ascertain, however, that there had been two unexpected deaths, which completely disrupted several changes in command. Every squadron needs both a commanding officer and an executive officer *and* it took four to five months of training time to complete the Replacement Air Group training and be fully certified in the A6. Casualties were running unusually high in Vietnam, especially among the senior guys, and there were simply not enough commanders in the lineup to fill the growing number of empty top slots, considering the losses we were taking. In my situation, for instance, we had a commanding officer, an executive officer, and one commander who was a prospective commanding officer. On his last flight, the commanding officer was killed in action, so the executive moved up. But then he was also killed in action about two weeks later. The new executive officer, who had just moved up, became commanding officer after just two weeks. That left me just beginning my A6 training as prospective executive officer, and the new commanding officer finished the new combat cruise without an executive officer.

My first obligation in A6 training was to complete survival school (SERE [survival, evasion, resistance, and escape]). It was an extremely arduous week in the woods of Maine. This was followed by instrument refreshers and then A6 ground school, also very complicated, because the A6 *Intruder* was a much, much more complicated system to work with than the A4 I was used to. My last phase of instruction was day flying, night flying familiarization with the aircraft, bombing at the local target, then a short deployment, generally two to three weeks, to Yuma, Arizona, for bombing and rockets. To wrap things up, I was given day and night carrier qualifications. Prior to completing the VA-42 syllabus, my squadron (VA-85) returned to Oceana from its combat cruise. My commanding officer had me start training with my squadron, only flying with VA-42 when necessary. VA-85 had a short turnaround, so we deployed to the West Coast NAS North Island, California, in September 1966 for several weeks of training. There are a number of procedures to follow when transitioning to and from targets in North Vietnam, so our air group spent a significant number of weeks training off the coast of California in simulated transportation routes like the ones we would soon encounter on Yankee Station. (Yankee Station was a designated rendezvous point out in the Gulf of Tonkin.) Just prior to our deployment, a handful of flights were arranged to take some of our crew members back home to Virginia for short visits with their families, as some would be gone for six months or more and some, like me, for even longer than that.

Once I returned to Virginia Beach, Louise and I, with Richard and Lisa, all spent much of that week on the beach, relaxing and resting, and just being together. There was nothing foreboding or ominous about that time I spent at home with my family. I didn't think it was any different than all the other carrier cruises I'd participated in. When it was time to leave, Louise and I drove together, and she dropped me off at the base, since the kids were still in school. I kissed her goodbye, and I promised I would be careful. The last thing she always said to me was, "Don't go too high or too fast!"

. . .

We got under way on November 6, 1966, with a stop at Pearl Harbor. Honolulu had changed so much since I was last there, and I couldn't even find my way to Waikiki Beach. We got under way again and headed for Cubi Point, Philippines, our last stop before joining the task force in the Gulf of Tonkin out at Yankee Station. The trip to Cubi Point was long, about a month all told, and we had to change the times on our clocks every day. We changed the date once as well, when we crossed the International Date Line. (If you're ever confused about which way to add or subtract the day, remember this saying: "When it's Sunday in San Francisco, it's Monday in Manila.") After those few days of R & R in Cubi Point, we headed into the combat zone.

En route to Yankee Station, we were visited by the Seventh Fleet staff. They were there to brief us on the current situation in Vietnam, mainly regarding the surface-to-air and air-to-air threats. We were also briefed on the rules of engagement and the areas of the combat zone considered off limits. Pilots were repeatedly reminded to adhere to the standard way of conducting war: *don't upset the enemy* and *don't upset their allies.* One of the really stupid rules, at least to me, involved watching Russian and Chinese ships go right past our carriers en route to Hai Phong Harbor with a huge load of munitions and surface-to-air missiles on board, while we sat by and did nothing about it. At this time, Hai Phong was, coincidentally, one of the off-limit places, so a Russian ship might go right by us and offload its missiles in Hai Phong, and you could be sure that they would be carried inland that very night so they could shoot us down with them the next day. If that makes sense to anyone, I must be insane. Nevertheless, we followed our orders.

Our aircraft carrier, the USS *Kitty Hawk,* joined a second carrier, and while operating on station, each carrier would fly for a twelve-hour period, with one carrier flying planes from noon to midnight and the other from midnight until noon. This would keep airplanes up and over North Vietnam around the clock. The targeting of all locations, including bridges, railroad tracks, manufacturing headquarters, and the like would originate in Washington and go through the US headquarters in Saigon. We normally had several hours to prepare for missions, and the A6 bombardier did most of the hard work anyway, as he was the one who would navigate us to the target and put us in position to attack. All significant targets in North Vietnam were heavily defended with antiaircraft artillery and, in some cases, surface-to-air missiles. We were well aware of that. There was a large paper map of North Vietnam tacked to the wall in our operations center, and around each target were pins with colored heads designating the the AAA, the 57 mm, the 85 mm, and 100 mm artillery we could expect.

USS *Kitty Hawk*. (US Navy Archives)

Grumman A6 *Intruder*. (US Navy Archives)

Some targets were virtually covered in pins. The A6 missions were flown night and day and in all weather conditions. Our A6 squadron usually flew alone; in fact, when we were on station that winter, we were the only A6s in North Vietnam.

We carried chemical bombs—that is, bombs with normal explosives but with fuses that start a chemical reaction that ultimately detonates the bomb. The time one of these took to explode was variable, and reaction times were unpredictable. My first flight involved dropping chemical bombs on roads in the

A JNA497 (A1AWA094) XV GOVT PD WASHINGTON DC 17A CAD

FLO 21

RADM AND MRS JOHN H BRADY USN (RET) REPORT DELIVERY DONT PHONE
PHONE 340-0848 3424 KINGSGRANT RD VIRGINIA BEACH VIR
I DEEPLY REGRET TO CONFIRM ON BEHALF OF THE UNIE STATES NAVY
THAT YOUR SON CDR ALLEN COLBY BRADY 542856/1310 USN WAS REPORTED
MISSING IN ACTION ON 19 JANUARY 1967 WHILE ON A STRIKE MISSION
OVER NORTH VIETNAM HIS AIRCRAFT WAS OBSERVED BY FLIGHT MEMBERS
TO EXPLODE ON PULLOUT FROM THE BOMBING RUN. THERE WAS ONE GOOD
CHUTE OBSERVED AND ONE WHICH FAILED TO OPEN FULLY. IT COULD
NOT BE DETERMINED WHICH CREW MEMBER HAD THE GOOD CHUTE. NO
EMERGENCY RADIO SIGNALS WERE RECEIVED AT ANY TIME. SUBSEQUENT
SEARCH OF THE AREA FAILED TO FIND ANY CHUTES ON THE GROUND.
IN VIEW OF THE ABOVE INFORMATION YOUR SON WILL BE CARRIED IN
A MISSING IN ACTION STATUS PENDING RECEIPT AND REVIEW OF A

FULL REPORT OF THE CIRCUMSTANCES SURROUNDING HIS DISAPPEARANCE.
YOU MAY BE CERTAIN THAT YOU WILL BE INFORMED OF ANY INFORMATION
RECEIVED REGARDING YOUR SON OR ANY ACTION TAKEN RELATIVE TO
HIS STATUS. YOUR GREAT ANXIETY IN THIS SITUATION IS UNDERSTOOD
AND I WISH TO ASSURE YOU OF EVERY POSSIBLE ASSISTANCE TOGETHER
WITH THE HEARTFELT SYMPATHY OF MYSELF AND YOUR SON'S SHIPMATES
AT THIS TIME OF HEARTACHE AND UNCERTAINTY. IF I CAN ASSIST
YOU PLEASE WRITE OR TELEGRAPH THE CHIEF OF NAVAL PERSONNEL,
DEPARTMENT OF THE NAVY, WASHINGTON DC 20370. MY PERSONAL REPRESENTATIVE
R CAN BE REACHED BY TELEPHONE AT OXFORD 42746 DURING WORKING
HOURS AND OXFORD 42768 AFTER WORKING HOURS. THE AREA IN WHICH
YOUR SON BECAME MISSING PRESENTS THE POSSIBILITY THAAT HE COULD
BE HELD BY HOSTILE FORCES AGAINST HIS WILL. ACCORDINGLY FOR
HIS SAFETY IN THIS EVENT, IT IS SUGGESTED THAT IN REPLYING

TO INQUIRIES FROM SOURCES OUTSIDE YOUR IMMEDIATE FAMILY YOU
REVEAL ONLY HIS NAME, RANK, SERVICE NUMBER AND DATE OF BIRTH

VICE ADMIRAL B J SEMMES JR CHIEF OF NAVAL PERSONNEL

(29).

The telegram my parents received when I was reported missing in action, January 21, 1967.

Flight log. The January 19, 1967, entry shows my flight before shootdown.

central regions of North Vietnam. Vietnamese women would sometimes jump on dropped bombs with bare feet to check the temperature. If a bomb was hot, they would run away, and if it was still cool there might be time to use a vehicle with a rope to drag it off and away from the road. Either way, this was obviously very dangerous to civilians, and I am sure there were some casualties. Of course, *my* only objective was to destroy the road as I'd been ordered.

On my very first mission in the A6, I dropped quite a few bombs without incidence, but then there was an ordnance rack malfunction on my aircraft that prevented me from releasing any more. I radioed the ship, and they directed me to Da Nang in South Vietnam, which was a Marine field. After landing, I was quickly told to put the plane in a remote area away from the field so that the explosive ordnance disposal unit could offload the remaining undetonated bombs.

Allen, Louise, Richard, and Lisa in 1966, Virginia Beach, Virginia.

My bomb load had both chemical and normally fused bombs so when the troops checked underneath the aircraft, whatever they saw caused them to walk away a safe distance to discuss their theories. I had my bombardier navigator disembark and follow them to find out what was up. He reported that one of my bombs

Lieutenant Commander Allen Brady, around the time of deployment to Vietnam, 1966.

remained armed and that we should both leave the aircraft until they could complete their job. I had no problem with that! After just a short time, the live bombs were safely extracted and we headed back to our ship, empty. Naturally, no one is ever allowed to land aboard an aircraft carrier with hung live ordnance, and in any situation where there were no suitable divert fields available, a pilot would have to eject and waste the plane. It was certainly turning out to be a frustrating mission, but it paled in comparison to what was still ahead.

The *Kitty Hawk* returned briefly to Cubi Point for about a week or two of golf and fun, but then it was back to work for me. By January 1967, I was perched in my A6 *Intruder* flying bombing raids over North Vietnam every single day. Every day was another day in the air, another day executing an otherwise normal set of orders on an uneventful day at work. Then, just past the middle of January, the weather started to improve, so a rather large air strike was planned for the nineteenth.

Part 4

Chapter 17

The Third Geneva Convention

Hanoi Jane

Because I was a commander, the Vietnamese went to a lot of trouble to keep me away from the junior officers. In their ignorance, they assumed that without experienced leadership the junior officers would fail to lead when left to their own devices. Nothing could have been farther from the truth, and the ones I knew were more than willing to step forward and take charge. Being kept away from the junior officers also prevented the senior officers from knowing more about the general population of POWs, and that was definitely the case for me for those first few weeks. As a senior officer, I intuitively felt responsible for what was happening around me, as I'm sure all those in my position did. I worried about receiving humane treatment not only for myself but even more so for the others I knew were there too. I was keenly aware that there were internationally recognized rules regarding the capture and containment of military prisoners as outlined in the Third Geneva Convention of 1949, to which the North Vietnamese were signatories and which specifically addressed prisoners of war. For example, according to this set of rules, a prisoner could be made to perform physical work, but the captor was to provide payment. As you might assume, this was hardly our experience. Other rules outlined the quality of food to be eaten, provisions for adequate medical care, communication with family, interrogation procedures, and proper emotional treatment while incarcerated. The following list details the conditions I experienced while in captivity at Hỏa Lò prison, but, from what I later learned, I can assume that conditions in other camps likely were very different, perhaps even worse.

- *American POWs must receive prompt and adequate medical care.*
  Democratic Republic of Vietnam (DRV): What little medical care was available was somewhat primitive, as would be expected from a war-torn nation

suffering such a significant number of casualties. After decades of conflict, North Vietnam was already stretching its resources to the max before the American POWs even got there. One American prisoner I knew of had a severe thumb infection and was taken to the prison courtyard, whereupon the thumb was just amputated. He survived, although we can be sure the procedure was not performed as precisely as it would have been at the Mayo Clinic. Surprisingly, the doctors appeared to do a relatively good job under the dire conditions nonetheless. In my own case, however, I fractured my L4 spine segment on shootdown but was never given X-rays, and I continued to endure back pain from that injury for all the years I was in prison. Not surprisingly, my injury healed improperly and still requires regular use of pain medications. In another incident, I had an infected inner ear, which a medic promptly scraped out with no antiseptic treatment and no sedation. Again, none was really expected. Among our ever-present worries were that we would contract a serious, life-threatening disease such as cancer. I think that if that had happened to one of us, he would have died over there. Thankfully, I am not aware of any POW who succumbed to any such conditions while at Hỏa Lò; however, some died of other causes.

- *American POWs must be allowed to write to their families within one week of capture.*

  DRV: Some POWs averaged two to three letters per year, and others were allowed none at all. The first few pilots and crew members shot down were permitted to write home almost immediately. The North Vietnamese government highly publicized their capture and, as such, was posturing diplomatically on the world stage. However, as 1966 approached and it became clear that the American bombing program would continue for some time, the North Vietnamese decided to stop extending that Geneva Convention–mandated "privilege" to all subsequent prisoners. I was not allowed to write to my family for the first four years following my capture, and then, over the remaining two years I was in prison, I sent and received a combined total of only about a dozen letters.

- *American POWs must be humanely treated and protected; reprisals against POWs are prohibited.*

  DRV: The North Vietnamese paraded American POWs through the streets in 1966, in an event called the Hanoi March. Civilian crowds were whipped up into a frenzy and told to throw things at prisoners in acts designed to inflict humiliation. As another example: many times, I was forced to write out statements thanking the camp commander at Hanoi for the "humane treatment," and withholding food and packages, receiving time in solitary confinement, and undergoing episodes of torture were the punishments for noncompliance to such an order.

- *American POWs are not to be held in "close confinement."*
DRV: Many POWs were held in solitary confinement for years without regular human companionship. I spent the first three months of my captivity totally alone, and in another stint I was completely alone for six months. Others, like Cdr. Leo Profilet, stayed in solitary confinement for four years or more, never getting the opportunity to learn the tap code or communicate in any way with anyone other than the prison guards until after prisoner reunification took place following the Son Tay Raid. Furthermore, many of the cells we lived in were no bigger than walk-in closets and were often shared by two people.

- *American POWs must receive adequate food to prevent loss of weight, and they must be provided with a normal, healthy diet.*
DRV: Fare provided to American prisoners in the Hanoi consisted of pumpkin soup, rice, bread, boiled greens, and pig fat, and we rarely received these in combination with one another. On just two occasions, Fred and I received a serving of new potatoes, but never any fruit while we were there. In many of the prisoners, this poor diet resulted in a condition known as scurvy. All POWs were underweight and suffered from malnutrition and dysentery for the duration of our time in the prison camps. On rare occasions when we were allowed to receive packages from home, our wives included packages of instant coffee to add to our morning pots of water, or perhaps they would send Lifesavers or Charms, which were delicacies, *if* we were allowed to receive them. During Vietnamese holidays only, we were given a dish called banh chung, sticky rice wrapped in banana leaves and tied with tallgrass, like a present. It wasn't so tasty.

- *Captors must allow American POWs to hold/attend regular religious services.*
DRV: This was not allowed to happen, with one exception. Following prisoner reunification after the Son Tay Raid, many of the POWs were placed together in a large room in Camp Unity. Some senior officers held an impromptu religious service when this reunification was initiated, and the prison guards allowed the event to take place. However, following its conclusion, some of those same senior officers were punished for this infraction by being removed from the group and placed back in individual cells. Group prayers were also prohibited, as was talking to one another, in general.

- *Captors must advise promptly the names of all POWs being held in captivity.*
  DRV: The DRV never released an official or a complete list of American prisoners until later in the war, at a point when the Vietnamese believed Nixon's promises that the war was about to be over. In preparation for that hopeful event, we were all given haircuts and instructed to fill out information cards for Red Cross workers, who were also anticipating our release. As it turned out, aside from our efforts at memorizing all of our own names, to my knowledge neither the North Vietnamese government nor the International Red Cross ever compiled an official roster until the war was over (and even then, there has been unending speculation that we still might not know if every American in captivity made it home). And then sadly, that hoped-for release did not come.
- *There are to be neutral inspections of all camps, and regular interviews of POWs are to be permitted without witnesses.*
  DRV: To my knowledge, there were no diplomatic inspections of our camps until just before our release in March 1973. I remember that morning seeing several people in civilian clothes and others in uniforms walking into and out of the building where we were being held, but no one spoke to us, and I am simply speculating that they were inspectors. Furthermore, the only interviews I ever submitted to were to camp officials and prison guards, and they were certainly never related to the quality of care I was being given. Our interviews were usually with guards, most notably a guy we called the Rabbit and others like him who gave us "quizzes" about our opinions on how the war was progressing, trying to get us so fed up with our treatment that we acquiesced to their belief that the United States was losing the war. I wouldn't have considered a meeting like that an actual interview; it was more like a session of intentional harassment, and, trust me, it never worked. The only other interviews I was ever aware of were staged propaganda performances—like the one forced on Jerry Denton early on in the war, when he was seen blinking "TORTURE"—and all of them were contrived to spin the message that the American prisoners were being treated well.

The North Vietnamese always defended their actions by maintaining that even though they signed the Geneva Convention (as Viet-Nam), the agreement as they understood it did not apply to any part of the existing conflict in Southeast Asia, simply because neither government had officially declared that war. Furthermore, they asserted that a state of war had not even been recognized by more than just one of the parties to the conflict (they were referring to themselves). The

American position was that Article 2 of the convention obviously pertained to the Indochinese conflict, since it clearly applied to "any armed conflict, whether the latter is or is not recognized as a state of war." The North Vietnamese also went as far as claiming that American pilots who were shot down and captured were not even prisoners of war but were "air pirates" or "criminals" who had broken Vietnamese laws and were subject to punishment for the crimes they committed.

In contrast to the DRV, the Republic of *South* Vietnam opened its detention camps to inspection by the International Committee of the Red Cross throughout the duration of the war. In fact, a widely publicized effort by Saigon in June 1971 to repatriate 660 sick and wounded North Vietnamese prisoners was initially accepted but later rejected by Hanoi, when only 13 of the North Vietnamese captives agreed to be repatriated and returned to their homeland, if that tells you anything!

As I mentioned, I didn't write to my family for almost four years, a blatant violation of the above agreements. The generally accepted reason I was finally able to send my letters had to do with a tribunal held in Stockholm, Sweden, prior to my capture. Even countries sympathetic to Vietnam's plight were critical of the North's refusal to let us communicate. British philosopher and Nobel Prize winner Bertrand Russell organized the tribunal, and representatives from eighteen countries attended it, many of whom were Nobel Prize winners predominantly from left-wing peace organizations. More than thirty individuals provided testimony at these hearings, including representatives from the United States and both North Vietnamese and South Vietnamese military organizations. It was purported that the North Vietnamese delegation boastfully claimed that an American POW named Nels Tanner admitted to them that many American pilots were opposed to the war in Southeast Asia and he gave the name *Tom Ewell* as evidence of a prisoner who would substantiate his claim. It turns out that *Tom Ewell* and some other names he gave were relatively unknown Hollywood actors and Tanner had completely contrived the whole story about dissent among the POWs. A reporter who was present to hear the testimonies wrote a scathing piece on the incident after returning home to the United States. He exposed the Northern Vietnamese's naïveté about the story and debunked their attempts to discredit American policies, which, of course, completely embarrassed their government. Needless to say, Nels Tanner, a man who was also a friend and VA-95 squadronmate, certainly paid the price for taking his shot at sticking it to the DRV.

Throughout the war, there were many such tribunals. Antiwar groups were in large supply, and their singular purpose was to collect anecdotal evidence that would vilify the US military. Of course, there are always serious transgressions to be found during times of war, on any front in any country, and considering the stress of close combat, it is disappointing but not often surprising that heinous errors in judgment sometimes take place. The My Lai (pronounced *me-lie*) Massacre is one of the most glaring examples of this point, and from what I know of it, it appeared utterly appalling. I have supported that suitable punishments be meted out, if the events as I understood them turned out to be true; however, I was not there and I cannot pass judgment on that unit's decisions. Furthermore, I strongly assert that anything illegal that might have ever taken place was not indicative of what I experienced as a member of the US Armed Services and should not be generalized to apply to our standard code of behavior. Throughout my entire career with the US Navy, I never witnessed, not once, a single incident in which a truly villainous act went unpunished, and, certainly, our mission was never to intentionally harm the innocent people in Vietnam. War is hell on everyone, and people undoubtedly behaved badly on occasion. But it was always incomprehensible to me that back home there was such hatred toward our military, in particular the American POWs, while we suffered inside the walls of an enemy prison cell defending America's resistance against Communism.

Regrettably, the most outlandish purveyors of the genocide propaganda campaign were two well-known American citizens. In the United States, there was an organization called the Vietnam Veterans Against the War (VVAW), which organized protests and hearings to malign the American military. The VVAW's most well-known events took place in 1970 and 1971, and its spokesman was future presidential candidate John Kerry. The VVAW organized a three-day march from Morristown, New Jersey, to Valley Forge, Pennsylvania, during which it simulated war atrocities against civilians, including mock rapes, murders, and torture, acts they claimed the US military committed, stating that American soldiers did those things *every day*. The Valley Forge event culminated with a rally featuring John Kerry and Jane Fonda on the same stage spewing their nonsense. Again referencing the My Lai Massacre of 1968, Fonda proclaimed, "My Lai was not an isolated event but rather a way of life for many of our military." She was referring, of course, to the highly publicized slaughter of hundreds of South Vietnamese villagers harboring the Viet Cong, a massacre led by Army lieutenant William Calley. It was a shameful blemish on our national reputation, and Calley was only mildly punished for his crimes, unfortunately. Still, for Fonda to extend that behavior to all of us and to claim it could occur on any given day in Vietnam or that, worse, it was standard behavior for those serving in the American military was simply beyond the pale.

In July 1972 in Hanoi, Fonda posed sitting in the seat of a North Vietnamese antiaircraft gun with its crew, the very people who shot us down from the sky with those same weapons and then tortured us once they had us in their prisons. She claimed that American pilots (like me) were bombing the dikes in the rice paddies, with the expressed intent to starve the Northern Vietnamese people to death, a complete fallacy. When the POWs returned home at the end of the war, after having been beaten and tortured by their captors for years and forced to sign confessions of war crimes, Fonda continued her maliciousness, calling us hypocrites and pawns. Her allegations questioned the basic truthfulness of our experiences as hostages and prisoners of war and called into question all that we claimed to have gone through. She called the American POWs liars and said we completely contrived our abuse and dishonestly misrepresented our prison experiences, asserting that "tortured men do not march smartly off planes, salute the flag, and kiss their wives!" But, in fact, we do. It's called returning with honor. Her comments echoed through our ranks.

Fonda reminds me of Iva Toguri D'Aquino, known as Tokyo Rose, another American who found herself in the middle of an international conflict. She was in Japan in 1941 when the Japanese attacked the United States at Pearl Harbor; she was stuck there during the aftermath, unable to return home to the United States. She was forced to make radio broadcasts to US troops, and her commentary included messages about anti-American propaganda. After World War II was over, President Truman had her brought back to the United States, where she was tried for treason, then, as a result of her trial, she lost her American citizenship. In 1976, not too long after he forgave former president Richard Nixon, President Gerald Ford also pardoned Tokyo Rose, but compare her offenses to Jane Fonda's. Tokyo Rose was *stuck* in Japan, whereas Jane Fonda went to North Vietnam freely. Tokyo Rose was forced to renounce her US citizenship, while Jane Fonda, in my opinion, should have had hers revoked! Instead, Fonda returned home to the United States and to her liberal Hollywood friends and never needed to be pardoned by anyone for any of the heinous offenses she committed, including the public degradation of the American prisoners of war.

Today, I believe America should never have a relationship with any country that once abused our citizens. Furthermore, anyone who took the positions Fonda did shouldn't be allowed to enjoy the freedoms of living in a country for whom she has never made a single sacrifice or given up a single day of her own freedom defending it.

Chapter 18

Uncle Ho

"I Want to Make for You Happy"

In spite of my experiences as a prisoner in their nation, I still believe that the people of Vietnam are very peaceful. If you understand their history, going back more than four thousand years, you can recognize that they have had to defend themselves from outsiders a great many times. When I studied geography as a kid, Vietnam was known as French Indochina, and in the early twentieth century, this region also included Laos and Cambodia. In fact, the area had been under French control from the 1700s to the early decades of the twentieth century.

To illustrate my point about their defensive nature and to show how the patience of Asian people appears to greatly exceed that of people in the West, I offer an example. During one of my "attitude checks" (interrogations), the camp officer stated to me that Vietnam had *always* been an independent country. I replied that it was my understanding that China had once occupied the country. He answered, "But only for 700 years."

After World War I, America grew concerned about the threat of Communism as it continued to spread throughout the eastern hemisphere. This accelerated dramatically at the end of World War II as the United States and the Soviet Union faced off in dominant opposition during the Cold War years. In fact, it was widely accepted that if left to its own devices, Communism would indeed spread throughout any neighboring countries, in a phenomenon known as the domino effect. We were assured, for instance, that if Vietnam fell to the Communists, so, too, would Laos, then Cambodia, and then Thailand, and so on and so on. We were reminded again and again that under the Vladimir Lenin regime, followed by the Joseph Stalin regime, Communism did in fact spread rapidly as the USSR sought world domination. Vietnam looked poised to follow suit, and we'd seen every important sign indicating that the Soviets planned to expand further into Southeast Asia.

On a smaller scale, Ho Chi Minh was also a merciless tyrant. Affectionately known as "Uncle Ho" by the Vietnamese people, Ho Chi Minh intended to propagate his Communist teachings in his own country, which had already been exposed to Communism in the years following World War I. Let me be clear though: not everyone was so enamored of him *or* his teachings. In 1933, he traveled to Moscow, where he attended and even taught classes at the Lenin Institute, absorbing the teachings of Communism. In 1940, the Empire of Japan also happened to be seeking world domination and was occupying his country when Ho Chi Minh returned to Vietnam to lead the independence movement against them and the French puppet government that was in place at the time.

Once home, he established and led the Viet Minh, the Communist regime in North Vietnam and, more importantly, an umbrella group purported to represent all groups that were fighting for independence. Then in 1945, following Japan's surrender to the Allies, Ho declared a Proclamation of Independence. He established the Democratic Republic of Vietnam and appointed himself chairman of the new movement, as Communist dictators conveniently do in times of chaos. Notably, he used US animosity to further his efforts against the Japanese, offering assurances that his motives were strictly aligned with the United States'. Clearly, no nation recognized Uncle Ho's new government, but it nevertheless received the attention of all nations (including the United States) that had interest in protecting against the rise of dictators, Communist or not. Then the French returned in 1945. On March 6, 1946, Ho signed an agreement with France in which Vietnam was to become an autonomous state in the French Union. In 1945–46, Ho and the Viet Minh collaborated with the French to massacre supporters of the Vietnamese Nationalist Movement in South Vietnam, who opposed Communism. The Communists suppressed all non-Communist parties but were still not able to secure a peace deal with the French. So, after French occupation before World War II and Japanese occupation during World War II, the Vietnamese now fought against the French in the First Indochina War. In 1954, the Vietnamese defeated the French, and the Viet Minh assassinated between 100,000 and 150,000 civilians.

The conclusion of that war resulted in the 1954 Geneva Accords. Vietnam was split into two parts, with the French regrouping to the South and the Communist Democratic Republic of Vietnam going North. There was to be a three-hundred-day period in which people could move freely between the North and the South, with the entire nation being divided at the 17th parallel. More than one million people moved south, while a much smaller contingency moved north. Then re-unification was discussed. The Viet Minh proposed that elections be held under the supervision of "local commissions," but the United States, with support from South Vietnam and the United Kingdom, vetoed this, in what was known as "the American Plan." The plan provided for reunification elections under UN super-vision, but, not surprisingly, the Soviet delegation and the North Vietnamese rejected this. Elections were never held. First, the North's population of 17 million exceeded the South's 14 million, and there were already many Communists in the South. Second, all opposition groups in the North were suppressed. Those speak-ing out publicly were later imprisoned in gulags or executed. Third, the North Vietnamese government launched rent-reduction and land-reform programs. These targeted peasants, who assumed, incorrectly, that if they were victorious in their fight on Ho's side, they would own their own farmland.

The Communists realized that the only way to unify their country under their terms was to defeat the South militarily. Have no doubt about it, Ho went to Moscow to meet with Stalin and Mao Zedong of China and to enlist their support. China was right in the middle of this but never got the heat they de-served. In fact, in one instance, in August 1967, when an A6 was shot down over North Vietnam, its pilot was killed but the bombardier/navigator, Bob Flynn, was captured and sent to Beijing, where he remained until we were released. Also, many American prisoners routinely saw bags of flour and rice from China sitting around our prison, so there was clear collusion.

The US government maintained its staunch opposition to any further spread of Communism and started to send in troops to thwart the North. It was certain that that no one would succeed against them in a conventional conflict. Perhaps in agreement with this observation, the Vietnamese strategy became prolonging the war until eventually the United States just relented and accepted the condi-tions of the North Vietnamese. At any rate, that's how the United States ended up involved in the war in Vietnam. Considering how it eventually turned out, the United States didn't seem to accomplish much, and we certainly underestimated Vietnamese resolve.

One day, as Fred and I were biding our time doing what we always did, a whole bunch of nothing, we were told that Uncle Ho had passed away. The camp offi-cers told us to be on good behavior, as the loss of Ho was very devastating to the Vietnamese people. Later, when we heard the bells ringing in downtown Hanoi during his funeral, we wondered if it was also our own death knell. Such a swift turn of events left us wondering what changes would come diplomatically and militarily, but as it turned out, Ho Chi Minh's death was a huge positive for the Americans in captivity. Our conditions seemed to improve slightly in the weeks that immediately followed his death. We still weren't able to talk to one another, but I sensed that we all felt more at ease, hoping that perhaps things weren't going to get any worse for us. In fact, our conditions actually improved a bit, and once, the guards even gave us small baskets insulated with wood shavings to keep our teapots warm. Fred and I felt like we were living high on the hog! Warm water in a heated teapot—it was unbelievable! At the time of Ho Chi Minh's death, we were living in the Stardust, in the half cell, the one where you could sit on the lower bunk with your back to the wall and easily put your feet on the opposite wall. I walked back and forth across those few feet so many times, I couldn't keep count. I don't know how many miles I walked during my years in prison, but I never wore out those rubber-tire sandals. In fact, there was still some good tread left by the time we got out, so maybe they were fifty-thousand-mile tires.

We also started receiving more packages from home. Next door to Fred and me was a classmate of mine who was living alone, and we learned through tapping that he hadn't received a package. Fred and I felt bad for the guy, so we decided to sneak him a piece of candy. We'd gone to wash up for dinner and on our way back to our cell Fred distracted the guard while I tossed a Lifesaver into the guy's cell, since he was gone and his cell door was wide open. That piece of candy bounced around that room and pinged off the walls as if I'd thrown a rock on a tin roof. Of course, the guard heard it, too, and knew pretty quickly that I did it. I knew I was busted, but, honestly, I thought the punishment would be minor. Was I ever wrong. The Bug came to see me. He was an officer in the Vietnamese Army who had frequent contact with the POWs and was one of the men who served up the orders for torture. He was pudgy and short, and North Korea's current leader, Kim Jong Un, resembles him slightly. He told me that he had to leave briefly to attend Ho's funeral, but he would be coming to see me once he got back.

Later, I was seated in front of the Bug and he pummeled me with questions, wanting to know how Fred and I knew the POW in the neighboring cell had not received a package. I decided to play the role of smartass and told him I thought Fred and I were such good prisoners that perhaps we might have been the only ones lucky enough to get a package. The Bug wasn't buying my story and didn't appreciate my humor, so three days of torture commenced.

I was placed in a chair facing a rectangular wooden table draped with a blue cloth, which prevented me from seeing underneath the table. I wasn't tied up at

"SPOOK"　"RABBIT"　"SPOT"

Hỏa Lò prison guards. Drawings by POW Lt. Cdr. Mike McGrath. (Reprinted by permission from John M. McGrath, *Prisoner of War: Six Years in Hanoi.* Annapolis, MD: Naval Institute Press, © 1975)

first; I was just made to sit still in the chair and not move. Day turned to night and then to day again, and I started getting tired and sore, my bad back ached. Twelve hours passed, then eighteen, then twenty-four, and I sat in the same position facing the same desk. The next day, they took my chair away and replaced it with a small sawhorse. By this time, I was seeing things that may or may not have been real. During the second night, I fell asleep sitting on top of the sawhorse and woke up hours later, bent completely over on my side at a ninety-degree angle. I finally fell completely off the sawhorse after several more hours in this position, so when the guards heard me crash to the floor, they came in and propped me right back up again.

After what I think was the third night, I started to feel dizzy and my mind began playing tricks on me. It was a foggy sensation and I saw things under the table I knew couldn't really be there. I remember sitting there, looking at the floor, and it was just bricks at first, but then suddenly they looked like glass and I could see into them. I could see things coming up out of the floor. I called the guards in numerous times to show them what I saw, yet there was never anything for them to see. Sadly, I also heard voices telling me we were going home the next day—cruel, untrue reassurances that my nightmare wouldn't last much longer. Still, I knew it wasn't right and that it wasn't possible. I knew I was hallucinating, and I started to suspect I'd been drugged. At any rate, it reached a point where they knew they had me beaten down, recognizing, perhaps, that this was it for me. The Bug came in and again told me to bow, and still I refused, saying, "No, I am leaving tomorrow." I swear, even now, I heard that voice telling me we were being released the next day. I was certain of it. So, I continued to refuse to comply and I refused to bow to him. The Bug left and returned with Flower Hat, asking me if I knew who he was. I said, "Yeah, I know him." Yet still I remained defiant, knowing I was getting myself into a real jam. They took me off to a small room, which had me leaving Little Vegas and going back to New Guy Village. They broke out the old leg irons and the dreaded ropes, and I got The Works.

After I was debriefed back in the States about this particular interrogation, obviously it was assumed that my delusions were caused partly by sleep deprivation. We all suspected then, though, and I suspect now that it was something altogether different. I know one thing for sure, I'd never felt that way before. The Navy officials who examined me said they'd gotten reports from other prisoners relaying the same experience.

After the torture, they dragged me, still in the irons, over to a table and told me to write out a confession of all my crimes, and the Bug said he would dictate for me. I was still feeling so disoriented and confused. He told me I would be writing to the camp commander to thank him for the kind and humane treatment I was receiving, then he told me to write, "I want to make for you happy." I was sweating from exhaustion, hurting all over, and yet, internally I smiled to myself, hoping to God they would send my confession out exactly as I was writing it. They were always warning us that if we did not cooperate they would publish our confessions. Oh, did I wish they would! When I finished composing my letter, the guards took me back to the quiz room and let me go to sleep. I'll never know how long I slept, but I still remember the voice that kept telling me I was going to be released the next day. When I awoke much later and felt like myself again, the disappointment I felt at comprehending my hallucinations about going home was more overwhelming than I can describe. Even now, any disappointment pales in comparison to that, and I haven't forgotten what it felt like in that moment when I realized those voices weren't real.

Chapter 19

The Cuban Program

The Other Fidel

It was known as the Cuban Program, and for many decades the US government asked the returning POWs not to discuss it. The 106th Congress held hearings on Thursday, November 4, 1999, some twenty-six years after my release, and the following declassified information was finally discussed openly. Until then, sketchy versions of the story of "the other Fidel" (a name coined by the POWs who knew him at the time) appeared in a handful of US publications in 1973, when Hanoi began releasing prisoners. Information continued to be leaked about "Fidel" until mid-1977, but it still drew very little attention. Now, newly released Department of Defense documents confirm that "Fidel" was indeed real, he was Cuban, and he tortured American POWs. (*Honor Bound: The History of Prisoners of War in Southeast Asia, 1961–1973* [Honolulu: University Press of the Pacific, 1998], Stuart Rochester and Frederick Kiley's excellent book, devotes thirteen pages to the "unusually intensive and prolonged operation that monopolized the prison's torture machinery for much of the year." I highly recommend it to anyone who wants to know all the gory details.) A two-inch-thick stack of documents declassified for those congressional hearings provided the extensive and gruesome details on the Cuban Program, including this observation from a 1975 US Air Force analysis of the reports on the topic: "This marked the first and only time that non-Vietnamese were overtly involved in the exploitation of American prisoners."

Sometime around August 1967, two men the POWs called Fidel and Chico showed up at the outlying camp known as the Zoo, a former French movie studio on the southwestern edge of Hanoi that got its name when the prisoners inside would make animal noises to amuse the gawkers who passed by the cells. It was clear to the prisoners that these two men were no ordinary visitors. When POWs were debriefed after they returned home, those who were held at the Zoo described Fidel as about six-foot-one, in his early thirties, muscular, ramrod straight, swarthy, and fairly handsome. They described Chico as lighter skinned, almost blonde, and a bit older, perhaps in his forties. Chico liked to play Spanish-sounding songs on the camp's organ, which was their first clue as to his nationality, and he often wore a beret with a visor, the type popular in Cuba at the time, and the same kind worn by Cuban leader Fidel Castro. Both men spoke pretty good English, though heavily accented, but while Fidel had full command of American slang (even the obscenities), Chico struggled. Fidel interviewed several POWs and then selected Col. Ed Hubbard and Col. Jack Bomar, plus eight other Air Force and Navy pilots and navigators shot down over North Vietnam. He segregated them in a block of four cells that the POWs nicknamed "the Stable." That moment of separation from the population is when the Cuban Program of torture began. In 2016, as I conducted research for this book, I read an August 20, 1999, news story from the *Miami Herald*, in which former Zoo POW Allen Carpenter said of them, "Under different circumstances, Fidel might have been an interesting guy, but I can't have anything but loathing for him" (available online at *Organización Auténtica O/A: Por una Cuba Cubana* http://www.autentico.org/oa09872.php).

Returning POWs told debriefers that Fidel loved direct hits to the face with tire strips, called "fan belts." He placed prisoners who were awaiting interrogation in cells next to his torture room, to make sure they could hear the screams of the guys being worked over. He threw POWs he'd just tortured in with new guys so that the new guys would see the results of his tune-ups. As the days passed, Fidel notched up the torture. Former Zoo POW Robert Daughtry also told the *Miami Herald*, in that same 1999 piece, "Fidel could get you squirming without even touching you," and "the anticipation of the beatings became more of a threat than the actual beatings. We got nervous to the point of losing our bowels when we heard the key in the lock."

In January 1968, a confident Fidel then selected a second group of ten POWs. One of them surrendered swiftly, aware of Fidel's reputation. Two other prisoners won the other POWs' admiration by engaging the man in friendly conversations that seemed to avert torture. But then, he found Jim Kasler, a man sent to the Zoo after already withstanding torture at another prison, and Earl Cobeil, an Air Force F105 pilot who acted somewhat insane and may have suffered a head injury when he ejected.

Fidel's month-long beatings of Kasler were among the worst episodes of torture any American withstood in Hanoi. He flogged him until his buttocks, lower back, and legs hung in shreds, and at the end he was essentially in a semi-coma.

Worse still were the abuses committed against Cobeil, whom Fidel accused of faking his craziness to avoid torture. For investigators, Colonel Bomar recalled hearing Fidel angrily vowing to the other POWs that he would break Cobeil into a million pieces. Bomar recalled that during one all-day torture session in May 1968, Fidel took a length of black rubber hose and lashed it as hard as he could into that man's face. Cobeil did not react; he did not cry out or even blink. Bomar told his debriefer that after a month of almost daily beatings just like this, Cobeil was bleeding everywhere, terribly swollen, and was a dirty yellowish, black, and purple mess from head to toe. This particularly vicious system of extreme physical and psychological torture was said to have been an experimental program to test domination techniques. Cobeil endured, as he told a *Miami Herald* reporter, "one of the most heinous and tragic atrocities in the Northern Vietnam American POW experience."

By Christmas 1967, four months after the Cuban Program started, all but one of the original ten had been tortured into "surrendering," which meant succumbing to any sign of submission that Fidel arbitrarily set, from bowing to a Vietnamese guard, to accepting an unwanted cigarette, to making written or tape-recorded statements that the North Vietnamese propaganda machine could use. Some of the ten were still beaten occasionally "just to keep us in line," Bomar said, but, ironically, those ten said they received better meals, more mail, and more time in the sunlight outside their dark and bug-infested cells at the conclusion of their initiation into the program than they had before entering the program. By the end of the Cuban Program, Fidel had tortured eighteen of the original twenty selected POWs. Two of them were never beaten. All of them besides Cobeil surrendered.

This man's service is officially recounted as follows:

COBEIL, EARL GLENN, US AIR FORCE, CAPTAIN
SERIAL NUMBER 364327201.
AGE 36, DOB 29 AUGUST 1934
US CITIZEN BY BIRTH
RESIDENT OF PONTIAC, MICHIGAN.
DATE OF LOSS: 05 NOVEMBER 1967
COUNTRY OF LOSS: NORTH VIETNAM
COORDINATES: 213000N 1051400E
STATUS PRISONER OF WAR
MARRIED   CAUCASIAN

After weeks of vicious beatings, unrelenting psychological torture, solitary confinement and forced electro-shocks, his mental and physical condition deteriorated progressively until his death in the Fall of 1967 in a cell at Hỏa Lò. His remains were returned to the United States on 24 March 1974.

With my confirmed knowledge of the Cuban Program, I could not in clear conscience ever forgive the real Fidel (Castro) and his brother Raul as they continued building their vicious regime. Just like Uncle Ho, those men were vicious criminals. I also watched the United States under President Barack Obama even attempt to extend diplomatic overtures to the Castros, to normalize relations with their country, and if this continues, it appears that American tourists will soon be allowed to travel there, keeping that monstrous Communist regime in power with American dollars.

I heartily welcomed Fidel Castro's death in 2016, and his brother's renewed intentions regarding improved relations with the United States disturb me greatly. When Cuba held elections in 2018 and chose its new president, Miguel Diaz-Canel, it seemed to finally signal the end of the Castro regime. But still, Diaz-Canel is simply another dictator of the Communist Party, and that government has always dismissed references to the atrocities of the Cuban Program and always denies any involvement in the torture of American prisoners. Most importantly, neither Fidel nor Chico has ever been positively identified or located, to my knowledge. For all I know, they are alive and well and living out their retirement in Cuba. Certainly, Earl Cobeil and the other victims of the Cuban Program deserve better.

Chapter 20

Your Blue Suit

Aunt Mary

In the fall of 1970, in an effort to become compliant with the international rules of war, and certainly to utilize us as propaganda tools, the Vietnamese government permitted many of the prisoners to begin writing infrequent letters home. I'd been a hostage at Hỏa Lò for about four years before they finally allowed me to write my first one. I knew I would never be allowed to ask my family directly, "How are peace talks coming along?" or "Has the CIA given you any new information?" because to do so might bait my wife, Louise, into sending me uplifting or helpful news, something my captors would absolutely not tolerate and would never have delivered to me anyway. I was, however, allowed to tell everyone back home "how well" I was doing, and soon I became adept at crafting benign messages about housekeeping items and safe subjects like the weather and golf. The prison officials, who spoke some English, needed to see approved drafts of each letter in advance, but then we were still required to formally rewrite each letter again as they looked on. This happened only rarely, about once every three months, so we had to be ready to go when it was our turn, and we had to work hard to make wise use of our opportunities when they came.

We used a couple of different methods. Our letters were always drafted on prison-provided paper, five inches wide by seven inches long, with writing space limited to seven lines. Prisoners were repeatedly warned not to make careless mistakes in judgment with regard to content when we were writing and were told not to get greedy with requests for, or delivery of, information from home. Even harmless news and current events were prohibited. Punishment for not following the rules was that our letters were simply not sent, an obviously disheartening consequence.

The first method I used required asking my wife odd questions that might not make sense to her at first, questions that I hoped would let her know that I was up to something. In one of my first attempts, I wrote, "How is Aunt Mary?" This certainly must have perplexed her at first, since I didn't have an Aunt Mary. If I am allowed to speculate, I would guess that conversations between my wife and Navy or CIA officials perusing the letter together likely went something like this:

"Do you have an Aunt Mary, Mrs. Brady?"

"No, I do not."

"Do you know anyone named Mary, Mrs. Brady?"

And here is where things must have started to make sense and she had it figured out. The Aunt Mary I was asking about was actually Mary Crow, Fred's wife. After a dig into still-missing POWs, the CIA likely pieced together that I was in the same cell as Fred Crow. Fortunately, Mary Crow and my wife knew each other, so with my subtle hints as proof, Mrs. Crow was notified that her husband was alive and was with me and the other American prisoners at Hỏa Lò. My wife wrote me back in confirmation, "I saw your Aunt Mary." That's when I knew she was in on it with me.

It was John McCain who first told me how to use another method of sending or requesting information using my letters. By 1971, newer prisoners were being allowed to send letters home pretty soon after their arrival at the Hilton, and by the time McCain found himself in the cell next to mine, he'd already sent a few of his own in this way, undetected. Using a different tactic, and with great skill and patience, we were also able to secretly spell out statements containing important information, camouflaged within the text of our letters. Here's how we did it: as we wrote our cursive strokes along the seven straight lines on our paper, we were careful not to let our words actually touch the lines, unless, of course a letter in a particular word was part of the coded message we wanted to send. It was rather difficult and extremely time consuming to craft a letter in this way, but, if you'll remember, all we had was time. So as I wrote to my wife, I rested the bottoms of select letters down onto the line in a way that did not stand out but still alerted my informed reader that I had a message to relay. In keeping with my desire to inform the Navy that Fred Crow was with me, and as I gained confidence in my work, I spelled out, "I live with Fred Crow." (This letter is on page 145; feel free to try cracking it yourself!)

Naturally, to the prison guards my letters read harmlessly enough, and usually any messages I tried to send would escape the language barriers that prevented

NGƯỜI GỬI (Addressor)

HỌ TÊN (Name in full):

Allen C. Brady

SỐ LÍNH (Service number): _542856_

TRẠI GIAM PHI CÔNG MỸ BỊ BẮT TẠI
NƯỚC VIỆT-NAM DÂN CHỦ CỘNG HÒA

(Camp of detention for U.S. pilots captured
in the DEMOCRATIC REPUBLIC of VIETNAM)

NGƯỜI NHẬN (Addressee)

HỌ TÊN (Name in full):

Mrs Allen C. Brady

ĐỊA CHỈ (Address):

3424 Kings Grant Rd
Virginia Beach, Va.

Above and facing page: The coded letter to Louise.

my captors from detecting the nuances of English. In other words, most of the time our letters got through easily enough. I have no idea of the path they traveled before finally arriving in the United States, but I would guess they were delivered first to a foreign embassy in Hanoi, perhaps the Swedish embassy, then possibly sent through other channels before finally making it to US officials in Washington, DC, and then on to Louise. I can't be sure, and it never occurred to me to ask her about these details. I still remain perplexed as to how they ever, miraculously, came to be in Louise's possession. I was just glad she was getting them at all.

NGÀY VIẾT (Dated) *5 October 1970*

Dear Louise and kids, I have no permanent injuries.

Louise dont worry about financial matters, car, house,

trailer etc. Any decisions you make are fine with me.

Richard, I know you are doing fine as man of the

house, help mom with the hard jobs. Lisa you were

very cute and grown up in your picture, help mom around

the house. I will be happy if you both do well in school. Love, Allen

GHI CHÚ (N.B.):

1. Phải viết rõ và chỉ được viết trên những dòng kẻ sẵn (Write legibly and only on the lines).
2. Gia đình gửi đến cũng phải theo đúng mẫu, khuôn khổ và quy định này (Notes from families should also conform to this proforma).

My wife acquired great skill in delivering important information to me using these clandestine tactics, and I was thankful for that, because I was absolutely starved for it. Surely, I can assume, other wives involved themselves in this task as well. Toward the end of the months when I was allowed to write to my family, my wife and I exchanged one especially important bit of promising news. My most memorable letter to her started the following hidden correspondence:

"Was I promoted?" I asked her, touching down just the right letters of my words hidden among the other mundane correspondence in the letter/line code. Only my wife would know how to respond: "I took your blue suit to the dry cleaners to be altered." She was telling me that yes, even in my absence, the US government had promoted me to captain, adding a fourth stripe to my existing three. It was the sort of news that got an air pirate through another tough day. I have to say, it was pretty impressive work; another testament to the immense sacrifices made by our families, most specifically our wives, who worked tirelessly for part of a decade to get us back home.

Chapter 21

Escape

Note in Ipana

One of the many outlying camps in North Vietnam was at the thermal power plant near Yen Phu in Hanoi. We called it the Dirty Bird Annex. When the United States announced that the Yen Phu plant and the bridge over the Red River in Hanoi were now on the United States' target list, the North Vietnamese reacted expediently. They placed approximately thirty POWs inside the power plant and announced publicly that they had done so. Furthermore, American POWs were photographed at the plant, so it was undeniable that they were there. The United States either didn't put all this together or chose to consider it irrelevant, but either way, they bombed the plant. On October 12, 1967, POWs George McKnight and George Coker hunkered down in their cell as huge explosions went off all around them.

It was the middle of the night, and apparently the prison guards were hunkered down somewhere, too, hiding. The two prisoners capitalized on their opportunity and picked the lock of their cell, then bolted out of the prison and ran brazenly through the streets of Hanoi until they reached the Red River. During that night, they floated twelve miles downriver, and as daylight approached they tried to hide under foliage in the bushes along the riverbank. Of course, a civilian soon spotted them, and they were taken right back to the prison. Later on, when we were all in Camp Unity, I saw Coker and I couldn't resist asking him about their escape plan. He humorously recalled that they floated downriver that night knowing it was a long shot, but their plan was to reach the Gulf of Tonkin. They hoped to steal a small boat somewhere along the way and head straight out to sea to find one of the US vessels operating nearby. However, since the Red River winds back and forth endlessly across the region, their trip was considerably longer. Who can ever know if they might've been successful under different conditions? In any case, I maintain a tremendous amount of respect for them for trying. I know nothing of the punishment they received, but I do know this: they did a tour in Alcatraz, and everyone knew that Alcatraz was, after the Zoo and its Cuban Program, among the most horrific places for a prisoner to be held in North Vietnam.

The second escape, this one from the Zoo, was much more strategic and required a great deal of advanced planning. To protect their fellow prisoners from any repercussions, should they be discovered missing, the two POWs involved, John Dramesi and Ed Atterbury, told very few about their intentions. According to rumors that circulated throughout the prisons, they believed it was possible to get out through an opening in the roof and then out of the camp under the cover of night. The men were successful at first, and their plan actually worked, initially. They ran as far as they could before daylight, and then they hid themselves. Of course, the North Vietnamese put a dragnet out for them almost immediately, and they were discovered the next day. Their punishment was extreme, and the camp commander at the Zoo was in a rage. He kept Atterbury captive there, but Dramesi was sent back to New Guy Village at Hỏa Lò for a long stint in portable leg irons. That variety locked onto the ankles and had one long iron rod laced though both ankle shackles so the wearer could not stand up or walk. Dramesi sat bracketed in those leg irons on the brick floor with his back against a wall and his hands cuffed behind him, unable to move around, for three solid months. The prison guards let him out of his cuffs only to eat. Miraculously, once he rejoined us, he *still* wanted to be a part of any escape plan the rest of us were plotting.

As for Atterbury, he was subjected to a fatal treatment with the fan belts, literally beaten to death. The other POWs in the surrounding cells could hear his screams as he died.

The camp authorities wanted to know every detail about how the escape had been planned, so they called in several other, innocent prisoners and tortured them as well until they gave up something, even if they had to fabricate stories. Of course none of the other POWs knew anything about any of it, yet all the men were beaten until they satiated the guards' hunger for information. Recognizing that I could easily have found myself in the same situation at any moment during those years, I always felt particularly sorry for men who were beaten mercilessly for information they didn't have.

I am proud to say that a dear friend of mine *almost* succeeded in his attempt to cross the demilitarized zone separating North and South Vietnam. Maj. Bud Day escaped from a small, no-name camp in the southern region of North Vietnam and traveled quickly through the jungle, knowing he was relatively close to the border, likely within two or three miles. He had to travel on footpaths because the thick jungles were impassable, which made hiding particularly difficult. Additionally, the B-52s were carpet bombing the area nearly constantly, and at least once they got close enough to permanently damage his hearing with their blasts. Bud told me that he spotted a US aircraft in a landing pattern near a friendly field, but that's where he ran right into the unfriendlies who proceeded to shoot him in the arm. He was taken back to his prison camp and put into the hands of another raging camp commander. Although his arm was initially set, as punishment he was strung up and they broke it again.

I knew Bud well, both in prison and in freedom. He was a mild, gentle man, but I can say with certainty that he was also the toughest man I've ever known in my life. He received the Congressional Medal of Honor for his service and for his heroic resistance. When Bud died in 2014, his body was driven through my hometown of Pensacola. The highway along the funeral route was lined for miles and miles with admirers and well-wishers from Fort Walton to Pensacola, a distance of over fifty miles. I miss him so much. Truly, where do we get such men?

To my knowledge, these were the only escape attempts. We all knew that even if someone had been able to escape from one of the prisons, without any outside assistance there was little chance of success. In a foreign land with a foreign language, stranded hundreds of miles from anything familiar, paired with the fact that we did not blend in at all, we had so little hope of breaking out of there. Still, as a result of these attempts, a prison crackdown was imminent. I don't know if it had anything to do with these attempts, but it certainly seems logical that they were a factor. Plus, the North Vietnamese realized definitively that we were communicating with each other, and the chatter among us, both spoken and unspoken, was undeniable to anybody with any common sense. They knew what we were doing, and by then we were deeply entrenched in our defiance. So they responded as they always did: with more torture and a crackdown designed to get us all back in line.

The camp commander at Hỏa Lò singled out the most senior POWs and included their unlucky cellmates, regardless of rank, and, as we say, "put the squeeze on them." The guards sensed that the excited talk of the escapes was spreading rapidly among us, so they came around regularly from that point on and checked our knuckles to see if we were tapping. Of course we were. But they also pieced together that the codes could be sent in many different ways. As such, after the crackdowns, we were no longer allowed to sweep the courtyard or engage in any other activity where we could use code. But be assured, we found ways around their new rules. This was one of the times when Jerry Denton's vocal code came in handy, and we had other ways, too, ingenious techniques developed by a collection of sharp POWs.

One significant part of the crackdown that followed involved eleven of the senior POWs and their cellmates, whom the North Vietnamese selected for torture to determine our methods of communicating. Subsequently, the eleven were sent to Alcatraz. This tiny facility was blistering hot during the summer, almost to the point of causing people to suffer heat exhaustion from simply sitting in their cells. The POWs kept there stayed for about twenty-five months, nineteen of which they spent in leg irons. That they survived this place at all under those conditions was nothing short of a miracle. When they finally returned to Hỏa Lò, we could see their pants hanging on the clothesline after they did their laundry. At the bottom of each leg was a permanent rust-colored ring, a stained reminder to all of the rest of us of their time in those horrible, rusty leg irons.

Jim Stockdale was one of these men, the Alcatraz Eleven. He was the senior ranking officer over all of the rest of us, and although there were four full colonels from the US Air Force in the prison, we had no idea they were even there until we were close to being released. The North Vietnamese knew Jim was a senior officer and just assumed he was to blame for most of our resistance to the camp authorities. They worked on him once for a long, long time, to get him to make a movie for their propaganda. They left him in his cell briefly to prepare and warned him that when they returned he would be forced to create the film. When they came back, they found that Commander Stockdale had used a wooden stool to beat himself in his own face so that they would not be able to film him. At that point, the camp commander commented, "My work is done," and they left Jim alone. Being the senior ranking officer was a heavy burden for anyone, especially in a POW scenario, and Jim did a truly heroic job. Like my friend Bud Day, upon his release from prison, Jim was deservingly awarded the Congressional Medal of Honor.

After the escape attempts and the harsh punishments that followed, the prison rules got much stricter. Naturally, we charged ourselves to get a good deal smarter. Fred and I became dishwashers for our building. We collected the metal dishes and took them to a shower stall to wash them. I use the term "shower" loosely, as there was no real shower. We simply used a cup to pour lukewarm water over ourselves when we washed. We did our dishes in these stalls as well. Anyway, this is where the guards made a critical mistake. Each building had its own dishwashing team, and we all used the same shower stall to do the job each time. We kept a wash rag over the door; it hung on a small ledge, and each team used the same rag every time. When Fred and I were taken to the stall, the guard closed the door and left us alone. We discovered that the rag had a long string wrapped around it. I unraveled that string and stashed it in my waistband and brought it back to our cell. When we looked at it closely, we could see small knots tied along its length. The string must've been pulled from someone's blanket. Whoever it was, he tied a series of knots in it, in perfect code. Two knots followed by three knots was the letter H. It was a rather long note, if you can believe that, and Fred and I marveled at the time it must have taken to construct that message. When we decoded it, the writer, or, should I say, the "knotter," relayed an incredible piece of information. As I remember, it said, "note in ipana stuck behind vat pipe rag in center no note on left incoming and on right outgoing." Ipana was a toothpaste in a red/orange tube, so on entering and exiting the room, we knew what kind of message was waiting for us. On our next dishwashing mission, the rag was on the left side of the door ledge. I reached behind the sink pipe, and there was a rolled-up toothpaste tube with a note inside, the tube was attached to the pipe with a piece of soap. Ingenious!

I imagine that a normal prison might have a diverse mix of many different kinds of people, some who bide their time in idleness and some who are always thinking aggressively and using innovation to keep motivated, which might mirror the general populace, too, if you think about it. It's why we have so few generals but a whole lot of privates. Anyway, I believe we had more generals than privates, which enabled us to keep our sanity simply by communicating with each other, outwitting the guards, and thinking of ways to frustrate our captors.

Chapter 22

The Bob and Ed Show

The Outer Seven

Back in 1953, when I first received my wings and went to Alameda, I moved into a room at the the bachelor officers' quarters. Across the hall from me were two other newly minted ensigns, Bob Schweitzer and Bob Valentine, both also assigned to VA-95, just as I was. They were really great guys, and we became pretty close friends. Bob Valentine served just a few years in the Navy after he finished flight school before moving on to go work in the private sector, for IBM, the leading computer manufacturer of the time.

Bob Schweitzer, however, made a career as a naval aviator, just like me. We ran into each other many times throughout our careers, and it was always a pleasure to see him again and to get caught up. Just prior to going to Vietnam, we lost contact, and I believe the last time I saw him stateside was in China Lake, when I was assigned to Michelson Laboratory. During that last visit, Bob and I met for drinks at the officers' club, and I clearly remember Bob saying to me, "Al, you are too smart and too valuable to go off to war. That's just for dumbasses like me!" I'd come to China Lake fresh from the naval post-graduate school, and, knowing the rigors of the training I'd been put through, Bob sincerely thought the Navy had invested entirely too much in me and that perhaps going off to war was better served by "dumb clucks" like him. I certainly did not agree with his assertion, but I let his comments go.

Fast-forward to 1969. Fred and I were lying in our bunks in the Desert Inn when we heard the blue speaker box come to life. Two POWs were heard talking to each other, going over their careers, their flying experience, and other personal information. They called each other Bob and Ed, and from the comments they made, it certainly seemed Ed was somewhat opposed to the war, which seemed extremely odd, considering where we all found ourselves at that

Bob Schweitzer, Louise, and Mr. and Mrs. Bob Valentine, in Sunnyvale, California, 1956.

moment. Fred and I listened in astonishment as Ed discussed his admiration of the antiwar group Students for a Democratic Society (SDS). At the time he was a prisoner at Hỏa Lò, Ed was a Marine Corps lieutenant colonel as well as an F4 fighter pilot. Ed droned on and on about his controversial opinions, and I grew increasingly uncomfortable because he certainly seemed to be taking the very public position that we, the Americans, were the bad guys in the Vietnam War. Fred and I agreed that Ed was certainly entitled to his own opinion, but, let's be real, the inside of a POW camp was most certainly the wrong forum to promote his ideas as American prisoners listened on, especially as he continued to draw a paycheck from Uncle Sam.

When Bob finally began to speak, he also talked about his early squadron assignments and his experiences flying in the ADs. As I continued to hear something familiar in his voice, it became more and more clear that I knew him. I remember thinking, the moment I figured out who he was, "Oh, no." Fred asked me what was going on, and I revealed that the man on the intercom was my old friend Bob Schweitzer. I felt in my gut that it was unlikely he'd turned on us willingly. I would've bet any sum of money that Ed Miller had to be the puppet master of the two, the primary culprit in this treasonous betrayal. As you might assume, the walls of the prison started buzzing with tapping. What we all heard over those blue speakers became known as "The Bob and Ed Show." It felt so disheartening and sad to listen to their abhorrent banter, paired with Jane Fonda's, whose words were once piped in over those same speakers as she relayed her opinions of our "misconduct"—all of which, by the way, was complete bullshit. When we listened to Fonda on occasion, again in silent astonishment, she spewed her venom at us, calling us murderers as we sat on concrete floors in damp, dark cells. She proudly claimed that she'd met personally with American prisoners who told her how well we were *all* being treated. She was, of course, speaking of Lt. Col. Ed Miller, Cdr. Bob Schweitzer, and another prisoner, Cdr. Gene Wilber. Their conduct, along with Fonda's, shamed and humiliated us all.

Bob and Ed's disappointing path began soon after their capture. Sometimes, small delegations of Americans came to visit the prisons in Vietnam. These groups were usually associated with left-wing organizations that were opposed to the war, and some of the visitors were actually parents whose sons were being held there. Most of the time you could assume that anyone who was permitted to visit was probably sympathetic to the North Vietnamese, and a visit to Hỏa Lò was all part of that government's propaganda. Naturally, it made sense that prison officials kept a compliant prisoner or two on hand, someone who would confirm our "good" treatment for the cameras. If a prisoner didn't cooperate with this request when it came, he certainly knew what would happen to him. Most of us instinctively took whatever punishment came rather than submit to their requests, but a small group of POWs, including Bob and Ed, plus Cdr. Gene Wilber and four others, did not, and none of them ever took a hard stand on the armed services' Code of Conduct that the rest of us adhered to. These men were known as the "Outer Seven," and they were, suspiciously, always kept separate from the rest of us.

Some weeks later, after I'd endured a good deal of torture for my "confessions," I was staying in one of the quiz rooms inside the cell block known as the Riviera. From where I was positioned, I could see parts of the courtyard through cracks around the door, and to my surprise, one day I saw Bob Schweitzer wandering around outside. I quietly called out to him, and he heard me and turned around. I beckoned him to come nearer to my cell until he was close enough to hear me talk, and then I whispered, "Schweitzer you dumb sonofabitch, what in the hell is wrong with you?" I didn't have time to give him our "plums," or our senior ranking officers' orders, or to say much else to him, because by then a guard came over and told Bob to move away from the Riviera.

Then once again, many months later right after the Son Tay Raid, Fred and I were in cell 8 of the Rawhide inside Camp Unity. The Outer Seven were being housed nearby, in a room we called Mayo, and at a time when the guards happened to be leaving us alone somewhat, I was able to call out to them through my back window and I asked for Schweitzer directly by name. The sound of my voice bounced off the shared wall, so everyone in Mayo must've heard what I said. I gave him all of our rules and regulations, reminding them all of our established protocol, and I *specifically ordered* Schweitzer to stop cooperating with the Vietnamese. He did not respond to me verbally, but I knew he was listening. Predictably, some time later the Vietnamese government ordered the Outer Seven to again participate in a variety of antiwar activities, including meeting with visiting delegations. This time, Schweitzer refused to cooperate. This frustrated the prison officials, and, not wanting his new attitude to spread to the other six, the guards removed Schweitzer from the group and took him to Building 7, across the courtyard, where at least thirty other prisoners were staying. Thus, the Outer Seven then became the Outer Six. Most of the senior officers were staying nearby in Rawhide, and when the guards opened the door to Building 7, Schweitzer was delivered to the other prisoners in the room, men who had listened to him spout his unpatriotic ideas.

Before Bob's arrival, a prisoner named Larry Guarino was the ranking senior officer, but Schweitzer now assumed the rank of most senior officer in Building 7. How ironic. When Guarino greeted Bob and started to make introductions, upon hearing Schweitzer give his name, he instinctively withdrew his hand. However, in spite of his enormous shortcomings, Bob Schweitzer was still the friendliest guy in any group, and no matter where he found himself, it didn't take long before he had everyone around him charmed. Larry watched over him as he was reintroduced into this new mix of men and guided him through that awkward and unusual set of circumstances. When another group of officers being housed in Rawhide was moved over to Building 7, Schweitzer was again moved out and into another building, and I did not see him again until after we were released and returned home.

After our return to the United States, several of the men in our POW leadership, including a very respectable man named Ted Guy, requested that several of those officers—including Wilber, Miller, and Schweitzer, plus a few others—be court-martialed for their behavior in Vietnam. However, the very top brass in DC thought that since our return was so uplifting, especially considering our motto, "Return with Honor," that they preferred to quietly retire the men and move on from the scandals of the Outer Seven. Sure enough, after we all returned home Lt. Col. Ed Miller was given early retirement. He then brazenly decided to run for public office in California, but a couple of POWs who had no intention of for-

Bob Schweitzer when he and I were serving in Seoul, South Korea, 1956.

giving him for what he'd done in Vietnam wrote letters about him to the media, which cost him his election. Miller, in turn, sued them, including a man named John "Spike" Nasmyth, for slander and defamation on his character. The United Services Automobile Association, more widely known as USAA, successfully defended Nasmyth and the others pro bono, which is the norm for that association's support for the military and its clients. And as a side note, former POWs learned definitively that Ed Miller was a member of SDS after he submitted his own publication, titled *The Vietnam War: A Documentary Reader* (Malden, MA: Wiley Blackwell, 2016), in which he recounts his staunch opposition to the war.

As for Bob Schweitzer, his story is a tragic one. When he was released from Hỏa Lò and returned to the United States, he settled in California. Just a short time after we all got home, I received a call from his wife telling me that Bob was driving down a mountain road and his car went over a cliff. Speculation takes us in many directions with stories like this, and there were rumors of it being a suicide, none of which were ever substantiated. I did know Bob well, and I believe he never forgave himself for things he did in Vietnam.

Chapter 23

I Will Give You Independence and Happiness but Not Freedom

Moon Landings and Movie Nights

The prison crackdown following the escape attempts finally subsided, and the guards returned to their post–Ho Chi Minh, laid-back ways, and our tapping and sweeping resumed with vigor. We often swept our brooms in code right past the other buildings and were able to establish contact with the guys inside pretty quickly. Soon enough after the sweeper made a communication attempt, the POW inside would cough twice, acknowledging that he was listening. The sweeper then first gave the occupants any changes in our roster, new building lineups, and the like, followed by other relevant information. When we were sending names, each name sent would get two coughs when it was received clearly, one cough meant "no" or a request for a repeat, and three coughs meant "I don't know." We shortened all our names and relayed rosters in a shorthand that consisted of one letter for the first name and two letters for the last name. For example, my code name was ABR for Allen Brady. I lived a short time with Al Brunstrom, whose code would also have been ABR—so we used ABRU for him.

When small visiting delegations from the outside met with particular POWs, the rest of us anxiously anticipated being able to glean some new and interesting information about what was going on in the rest of the world. On the return of an interrogated prisoner, a tapping session ensued, asking the prisoner if he learned anything interesting. Even *I* recall going in for a session with the Bug once and desperately craning my neck to get a glimpse of the cover of the *Time* magazine sitting on his desk. When a prisoner being quizzed was later returned to his cell, the walls would begin vibrating with taps like, "Where did you go?" to which he would respond "QBUG," our shorthand for "I was getting quizzed by the Bug."

Publicity photograph of the Apollo 11 Moon landing crew, 1969.

Once, when a visiting group was with one of our prisoners, a quiz session revealed that a rather big event had taken place back home in America on July 20, 1969. The United States put a man on the moon. Of course, the prison officials tried their hardest to keep this news from us, to deny us the opportunity to have our American patriotism reinvigorated. Previously, via our little blue box, the North Vietnamese had made a huge deal about the Russians being the first to put a buggy on the moon, but we knew that since most of the Vietnamese population had no TVs or radios, they would never have been able to find out about the United States' accomplishments anyway. It seemed so petty of them to try to rob us of our joy.

This kind of manipulation was pretty standard, but like with everything, we defiantly fought back against the North Vietnamese's attempts to chip away at our nationalism. Periodically, we were called in to the quiz room by a camp officer for an undeserved attitude check; during one of my quizzes, the prison officer started to denigrate the United States, just to make me angry. When I finally had the opportunity to respond, I asked him why Communists always had to wall in their own people and why they had to shoot them dead when they tried to escape. I pointed out that everyone knew this was the conduct of *all* Communist countries, including East Germany and North Korea. The officer responded that we were not discussing other countries. As you might guess, I stayed in the quiz room for quite a while for my back talking.

After I'd been in the Hilton for about four years, we also started to receive irregular packages from home, besides getting to write letters to our families. The first couple of times I just picked up the package and signed a receipt for it. Simple enough. Another time, however, they gave me a form and a blank sheet of paper and told me that before I could get my package I had to copy the words on the form onto the blank sheet of paper, verbatim. We were always suspicious when something out of the ordinary like this happened, and sure enough, I was asked to copy the title on letterhead that read, "The Democratic Republic of Vietnam" and a more disturbing phrase, *"Independence, Freedom, Happiness."* Fred and I wondered if everyone else was being asked to copy that same malarkey and guessed probably not, so we decided not to risk it. We were called in to get our packages, and when we performed our transcriptions as directed, we included some slight editing. When the Rabbit looked at it, he said we'd left something out. We stared back at him defiantly and answered, "It looks OK to us!" whereupon he went ballistic, screaming at us and telling us our packages would be sent back. He kicked Fred out of the room and put him in the Mint at the corner of Thunderbird and Desert Inn, and he put me, alone, in a dark room in some unknown part of the prison. After a week of solitary, I was called back in with a different officer who asked me why I didn't fill out the form completely and why I wouldn't agree to comply. I told him, "I will give you *Independence* and *Happiness* but not *Freedom*." He shrugged his shoulders dismissively and then had me rejoin Fred in the Mint. We stayed there together for another week and then were finally sent back to our old cell in the Thunderbird. When we got back online, the guys asked where we'd been for so long and why. As it turned out, Fred and I were the only ones in the whole group who resisted their request to write that nonsense and were the only ones who went without packages. Boy, were we stupid!

Once, I learned we were going to be allowed to watch a movie in the courtyard, Vietnamese style. I hadn't been in the Thunderbird very long when the message came through the wall that it looked like movie night, and I was stunned to learn there was such a thing. I wondered how the prison guards planned to get us all together in the same place and still keep us from communicating. Just as it began to get dark, we were brought out cell by cell, building by building, each of us carrying two blankets. The guards tied together a large number of bamboo stakes about four feet high and five to six feet apart. When our blankets were draped

Above left: Commander Ken Coskey;
above right: Colonel Carl Crumpler; *left:*
Captain Byron Fuller.

over the lines connecting the poles, these formed small cubicles. The prisoners
inside these blanket tents could not see over the tops of the blankets if they were
sitting on the ground, and the guards were everywhere, anyway, but there was
still a lot of coughing and whispering. When the flick finally started, to no one's
surprise it was a poorly made black-and-white propaganda film showcasing the
glorious superiority of Communism. Ha! And I thought we were going to get to

watch *The Graduate* and eat popcorn. Although our big night at the movies was disappointing, it was still nice to get out of our cells and breathe some fresh air.

Around the middle of 1970, in a miraculous turn of events, the authorities at Hỏa Lò decided to allow some very limited visiting among the POWs. Now, Fred and I had been tapping with the guys in the cell across the hall for some time, and we already knew that the occupants were Ken Coskey, Byron Fuller, and Carl Crumpler. When the guards opened our door that day and when the cell doors across the hall also opened, we saw the guards watching us in great anticipation. I think they wanted to see a lot more emotion than they did. I spotted Byron Fuller first. He was a Naval Academy classmate, and I knew him very well, not to mention we'd been in constant communication with one another since being placed in the Desert Inn. When I saw him, I simply said, "Hi, Byron." It probably wasn't the joyful and elated reunion the guards were anticipating, but it wasn't exactly a reunion, either, since we'd been right there together, tapping and communicating the whole entire time. Ken Coskey had been the commanding officer of my old squadron, but he and I had never actually met in person, in spite of tapping with each other for many months. It was good to finally shake his hand and see his face. Carl Crumpler was an F4 pilot I'd also never actually had the pleasure of meeting, so in that respect, our reunion and introduction were nice. What a great guy! For those few weeks before the Son Tay Raid, we sometimes enjoyed meeting and talking and laughing with each other in those hallways, face-to-face when the guards allowed. Even if it was just briefly, sharing stories with each other instead of just telling the same old tired tales to our cellmates over and over again was indeed wonderful.

Chapter 24

Living with Prosperity

Rawhide Theater

Sometime in late November 1970, after I'd been moved several times—from the Thunderbird, to Heartbreak, to the Gold Nugget, and to the Desert Inn—I was parked at the Stardust for a short while. I settled into cell 8, anticipating another long stay in tight quarters. Life was so mundane in those days, so I cannot even recall any good stories to tell, except for one. One day while we were biding our time, a guard came to our cell and told Fred and me to roll up our possessions, that we were being moved again. We were blindfolded and led on what seemed an unusually long hike. We finally stopped walking and were directed to enter a small six-by-eight-foot cell with two concrete bunks, which meant two people to a tiny cell again, in a larger section of the prison we would soon come to call Camp Unity, for reasons that will become obvious. We were placed in the smaller group of cells we called Rawhide, the same cell block where I had contacted Bob Schweitzer back when he was with the Outer Seven. A little later, after fourteen of these cells were filled with newly shuffled POWs, we were strip-searched. Unfortunately, poor Fred had held on to a gadget he'd received in his last package, and it was stashed in his waistband. The guards considered it contraband, so he was taken away and put in a cell separate from the rest of us, over in Heartbreak Hotel.

We all had mosquito nets in our cells that were held on to the walls by pegs driven into the concrete. POW Howie Rutledge was next door to me in cell 7 and he was designated as our "communications officer." I asked him if their cell had the same kinds of pegs pinned to the walls as ours did, and when he said yes, he and I got to work. We constructed a hole in the wall between the two cells, and after Howie found a long, thin stick lying nearby, we rolled a note around the end of it and slid the stick through the hole back and forth to each other. We were as busy as those ants Fred and I used to watch back in the old days. Inspired,

Howie also wanted to drill through the wall into cell 6 so we could send written messages-on-a-stick to the guys over there, since this method was turning out to be so much faster than tapping and certainly safer than whispering. We kept pretty busy at this task, and it seemed strange how unconcerned the guards were acting; they were totally leaving us alone and didn't appear to care even when they noticed us whispering between the cells.

By the next day, Howie and I had communication going all throughout all the surrounding cells. Jim Stockdale was still the senior ranking officer, since the four full colonels—Norm Gaddis, John Flynn, David Winn, and James Bean—were not with us. Fred Crow still wasn't there either. He remained in Heartbreak Hotel, but it still butted up against the side of a cell that shared a wall with the rest of us, so we quickly established communication with him too. There was just one drawback to building these lines of communication: where the holes were. At the end of the room we were in was the "throne" we used for going to the bathroom. We sat on the throne to do our business, and the waste dropped straight down a hole and into one of two large round metal buckets underneath, and the buckets had no tops, of course. The throne had an opening underneath on one side so a prisoner could access and empty the buckets as needed. Of course, this hidden under-area was a prime location for secretly drilling our holes through the walls. The act of drilling could be noisy, so going underneath the toilet areas was helpful because it not only muffled the sound, it also kept the person drilling out of plain sight. It was obviously an unpleasant area to work in, to say the least, and this humble writer spent more hours under there than he wanted. Fortunately, we got our new transmitting station online rather quickly, and although I got no medals for my service, I got an *attaboy* from Jim Stockdale.

As a much larger group, we often crafted some rather entertaining ways to pass the time. A couple of the guys told us they were able to perform reenactments from movies they'd seen back home in America, and they enthusiastically volunteered to do this for everyone. Thus began "Rawhide Theater." While I listened to them through the wall, I could mentally see the movies as they performed them on the other side, and we enjoyed hearing reenactments, perhaps from Leo Profilet or Jim Mehl, playing Steve McQueen in *Nevada Smith*. One member of our cast, Jack Finley, turned out to be an impressive whistler, and, thus, we found ourselves enjoying *The Sound of Music*, with Jack providing the background music. It was one of the only deeply happy memories I can recall from those dark days, a definite morale booster after so many years of suffering silently.

Then, things changed dramatically. After we had spent just a few days inside Camp Unity, a guard came through Rawhide flinging all the cell doors wide open. At first, we weren't sure what we were supposed to do. We began peeking our heads out, timidly saying hello to one another, and before we knew it, there we all were, dozens of us, standing in the middle of the hallway hugging and embracing and shaking hands like old friends being reunited. The guard pointed for us to go outside the building and sit down on the ground and wait. We did exactly as we were told, and soon the Bug arrived and asked us if anyone knew what was happening. We all said, "Yes! We are being released!" and then of course he gave us his usual response, the same one he always gave, "You never going home!!!" Then he lectured at us that we must behave. He was quite obviously not acting like himself at all, and he continued acting strangely as we tried to figure out what was going on. We were told to rise and follow him once again, and we walked as one large group back over to Building 7. Then the Bug opened another large door and put us all inside a pretty sizable room. I counted forty-seven of us in that one space. FORTY-SEVEN! In the four years I'd been in prison, I'd only ever seen about ten other POWs, at sporadic times and never all at once, so to be in a crowd of that size was overwhelming. I could try to describe it by saying I was overjoyed and so happy, but even those words seem inadequate to try to explain what it felt like to be in the same place with everyone else, so many other Americans, finally. I'm not sure any of us slept that night.

The room we were in was a large, rectangular-shaped space with an odd, raised platform built into its center for sleeping. This platform was about a foot high at the outer edges and peaked upward toward the center. In other words, each of the sides sloped up toward the middle so that when we slept on them, our feet pointed downward and our heads remained slightly elevated. Boy, they thought of everything at the Hilton! Somebody in our group found a few broken pieces of terra cotta roof tile, which made excellent writing instruments or, in our case, drawing utensils. We started to sketch a very large map of the United States directly onto that concrete platform where we slept. People were constantly walking back and forth around the room, and it was a fairly good hike if you made a good number of rotations, and prisoners almost constantly made pit stops to add something to the drawing. With forty-seven of us in the room, we represented a good number of the fifty states, so as each person walked by the large map, he would suggest certain changes to the details as we continued drawing each state, especially the ones we were familiar with. I'd lived in Connecticut, my mother's home, so I certainly had a responsibility to do my part to make sure her state was drawn accurately. When we finished, we'd created an almost perfect map of the whole, beautiful United States. Some of the guys then began to scratch harder and deeper into the surface of the concrete, which left a glorious, permanent map of

America inside the walls of that awful prison, a place that tried so hard to make us question why we were there in the first place. In fact, the more time we spent inside those walls, the more resolved we became that our efforts to defeat Communism were justified, a fact clearly substantiated by the drawing we left behind for them in that room, which would last long after we were gone.

In spite of our improved social situation, we still had rules. The Camp Unity authorities told us not to congregate in large groups and not to have any one person address a large group. I don't know what they were afraid of, because we were still certainly outgunned even when we were together. We were told to eat in small groups and to keep fairly spread out. However, one unremarkable Sunday approached, and someone from our group asked the prison guards for permission to hold church services. This was summarily denied, of course, in spite of the mandates of the Third Geneva Convention. Nevertheless, a member of our group suggested that we should do it anyway, and I thought, *Oh boy. Here we go.* The church service was allowed to proceed, but at its conclusion, the guards came in with a list of our most senior officers, and they were removed from the group and did not return.

Instead of teaching us a tough lesson, as I am sure they intended, this punishment caused indignation and anger among many of us who stayed behind. In fact, some in our pack decided we should show our displeasure by following Bud Day's lead and arrogantly singing "The Star-Spangled Banner" as loud as we could. So we did. Soon, each of the other buildings and all of the occupants of their cells chimed in together, so that at one point the whole prison sang, in unison, a loud and resounding rendition of America's national anthem. We followed up our serenade with a session of the stare-and-glare game whenever the guards came in to check on us, which definitely intimidated them to the point that they finally wouldn't even come into the room with us. I wasn't really in favor of any of these antics, because I couldn't see any good outcome from them, and of course I discovered that my hunch was correct.

A few days later, the guards came in with another list, this one containing the names of the commanders and lieutenant colonels, myself included, and we were also marched out and sent back to Rawhide, the cell block with the small cells, only now, instead of two prisoners per cell, we had four. Two of us slept on the concrete bunks, and the other two slept on the concrete floors with the spiders and the rats. There was also nowhere to hang our mosquito nets, so you can imagine how those evenings passed. Two weeks later, the guards came back and retrieved us and spread us back out again so we were returned to the "luxury" of two per cell. It became clear that with every decision we made, there was a consequence that had to be weighed.

I won't say that I thought anyone made any errors in judgment for those acts of defiance, because no one can judge the mentality of men in those kinds of situations. But I believed that if defiance was the way we chose to respond to our new freedoms, gambling with the luxuries that for years we'd only dreamed about often wasn't really worth it. Jim Stockdale predicted this exact phenomenon. A few months prior to the prisoner reunification in Camp Unity, when Fred and I were still in the Stardust, I'd tapped a little with Jim. By then, he'd finished his ordeal over making the propaganda film (the one he avoided by beating his own face with a stool) and he told me he thought our conditions were going to improve. But, he also told me quite frankly that many of the men among us would have difficulty "living with prosperity," if that actually happened.

A fairly well-known episode took place during our time in Camp Unity, related to a hunger strike staged by our leadership. Our senior ranking officers often took turns being in charge, and this gave people like Jim Stockdale and Jerry Denton somewhat of a break from the burdens of constantly leading our group. Once, when Denton was the senior ranking officer, Fred and I learned of a planned hunger strike. In spite of our constant communication, sometimes some of the prisoners were simply not in the loop about what was going on in other parts of the prison. I admit it, I was not a big fan of the strike. Fred and I learned of it through the walls, and, of course, if Denton wanted the population of prisoners to make a unified statement of protest, we would certainly comply with his orders. Privately, however, Fred and I were frustrated, thinking how incredibly unbelievable it was that after already being malnourished and quite underfed, Denton was now having us go completely without food. I don't believe Jim Stockdale would have asked this of us, but I knew enough about Denton to know the resolve he possessed when something was important to him. To be honest, I never knew anything about why he called for the hunger strike until I was already writing this book, when I read US Congressman and former POW Sam Johnson's memoir that detailed the event (*Captive Warriors: A Vietnam POW's Story* [College Station: Texas A&M University Press, 1992]). I discovered, to my surprise, that Johnson was placed in solitary confinement for an extraordinarily long time and Denton's hunger strike was an effort to get Johnson and some other prisoners released. Fred and I never knew this. After I learned this, it did seem to me that our efforts were justified and that Denton's orders fell in line with the demands of being in charge. Apparently, they also succeeded in garnering Johnson's release from solitary.

We found ourselves all living together, *finally,* playing card games, putting on theater shows, giving lectures, and the like, and the guards were leaving us alone. It seemed the torture had finally ended too. It was bizarre, but exhilarating and wonderful to have so much normalcy, if you can call it that. But so many of the men in our group, victims of the Cuban Program and the men who were tortured for the Zoo escapes, for example, were so full of hatred and bitterness. That could certainly be expected under the circumstances. No one was ever criticized for their actions in this regard, and we remained brothers in arms as we continued to play the hands we were dealt. It was certainly okay with me if, given a bit of room to stretch out our emotions, some of the men around me needed to get some things off their chest. I'd spent my time in the ropes, too, as well as in solitary just like everybody else, and I can confirm that it does a number on your soul. I did not endure the Cuban Program or the Zoo reprisals, but I can certainly imagine what those events did to the men who lived through them. Lashing out sure seemed justifiable, and I expected it, but it was hard to be dragged out and punished for simply following orders. Indeed, war is hell on everyone.

Chapter 25

Son Tay Raid

Operation Ivory Coast

We found out about the Son Tay Raid while we were in Rawhide. Turns out that it was the Son Tay Raid that caused the North Vietnamese to move us all into Camp Unity in the first place, and that's also when they finally closed all of the outer camps. It was my understanding that the Son Tay POW Camp was built to house about sixty-five US POWs between the late 1960s and late 1970, as was another camp, ironically named Camp Faith. Apparently, the prisoners placed out there were writing home pretty regularly and somehow hinted to their families as to their location near the town of Son Tay. Once this was known, the chairman of the Joint Chiefs of Staff authorized an inquiry into the feasibility of an attack on the prison, with the objective of freeing the Americans being held there. It was determined that a coordinated joint night attack held a reasonable chance of success.

The code name for the mission was Operation Ivory Coast. Overall command was given to Brig. Gen. LeRoy Manor of the US Air Force, with Col. Arthur "Bull" Simons of the US Army Special Forces actually leading the raid. Simons recruited 103 volunteers from the 6th and 7th Special Forces Groups to assist. A full-scale replica of the Son Tay camp was constructed at Eglin AFB in Fort Walton, Florida, and the rescue group trained by simulating the attack more than a hundred different times. To ensure security, however, the volunteers were not informed of the target location until the day of the attack.

The group members honed their skills, and the mission was to be executed somewhere between October 21 and 25, 1970, when conditions included the ideal moonlight and a clear sky. Manor and Simons met with Adm. Frederick Bardshar to establish a diversionary mission to be flown by US Navy aircraft, including contrived bombing missions to be flown specifically to distract the attention of the North Vietnamese. For a reason still unknown to me, following a meeting between the commanders and Secretary of State Henry Kissinger at the White House, it was determined that execution of the mission would be delayed by a whole month, targeting the end of November instead. Finally, on November 21, 1970, all the pieces were put into play. The mission was positioned to execute out of Thailand.

The Son Tay Raiders flew at night in helicopters into North Vietnam through valleys below the mountain ridges, which was pretty hairy. For the raid, Simons selected a force of Green Berets, split into three assault groups. The plan was to crash-land inside the compound, then blow a hole in the outside wall. A twenty-man group provided security against any North Vietnamese reaction. The first chopper successfully landed inside the camp at 0218, and the assault team jumped from the chopper and took out all the guards before securing the compound. However, after searching the entire camp, to their horror and disappointment they found no POWs present. Disheartened, all personnel were recovered and returned to base safely, but empty-handed. To make matters worse, Colonel Simons accidentally landed about a quarter of a mile away at another nearby compound, one that turned out to be a base for Russian and Chinese military advisors. A firefight ensued, and it was estimated that an additional hundred-plus enemy troops were taken out. One American commando was wounded in the leg and another broke his ankle jumping out of a helicopter, but other than that these men were returned safely to base.

Certainly, there was an intelligence failure somewhere. The problem was blamed on Washington, DC, where the mission's high classification prevented the free flow of information among various essential departments of the Pentagon. We know that prior to the raid, a few POWs received coded letters asking for the location of "the New Son Tay," which clearly revealed that the POWs had transmitted messages that they'd been moved prior to the raid's execution. Still, in spite of its failure, and in spite of the soldiers' failure to spring any prisoners, the mission was superbly executed by a group of highly motivated, courageous men. I will never deny thanks and gratitude to anyone who was trying to get those men out or to get any of us out of there. Selfless service. Men putting their own lives on the line to help save ours.

Anyway, information about the raid made its way on to us in the prison in several different ways. Some of the guys received packages from home that contained tidbits of information about it. Later on in our captivity, several B-52 pilots and crew members were shot down and placed in Hỏa Lò with us, and they also told us what happened. Once just a few of us knew about it, the tapping superhighway took it from there. We were thrilled to hear of it, proud of the meticulous nature of the execution, and happy to know that our government was still trying its best to get us out of North Vietnam.

Chapter 26

Release

March 4, 1973

We were moved again. This time we settled into Mayo. It was another good-sized room, and it held "only" about twenty POWs, although that was still a great improvement from our days in Rawhide. The room had our bunks placed neatly around its perimeter, and there was an open area in the center, the opposite of the setup in Building 7. Any church services we were allowed to participate in were held with everyone staying seated on their beds, because the guards continued to try to keep us from congregating in large groups. Still, we remained all together and enjoyed our own walled-in courtyard.

Those walls were high, though, and sometimes hindered the easy flow of information, but we managed. When we were able, we communicated with neighboring courtyards by having one POW hoist up another so he could look over the wall and see the buildings in other cell blocks. On a few occasions we used hand signals to communicate messages to nearby buildings; our sign language consisted of making all twenty-six letters using the fingers of one hand. This was not your standard sign language. In fact, the sign for "Q" was what most would recognize as "the bird." In addition, when POWs were in the big courtyard, it was pretty easy for a prisoner in a next-door cell block to linger around his courtyard wall and simply toss a note into another yard. Again, the guards were ignoring us anyway, so we settled into a much more normal, less stressful routine. It was particularly nice in those days, too, because we could actually see the faces of the people we'd been only tapping with for so many years. As was becoming the nice, new norm with prosperity, pretty soon the door to the courtyard was even left open during the day, and we got some refreshing time outside in the sun on a regular basis.

Still, I was slowly approaching the end of my sixth year in that dump. I don't mean to make light of those later years, which were by all definitions still difficult, but it was hard to deny that they were so much better than my first four years. We no longer spent our days by ourselves inside of empty cells, and we were being allowed the human interaction we so desperately craved. By comparison, it did sometimes seem like life was tolerable, in the event that the Bug was right and we really were never going home. But I never let myself forget that this was still a prison and I was still being held against my will in a foreign country for what was turning into an excruciatingly large chunk of my life.

One of my really good days was the day they put a South Vietnamese A-1 pilot into the cell with us. His name was Nguyen Quoc Dat, but we just called him Max, or Dat (pronounced *dot*). He was a young man, very friendly, and he spoke fluent French, English, and, of course, Vietnamese. Max told us he'd gone through flight training in the United States and learned to fly the ADs just like I did. He and I spent a great deal of time together during those months in Camp Unity, so there were plenty of opportunities for us to learn from each other. We whiled away many hours practicing French together, not that I needed to learn French—I'd had four years of it in high school and college—but what else did we have to do? With Max's help, I compiled a respectable little handwritten dictionary of English-French words, and I still have that little book to this day.

On the night of December 18, 1972, the wailing sounds of an air raid started up, something we'd gone for years without having to endure. It had also been a good, long while since the bombing raids rattled us like they had in the old days. But this night, things seemed different, much worse. It's difficult to describe the terrifying and ominous booms of an incoming bombing attack, but suffice it to say that when you're hearing those sounds, you think *The End* is coming. In the past we'd often heard jets screaming overhead, too, followed by the antiaircraft guns trying to blast them out of the sky. It was so loud, and it always sounded uncomfortably close. There was also a distant growl, like rolling thunder approaching, and then the sound of large, booming guns, followed by a high-altitude muffled explosion. We normally wouldn't have worried about all of these things going on around us, but this particular night we got increasingly nervous because the explosions were getting progressively louder. It was the sound of wave after wave of aircraft dropping a slew of bombs all around us. As the bombs got closer, the plaster started falling off the walls. Most of us were pressed up against the room's perimeter, saying little prayers. One string of bombs landed so close, I thought, *If there's one more, we're done.*

The next day, the camp commander came in and told us to behave and not to harass the guards, as the situation was very serious. We also learned that as a result of the bombing raids we now had no running water, so we had to conserve and ration while water was brought into the prison by hand. Great.

The night of the eighteenth was the worst of that bombing mission, but still, this went on for several days, as I recall. As you might guess, before long we had several B-52 pilots and crew members joining us in the Hilton, and we knew they were coming because we'd seen at least one B-52 go down. Naturally, we were glad to see the pilots walk through our doors alive. I don't recall how many bombers were in each attack, but they flew in groups of three, each dropping seventy-eight five-hundred-pound bombs. Being able to watch the situation escalate boosted our morale, and I honestly didn't believe the North Vietnamese could endure much more. In several previous attacks, the guards would've been in the court-yard shooting their rifles into the air at our jets, but now even *they* were building bomb shelters. Everyone appeared quite frightened, which got our attention.

A fairly short time after this bombing sequence, a few of us were called in to the camp commander's office, whereupon he told us that an agreement had been reached in Paris. The United States would commence withdrawing one quarter of the five hundred thousand troops it still had in South Vietnam every two weeks for eight weeks. We were told that the POWs were to be released in the same way and that the first group of prisoners would get to go sometime in February, on the twelfth, as it turned out, about two months away, and these prisoners would leave along with the sick and wounded. The second group, which included me, would go two weeks later, and so on, with the POWs going home in the order in which they had been captured. There were a few excep-tions to this rule, of course. Ed Miller and Gene Wilber of the Outer Seven were allowed to leave with the first group, a clear indication that they were given preferential treatment for reasons that were pretty clear to everyone.

End of February 1973.

Prisoners in the second group, which included me, were fitted for release clothes, and on the evening before they were to depart, the members of the first group even stopped by to say goodbye to us. As I hugged them goodbye and wished them well, I allowed myself to believe it was actually happening, finally! I saw American prisoners leaving on buses, on their way to get onto airplanes, and I knew my turn would come soon too. The departing POWs even asked if we wanted them to call our families. It was surreal; I couldn't believe any of it could be real. We talked about what it would be like to leave that prison, we talked about

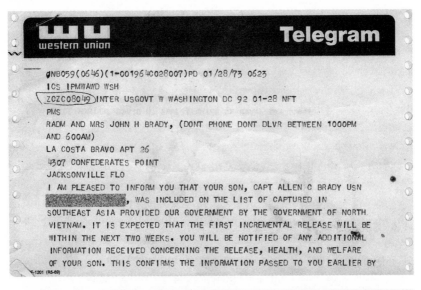

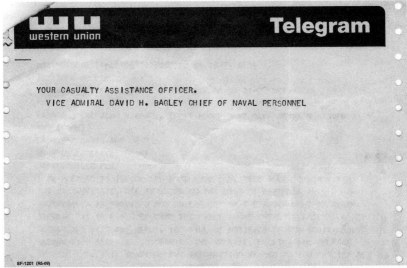

January 28, 1973, telegram to my parents informing them of my anticipated release.

what we wanted to eat, who we wanted to see first. On the night before my big day arrived, the guards moved us into yet another building. It was impossible to sleep, and the hours ticked away more slowly than I can possibly explain to you.

At some point in everyone's life, there comes disappointment. Sometimes, the disappointment is so profound that we ponder the advantages granted to others compared to our own hardships. Many times, I'd even heard myself saying, "Life's not fair," but my group was about to endure a disappointment like none we would ever experience again. When morning arrived and no one came for us, I didn't worry too much at first. Several groups of military officers from an assortment of different countries came to our room, however, and looked in at us, but none of them spoke. Finally, later that afternoon the camp commander ordered all the remaining POWs to come out to the courtyard so he could address us. He said that the United States had not lived up to its side of the agreement and that all releases were to be stopped immediately. I will leave it up to you to imagine how it felt to hear that, because my words cannot adequately describe it. Richard Nixon also stopped withdrawing US troops from South Vietnam, he stopped clearing the mines from the rivers and harbors, and he prepared to call in the B-52s again. All parties to the conflict rushed back to Paris and continued to work out their differences posthaste, but it didn't matter to me as I listened to their excuses. I don't remember how long the camp commander droned on, or how long the peace talks took, and I didn't even care, as I was in a daze of anger and frustration.

March 4, 1973.

Again we were cleaned up and dressed. This time, the guards came for us and told us to follow *quickly*. We boarded buses and headed for the Gia Lam Airport, and I still waited around every turn for the disappointment to come. After crossing a bridge across the Red River, we stopped and were told to disembark. My pessimism got the best of me once again, and I thought, *We aren't going home.* Instead, they put us in a small building and gave us each a few cookies and a bottle of Vietnamese beer. Then, back onto the buses we went, and soon we rounded a corner, when I saw the most magnificent thing I've ever laid eyes on in my entire life. There they were, several C-141s with "US AIR FORCE UNITED STATES OF AMERICA" stenciled on their side.

We disembarked from the buses and got into a line. No one spoke a word. When my name was called, I walked up to a table and there was a Vietnamese man with a US Air Force officer standing behind him. I saluted the officer, and then out of nowhere someone approached, took me by the arm, and quickly led me to the aircraft, and I boarded. A flight nurse approached me, stood perfectly still in front of me for just a moment, then hugged me tight. I remember how good she smelled. Still, no one said anything. The air was tense, everyone was nervous. The aircraft was spacious, and we each had both a seat *and* a bunk.

When the plane was full to bursting, we cranked up, taxied out, and lifted off the tarmac. Even in the air, everyone was still quiet. Then the pilot came on over the intercom and told us that we'd just left North Vietnamese air space.

And then it was bedlam.

Everyone jumped from their seats and bounced up and down, cheering and hugging each other, whooping and hollering. March 4, 1973. The happiest day of my life.

At that moment, I decided to let myself believe that perhaps, just maybe, that other shoe wasn't going to drop after all. They offered us a wide array of pornographic magazines, and I noticed one of the guys as he opened a *Playboy* and then I watched him put it back down, looking somewhat embarrassed. I guess some of us weren't ready for the outside world yet.

All I could really think about was my future. My wife, my kids, my parents, my career—what was going to happen, moving forward? There were so many decisions for me to make, and yet I felt totally unprepared and ill-equipped to consider what my life back home might be like now, 6 years, 1 month, and 13 days, or 2,236 days, since I'd last lived as a free man. On the plane ride home, I decided that after all I'd been through, I did not want to put myself in danger anymore, so I made up my mind in those hours that I would not fly as a pilot ever again. That being decided, when our pilot invited each of us to come up to the flight deck, I availed myself of the opportunity and went forward. When I positioned myself between the pilot and the copilot, I looked out at the beautiful blue sky, those same white clouds I had admired throughout all my years of flying for the Navy, and a gorgeous turquoise sea. It took about a microsecond to change my mind, and as such, it became clear that my next task had to be to find a flying billet, which would not be easy, since there were very few of them available for captains.

After all, I was still a Navy man.

Chapter 27

Homecoming

Escape Artist

We landed at Clark AFB in Manila, Philippines, after a short two-and-a-half-hour flight. There was a small crowd of military sorts gathered, mostly service dependents, and some were holding signs welcoming us home. It was undeniably moving, and I was touched that they even knew who we were and where we'd been all those years. We waved at everyone but didn't have a chance to address the crowd before we were assigned to the bachelors' quarters on base. The US government had already sent for our uniforms, which our families had provided, with our new ranks adorning them. Other than being a little loose, mine fit like a glove. We were told we could eat anything we wanted: milkshakes, hamburgers, steaks, et cetera, just no booze until we made it home safely. We were allowed to call our families, and I placed a call to Louise. She tried very hard to act as normal as possible as we spoke, but the strange circumstances of our conversation were tough to ignore. I spoke to my very grown-up thirteen-year-old daughter Lisa, who had been not quite eight the last time I saw her. She broke down in tears as we spoke, and I knew it was a lot for a little girl to grasp. My son, Richard, who had been eleven when I was shot down, was seventeen when he first said hello to me on the phone. Although I knew I was still somewhat of a stranger to him, he was refreshingly easy to talk to.

We had a couple of days where we did nothing but sit through a series of physical exams. Then, after a few more days in Manila we boarded another C-141 and headed for Hickam AFB in Honolulu. When we stopped to refuel there, we were again allowed to disembark. During the layover, we were still kept away from the press, in a small private room, but we were allowed to go out to the main room of the operations building if we had visitors, and in that case a Marine had to come in and escort us out. To my elation, I had a few people

On the plane from Hanoi, Vietnam, to Clark Air Force Base, Philippines, writing speeches with a Navy official. Swede Larson is seated to my left.

who wanted to see me. First was my air wing commander from the *Kitty Hawk*, Cdr. Royce Williams. Second was my former commander, "Davy" Crockett, an officer I served with on the carrier division staff. Third, I got to see Chief Petty Officer Abrigo, whom I'd gotten to know way back in the 1950s when I'd helped him change his rate from steward to yeoman.

And finally, I met a pretty, young flight attendant who had been wearing my POW bracelet. What is a POW bracelet, you ask? Well, I had the same question. I learned that during our captivity a student group in California, with the help of some POW wives who started the program, supported us by selling metal bracelets, each with the name of a POW etched on it. For the duration of the war, over 5 million bracelets were mailed all over America to people who wrote in to their local newspapers and asked to receive bracelets inscribed with the names of prisoners being held in Vietnam. According to this flight attendant, the local Honolulu paper had printed our names and relayed the news to the public that we were arriving that night, so when she saw my name and recognized it, she came to see me, adorned with her bracelet to welcome me back.

On our flight back to the United States, I was seated next to POW Jack Fellowes. When we took our seats, Jack asked me how I liked the flower lei that

One of my returned POW bracelets.

his friends had given him in Honolulu. I said it looked fine, but then Jack said, "No, look closely." I pushed aside the flowers and saw where his friends had tied a number of miniature whisky bottles around the interior. Jack had defeated the authorities once again, just like we'd all done when we were back in Hanoi. We both knew we would probably have to give speeches when we arrived home, so we each saved ourselves one whisky mini for calming our nerves.

The next morning, as the sun came up and peeked into the airplane windows, the flight deck woke us up to tell us that we were over the Golden Gate Bridge. Our pilot even did a 360 so we could all see it. Then we learned that our flight was part of a project being called Operation Homecoming. We also learned that the pilot of a nearby passenger plane asked the FAA for permission to vector his aircraft to a certain area so it could get nearer to us, and he would tell the passengers on the other flight who we were and that we were coming home. The pilot on that flight was then granted permission to fly his plane at a lower altitude so we could pass right by each other. As we passed, our pilot told us that those other passengers were looking out their windows and screaming and clapping for us.

We weren't sure what to make of it all. It seemed that there had been nothing but bad news about the Vietnam War while we were in prison; we'd heard only from people who hated us; and we'd been forced to listen to so much propaganda from the antiwar left—things like how some young Americans were hiding out in Canada to avoid the draft. We all knew about America's reaction to the My Lai Massacre and similar incidents, and we were repeatedly disheartened to hear about the negativity that lingered around the United States' involvement in the war as a whole. So no, we certainly never expected a warm welcome home, or any welcome at all really, if I'm honest. To be fair, I thought instead about what the American public would expect from us when we returned. Did they think we were going to be bitter? Did people want an apology of some sort? Did they assume we'd turned antiwar or anti-American? It was as if I were being forced to get reacquainted with my own country.

As a blessing to all of us, it was a relief for us to hear that during the earlier February release, when Capt. Jerry Denton walked off the plane containing the

Arriving at NAS Oceana, saluting the commanding officer.

first group of prisoners in Manila, that morning he spoke honorably for all of us. He'd been the first POW out of Hanoi, and millions of people saw and heard him when he addressed the crowds on our behalf. He made a short, simple speech: "We are proud to have had the opportunity to serve our country under difficult circumstances. We are profoundly grateful to our commander in chief and to our nation for this day. God Bless America."

Many people stayed up all night watching television to see the planes come in, even when the time differential might've been up to twelve hours, depending on where they lived in the United States. I was so touched. We landed at Andrews Air Force Base in Washington, DC, and there were five of us heading on to Norfolk, Virginia, so we had our own C-9 (DC-9) waiting for us. Someone asked who was the senior officer of the five, and I said, "I am." The pilot of the C-9 told me that the weather was terrible at Norfolk, and I either had to take a chance in the air or they would arrange for cars to drive us there. I told them without hesitation that I was ready to fly, so we took off and headed to Norfolk. As we got closer, the pilot called me to the cockpit and told me that Norfolk was zero-zero for visibility but NAS Oceana was at minimums. Again, I just wanted to be home, so I told the pilot to go for it, which he did, and we landed safely. The amazing thing was that with less than thirty minutes' notice, most of the Navy base had turned out

Arriving at NAS Oceana.

Allen watching Jack Fellows salute the commanding officer of NAS Oceana.

Red McDaniels (saluting), Mike Christian, Jack Fellowes, me, commanding officer of NAS Oceana.

Oceana, Virginia, 1973, me, Jack Fellowes and the commanding officer of NAS Oceana.

Louise (*second from left, rear*) being escorted to meet me.

Louise, Lisa, and Richard meeting me at Oceana.

to greet us. Some even had signs. We had to coordinate with the admirals and other dignitaries who were arriving, plus our family members who were being transported to the Portsmouth Naval Hospital, our final destination. We cooled our heels for about a half hour, then loaded into the cars waiting there for us. Another pleasant surprise awaited us on the drive over: there were people standing along the freeway, even in the bad weather, with signs welcoming us home.

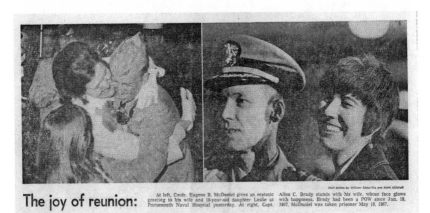

The joy of reunion: At left, Cmdr. Eugene B. McDaniel gives an ecstatic greeting to his wife and 10-year-old daughter Leslie at Portsmouth Naval Hospital yesterday. At right, Capt. Allen C. Brady stands with his wife, whose face glows with happiness. Brady had been a POW since Jan. 19, 1967. McDaniel was taken prisoner May 19, 1967.

Louise and me as featured in the *Ledger-Star,* March 8, 1973.

Virginian-Pilot,   Thursday, March 8, 1973   A19

Capt. Brady is greeted by his son, Richard, 17, and daughter, Lisa, 13.

Seeing my children. *Virginian-Pilot,* March 8, 1973.

Later, we learned the local TV station had tracked us in the air during our flight and kept everyone up to date with our location.

When we finally reached the hospital, officials stopped us just around the corner from the entrance and told us to wait to be called. Jack Fellowes and I decided that was the appropriate time to polish off what remained of the leis. With our warm courage, we made our way through the entrance and were met with bright

THE SECRETARY OF DEFENSE
WASHINGTON, D. C. 20301

MAR 8 1973

Captain Allen C. Brady, USN
c/o Homecoming Processing Team Chief
Naval Hospital
Portsmouth, Virginia 23708

Dear Captain Brady:

All of your friends in the Department of Defense join a grateful nation in welcoming your return to the United States. For 74 months you have experienced one of the most trying ordeals that an officer in the United States Navy can be called upon to endure on the Nation's behalf. We will not readily forget that ordeal though few of us will ever fully comprehend the test of strength, faith, and patience that has been required of you and your family.

Everyone involved in Operation Homecoming is ready to do everything possible to assist you. Though all America is relieved and joyful at your return, you can be certain that we will not rest until we have achieved the best possible accounting for your compatriots listed as missing in action.

You and your family have the heartfelt best wishes of Mrs. Richardson and myself for success and happiness in the future.

Welcome home,

Elliot . Richardson

A kind letter from Secretary of Defense Elliott Richardson, March 8, 1973.

Louise and me outside of my hospital room at Portsmouth Naval Hospital in Portsmouth, Virginia.

lights and TV cameras. A group of admirals came in with our families. Naturally, there was the ubiquitous microphone and we were each expected to give a short speech. We all mentioned how grateful we were to be home and hoped that the remaining POWs would soon be released. We shook hands and received congratulations from our well-wishers, and then I was finally able to see my family. I would have passed my own children on the street without recognizing them. They'd changed so much.

After meeting with the admirals and other dignitaries, we were taken to our hospital rooms. The commanding officer of the hospital was a rear admiral and a doctor. He ordered one whole floor in one wing of the hospital emptied of its patients to make room for us. Our rooms were furnished with couches, chairs, dining tables, et cetera, and were completely set up with normal bedroom furnishings. It was very nice and plush, and I got the uncomfortable feeling that the CO did all this with a much longer stay in mind, one longer than what *any* of *us* desired. Our wives were allowed to stay as often as they liked and to come and go as they pleased, but the kids were made to go home each night. We learned that the reason for this extended supervision was rooted in an unfortunate event that occurred with the first group of returning prisoners. One man was unable to

Louise and me greeting the rear admiral in charge of my hospitalization and recovery at Portsmouth, 1973.

The rear admiral in charge of the Portsmouth Naval Hospital, me, Jim Mulligan, Jerry Denton, Jack Fellowes, and Mike Christian, Portsmouth, 1973.

reconcile with his wife and was so devastated to learn that she had divorced him while he was gone that he committed suicide. This occurred at a different hospital and under different conditions, but our CO wasn't going to let anything like that happen on his watch. As such, even though we thought we were finally free men, it turned out that the US government intended to keep us right where we were for a bit longer, and since we were still in the Navy, we didn't have much choice. We were not allowed to leave our hospital wing without a Marine escort, not even to wander around the hospital and get some exercise. But let me tell you something. They clearly underestimated our craftiness in outmaneuvering guards.

Each of us had an assigned officer throughout our days and days of debriefings. We also had heavy schedules of doctor's appointments. My assigned officer went by the name of Lt. Cdr. Sid Beaver. After a couple of days of getting to know Sid, I told him that although I was never able to escape from Hỏa Lò, I was pretty sure I could get out of that hospital. I could see that what I said really terrified him—he took his job seriously, and he knew I wasn't playing around. He weighed his situation and realized that if he helped me and got caught, his career was over; if he didn't help me, he also had to live with that too. So together, we hatched a plan. That next Sunday, he came in when there was only one Marine guard on duty. Sid double-checked to make sure the door to the stairwell was unlocked, and then we snuck down the stairs, ran to his car, and took off. Louise had been alerted to our plan, and she stayed home waiting for us. I hadn't seen the house she bought while I was away, and it seemed smaller than I imagined, especially since she'd written to me in prison about how much it cost! Sid closed all the windows and blinds in the house and kept peeking out as if there would be an ambush at any moment, the Marines with their guns blazing and all the flashing lights! To keep Sid from having a stroke, I agreed to leave after thirty minutes if he would just relax, and, thankfully, he did. He and I successfully snuck back up to the POW floor a little later without ever being missed. Mission accomplished, escape successful.

After a couple of weeks, the folks in charge said I could go home, but only for the weekend. Before leaving, I was dosed up with anti-parasite medicine, which is essentially a poison, and it made me sick as a dog. As a result, I came back to the hospital after a pretty disappointing weekend, conveniently feeling much better by Sunday evening, when I got back and settled into my hospital room. The North Vietnamese didn't corner the market on torture or stomach woes, it seemed. After another week, I was formally released from the hospital for good. For most of the rest of that year, I was asked to check in on occasion, but I only had to show up for scheduled appointments. The Navy wanted to give us all the

Honorary Parade at the US Naval Academy, 1973.

Honorary Parade at the US Naval Academy, 1973. Mike Christian, Jack Fellowes, an unidentified Navyman, me, and the admiral who received us.

Florida congressman Bob Sikes with Louise and me in Washington, DC, 1973.

Me (*second from left, in civilian clothes*) with Byron Fuller in dress whites (*fourth from left*), and Florida governor Lawton Chiles (*second from right*), Washington, DC, 1973.

time we needed to unwind and relax and think about what we wanted to do next, and what we wanted to do with our future. Did I want to go back to active duty or retire? I had so much to think about. I believe most of us stayed in the Navy, and I chose the same.

Fairly soon after our return home, I got a call from the New York Mets, saying that their organization wanted to invite a couple of the POWs to attend their opening day game and throw out the first pitch. I think they were playing the Yankees. They kindly offered to fly Louise and me up there and put us in a hotel, all expenses paid. They brought us to the ballpark to give us a tour, and we had lunch in a special VIP room, and then that night, the evening before the opening game, they held a cocktail party in our honor, hosted by the Mets Booster Club. The next day, we were given the agenda, which culminated in a rather elegant and delightful dinner, to be attended by all of the POWs, all of us staying in the same hotel.

That evening as we dressed for dinner, I was sitting on my bed waiting for Louise to get ready, and all of a sudden I heard a tapping noise on the hotel room wall, set to the "shave and a haircut" tempo, the calling card of a tap-coder trying to establish communication. The second I heard this sound, I returned his call in kind, tapping the "two bits" part, reassuring him, "Hello. I'm here. I'm listening."

Part 5

Chapter 28

Matwing One

A Changed Man

After being released from the hospital and given a clean bill of health, I was temporarily assigned to the A6 Replacement Training Squadron, still in Oceana, Virginia, to get refresher training in a plane we called the A6E, a newer version of the A6A. I was so happy to see that the training squadron commanding officer was an old shipmate of mine, Sam Sayers, from back when we flew A4Bs in Attack Squadron 34 at Cecil Field in Jacksonville, Florida. He was also in VA-85 when I was shot down. My training consisted of ground school to re-familiarize me with all the aircraft systems and the carrier landings. I was also getting briefed by the current Matwing (Medium Attack Wing) commander, Capt. Herm Turk. The aircraft maintenance systems had changed substantially since I'd last flown, so it was a lot for me to absorb. Soon, Herm got his orders to the Philippines, and I received mine to relieve him, so a change-of-command ceremony was planned. For this level of promotion, we held a fairly good-sized ceremony; with several flag officers present, Herm and I both gave speeches. Even our congressional representative was present. The next day, I went to work and was pleased to see that I even had my own parking spot, my first ever since entering the Navy. Then, to get acquainted, I held a meeting with the commanding officers of the squadrons under my command.

This assignment was different, mostly in that I was in charge of a lot more people and the job was more complicated than any I'd served in before. One day we received a message that one of our A6s at sea in the Mediterranean was involved in a midair collision. The pilot was killed, but the bombardier/navigator survived. Protocol required me to get into an official car immediately, accompanied by a doctor and a clergyman, and drive over to notify the widow before she heard it from some other source. We went to her house, but no one was home.

A Navy wife from across the street saw us from her front window and of course, she guessed what was going on. She approached and invited us to wait at her house until the pilot's wife returned. We shared with her what had occurred, and she did not envy our task. Finally, our widow returned, and, thankfully, someone was with her. We again went to her front door and knocked. When she opened the door, I asked if I could come in, and she looked confused but said yes. Then she saw the others with me and pieced together why we were there. She dropped straight to the floor and howled. I will never forget it. This is why we bring a doctor with us, and he quickly attended to her. When she settled down, I answered her questions to the best of my ability. There was just no easy way, then or now, to do that particular job.

In my long career, I'd known many friends and shipmates who'd given that ultimate sacrifice, and I knew the grief their families felt when told of a tragic death, but this was my first time notifying someone's wife. I know that when I was shot down, my wife also received "the visit." My parents simply received a telegram. However, in both cases, a casualty officer was assigned to keep my family members informed as events unfolded, and it's one of the more somber responsibilities of people who serve as squadron commanders. In this case with this widow, my squadron commander was deployed, so I was tasked with this incredible responsibility. The pilot's parents were also notified, and they came to Oceana to attend their son's memorial service. I did my best to console them, and they were glad that their son had achieved his lifelong dream of becoming a Navy pilot and that he died honorably. Make no mistake, it is a career where danger is always lurking.

While also on this tour, I was informed of a situation where two of my aviators and a very expensive aircraft ended up in the ground. I was at home when I got a call from the squadron duty officer informing me that an A6 was in trouble over the field. The landing gear had been cycled up and down several times, but instruments still did not indicate "down and locked." The crew members were two nuggets (a new pilot and bombardier/navigator) who had requested a tower flyby, but with it being dark outside, the tower personnel could not tell if their gear was down. The tower had another aircraft in the area fly underneath the A6 and see if the gear was locked down because the pilot still couldn't tell. The landing gear indicator reads up, down, or what we call "barber-poled." This does happen occasionally, however, as I was told, their low fuel light had already been on for quite a while. It seemed to me, in fact, that it had been for *too long a while,* and in an A6 you simply don't have that much time before you're on dead empty.

I told the squadron duty officer to land them ASAP, but at that exact moment, the nuggets reported that their engines had quit and they were ejecting. Now, it was hard for me to imagine how this disaster happened so quickly and why in the world they didn't just land their plane wheels-up. Regardless, we still found ourselves in the middle of a terrible disaster. Fortunately, no one was injured, but, still, our aircraft was gone. I received the completed accident report and decided to pull their wings and transfer them to shipboard duty. If it was their lifelong dream to be Navy pilots, I'd just ended it for them in a nightmare of unfortunate events.

All things considered, those difficult years during my commands in the Navy didn't seem too stressful compared to being in prison. In fact, one might think that in my new, prestigious command, with my loving family intact, everything should have picked right back up for me quite normally, happily, and easily. But those six years in Vietnam had a larger effect on me than anyone could have anticipated, certainly more of an effect on the subsequent behavior of all POWs than we were able to predict. We came back changed men. Harder in some ways, numb in others. It takes some extended time to observe how people who have been under severe stress will learn to cope with their normal lives again, thus the diagnosis of post-traumatic stress disorder (PTSD) evolved, but it was difficult back then for me to admit that it's very real.

I didn't see that I, too, was deeply changed after I came home. I didn't sense those differences in my demeanor at the time, but now I recognize that, for example, I'd grown less critical of practically everything and mundane irritations just did not affect me. I didn't let myself get wound up about *anything,* which sounds great in theory, but I was still a father. As Louise and I tried to create our "new normal" life together, those changes in my personality caused me to disengage from disciplining my children, for example. I didn't see the importance of forcing Richard to brush his hair, because to me, it was such a petty thing. When I wanted to go outside and work in the yard, Louise would beckon me back inside to rest and relax. She was always doting on me, urging me, in the most attentive ways, to be kind to myself, and that was wonderful, but after returning from prison I was a person who just didn't like to be told what to do, no matter how kind and thoughtful the request. Quite plainly, I'd forgotten how to be a husband and a father in almost every way, as many POWs would attest to. As a result, Louise and I ultimately divorced after my return from Vietnam, and I maintain, with sadness, that it was all my fault.

Chapter 29

A New Life, a New Navy

Sailing

Before my Matwing tour was over, a lieutenant from VA-35 came over to my office and told me that the commanding officer of the newest carrier undergoing sea trials wanted to invite me to fly out and test out his Carrier Control Approach Unit. This new aircraft carrier was off the Virginia Coast and had no air wing aircraft on board. The CO was a classmate of mine, Brian Compton, and he was a nuclear engineer among other things, including an A4 squadron commander during the Vietnam War. He'd also been with the ship all during its construction. A couple of squadron pilots and I headed out to test our skills. It was a beautiful day, and the carrier was one of the largest in the whole fleet, if not the largest. The deck was enormous, and each time we made an arrested landing (using the plane's tailhook to grab the wire on the aircraft carrier deck), we could simply taxi to the catapult and launch again. I got ten traps (arrested landings) during that day, and that's the only time in my career that I had my own carrier all to myself for an entire afternoon.

Near the end of my tour, I received a message from my A6 cohorts at the Pentagon that I should send a message to the Chief of Navy Operations (CNO) expressing my support for the A6 Acquisition Program so that the Navy would continue extending A6 production, as there was no other aircraft in the fleet at that time as capable as the A6. Time was of the essence, so my staff drafted the message directly, and boldly, too, I might add, laying out the requirements I wanted. I included the whole chain of command in my message—that is, the commander of Tactical Wings–Atlantic and the commander in chief of the Atlantic Fleet from two- through four-star admirals—but my memo still went straight to the CNO, *all* the way to the top, without stopping anywhere along the way. The next day, I received a phone call from a two-star admiral who worked for a four-star admiral, asking me what the hell I thought I was doing. Adm. Isaac Kidd Jr., his superior, was widely known to be a hard-ass, and they were all afraid to even show my memo to him, but, of course, they had to.

In hindsight, yes, my message should have been sent via the chain of command, but my logic was that it would've taken months. As you might expect, my message stepped on a good many bureaucratic toes, which, in turn, upset a lot of brass. My only excuse was that as I had been a POW for so long and had to act alone on so many occasions, perhaps I needed to consider that maybe I was ill-equipped to work within a complex bureaucracy. I was called into the office of the commander of Naval Air Forces–Atlantic, which was headed by a vice admiral. He was a good guy, and he saw my pain. He said I shouldn't be so pressured by my cohorts in the Pentagon and that I needed not worry about doing permanent damage to my career. Still, my actions didn't help the A6 program, it seemed, because it was not extended. With that disappointment, I decided that it was time for me to move on before I wreaked any more havoc.

Toward the middle of 1976, as the two years in my present assignment drew nearer the end, I received orders to Pensacola, Florida, to be the chief staff officer of the chief of Naval Education Training and Support. A few months before detaching, I used some of my savings from my Hanoi incarceration to buy a forty-one-foot Tartan Offshore Cruising Ketch. I got the boat commissioned with the help of Bill Seifert, a super guy from Tartan Marine, who was knowledgeable about all phases of yacht construction and sailing, including racing. We finally got my boat commissioned and took a trial sail and were delighted when everything worked to perfection. I'd learned to sail way back at the Naval Academy and during active duty had rented sailboats occasionally, so I still had the magic touch. With my son, Richard, and a friend of his, plus two officers commandeered from my old staff, I headed out of Pungo, Virginia, down through the Dismal Swamp Canal, past Elizabeth City, and into the Albemarle Sound as we headed south on our voyage to Pensacola.

By this point, I was not only divorced but also essentially homeless and would be so for the next six years. Back in Hanoi, many of the prisoners had often talked about cruising when we got home, but I was determined to actually pursue it. From the Albemarle Sound, via the Alligator River to Pamlico Sound, we continued until we reached Morehead City, North Carolina, arriving there about two or three o'clock in the morning. We didn't get off the boat other than to walk around the commercial docks a bit. After a day spent resting, during a drizzle of rain we headed out, with Hilton Head, South Carolina, as our target.

Westerly *Centaur,* 1973, my first sailboat.

Another three nights at sea passed, and we arrived off of Hilton Head and headed into the marina, with its simulated lighthouse. The tide was over eight feet, which we weren't used to, so we waited for slack water. After another couple of days' rest, we headed back out toward the naval base at Mayport, Florida, just a few miles from Jacksonville Beach near the entrance to the St. Johns River, the longest US river to flow from south to north, at about 310 miles long.

We entered the St. Johns River just as the carrier *FD Roosevelt* was getting under way. It was no problem for me to navigate alongside the ship, but for one of the yardmasters, a yard patrol boat that clearly didn't want me there, it was *quite* a big deal. The yard patrol boat came toward us, telling us over a loudspeaker to leave the area immediately. What he didn't realize was that a couple of months prior, I had been at a commanders' meeting in Norfolk and I met the Mayport Naval Station's commanding officer. I told him I would be coming his way via Mayport, and he said, "Fine, come on," and gave me permission to dock at the flag pier. So here I was doing just that, as an invited guest, or so I thought. Still, the patrol boat grew more aggressive about ramming me and threatened me with all kinds of crimes. I ignored him and proceeded right up to the flag dock. At that point, a small platoon of Marines showed up with their weapons drawn. I told them, "Take me to your leader!" whom I hoped was still expecting me.

The *Tartan,* 1976.

Fortunately, the commanding officer's office overlooked the harbor, and he was watching us the whole time, laughing his ass off. He said he'd totally forgotten I was coming and apologized. He turned back the Marines, and we commenced an enjoyable stay of about four days.

Back at the Matwing, we had a turboprop twin engine aircraft that often took bombardier/navigators up for training. Before we ever left on our cruise, I'd requested that the new commander schedule one of those training missions down to Mayport and back to pick up my two crew members who had accompanied us. Just as my sailing crew and I entered the Mayport Harbor that day, right before the angry Marines arrived, we all looked up and, sure enough, our aircraft flew overhead and landed at the adjacent airfield, ready to pick up my guys. It was a well-coordinated mission!

My parents were also living in Jacksonville at the time, so the commanding officer arranged for them to have quarters at Mayport so they could visit with Richard and me while we were in town. We took them sailing, accompanied by Mayport's retired former commanding officer, a man who had been on the Eniwetok project with me and who still remained a good friend.

While in Mayport, my daughter, Lisa, who was seventeen, and our next-door neighbor flew in from Norfolk and joined us for the next leg of our odyssey. After briefing my new crew members on their job functions, we pressed on toward Miami. The weather continued to be marvelous, and we cruised for another three days and nights before deciding to stop in Fort Lauderdale. After a good night's rest, we headed for the Miami area, but then things took a scary turn. On my chart the route looked easy, but I advised everyone I met thereafter not to head down the Hawk Channel at night. It was dusk when we started out, and I had two of my lookouts positioned forward to keep track of the markers. We missed one, then another, then we didn't see another until after midnight. Then, as if things couldn't get worse, we encountered a massive thunderstorm with strong crosswinds, with driving rain and lightning. I was *dead reckoning,* or navigating by course and speed alone, and steering about a ten-degree cut to windward to account for the strong crosswind. After about an hour, the storm moved on and we spotted a light off the port bow. It was the light at the Hen and Chickens position on the reef separating the Hawk Channel from the Florida Straits. Thank goodness! I would like to think our survival was due to my superior navigational skills, but I think someone up above was probably just looking out for us.

We pulled into the Navy marina on Boca Chica Key, and, as it turned out, a former POW happened to be the executive officer at Naval Air Station Boca Chica. He sent a car for us, to help us get a slip as well as to get our bearings at the Kings Point Marina on Stock Island, the next Key between Boca Chica and Key West. That very next day we got under way and moved the boat to Kings Point Marina and decided to take a few days' rest. At this point, Richard's friend left and headed back home to Virginia, as did our next-door neighbor from Virginia Beach. That left Richard, Lisa, me, and another friend. I was able to get a couple of rooms at the bachelor officers' quarters, and one of the rooms was actually a VIP suite, so we were in pretty good shape. It was July, and it was great to have air-conditioning and to be able to sleep in a real bed with sheets and take long, hot showers instead of two-gallon ones.

From there, the plan was to sail to the Dry Tortugas and then directly to Clearwater, Florida, where I was going to have air-conditioning installed on my boat at the Ross Yacht Yard. On the way to the Dry Tortugas, we crossed over an area called the Quicksands, so named because as the sand shifts, soundings on the navigational charts are unreliable. It was a truly beautiful place; the water was clear, and the bottom was pure white sand. When you looked ahead of your position, the refraction of light gave the impression that the water was much shallower than it actually was. There wasn't a lot of wind, so we motored cautiously for a couple of hours until we were clear of the shallows. This was the same area where in 1985 Mel Fisher would discover the wreck of the Spanish ship *Atocha*, which was destroyed and sunk in a hurricane in 1622. (The treasure Fisher discovered netted forty tons of silver bullion, as well as coins, jewelry, and countless artifacts. Unfortunately, the State of Florida sued Fisher for the loot, and he eventually had to forge a compromise and share his booty. Much of that treasure is now on display in museums throughout Florida, and Mel Fisher's Treasures continues to search for sunken ships throughout Florida.)

Having survived Quicksands, we continued on our way, finally sighting the Rebecca Shoals marker. We made a turn to port and ultimately spotted the massive Dry Tortugas National Park. This park is only accessible by boat or sea plane, and its Fort Jefferson remains the largest all-masonry fort in the Western Hemisphere. Once we entered the protected harbor and anchored, a park ranger motored out to our boat to welcome us and to give us a copy of the park regulations. There were plenty of lobsters to see there, but we weren't allowed to catch them. After two days, we were ready to move on, so we jumped into the water several times to swim and enjoy the serenity of a truly beautiful, magical place, and then we prepared to set off again.

On the morning of our third day, we set sail for Clearwater, about two hundred nautical miles as the crow flies. Again, the weather was good, as it usually is during the summer unless a hurricane rears its ugly head. We moored at Ross Yacht Yard, where work began on the badly needed air-conditioning. In the interim, I called up an old squadron-mate and he had us over to his house for a few nights, and we enjoyed *his* air-conditioning. Finally, once the installation on the boat was complete, we headed for Pensacola, a two-night passage. When the wind lightened, we motored on, but the second day at sea we experienced a leak in the engine's freshwater cooling system. Of course, it was in a location I couldn't easily reach without a special tool, so we sailed on. The wind picked up significantly, and during that last night we boomed along at six knots, in sight of the shore lights. I had no LORAN device, and GPS hadn't been invented yet, so I had to rely solely on a sextant and sunlines to navigate. Celestial navigation has practically become obsolete since GPS technology has evolved, but I think it still has its unique and special uses, especially on a long voyage.

Upon arrival in Pensacola, I was to relieve Capt. Glen Hatch as chief staff officer for Chief of Naval Education and Training Support, and he was glad to see us coming. I called him on the VHF radio to rendezvous. He led us into the Naval Air Station Pensacola marina, which was tricky since there were no markers and there were shoals everywhere. As we came into Pensacola Bay I had Richard down by the damaged engine, tasked with adding water while we motored in. After pulling in to our slip, we all drank a beer and reflected on our long trip. I knew that in a couple of days, I would be back at work sailing . . . a desk. Ugh!

Chapter 30

Retirement

Salty Old Sailor

The staff of the Chief of Naval Education and Training Support was located at Ellison Field in Pensacola, which in prior years had been a helicopter training base. Shortly after my arrival in 1976, I was asked to be the keynote speaker at the chiefs' annual banquet. It was an honor for me to be invited, and of course I accepted. When I stood at the podium to begin my speech, I looked out at all the chiefs in the audience. I'd never seen so many gathered in one place at one time, and, very tongue-in-cheek, I asked them, "If you're all here, who's running the fleet?" In my speech I reflected on my anticipated retirement, and I congratulated the staff members on their good work. I joked that I used to terrify myself at five hundred knots regularly, and now I was doing it at five knots only occasionally. I poked fun at the dangers of my career by saying, "Navy flying involves hours and hours of boredom interrupted by brief moments of stark terror." This speech was one of my last public addresses while still on active duty, and it was strange to hear myself discussing the end of what had been my long and rather eventful Navy career.

The following spring, I took two weeks' leave, having made plans to sail with a small crew first to the Dry Tortugas and then on to Key West. The first day and night were beautiful sailing days, but then I picked up a strong southeast wind from a persistent high pressure system. At one point, I took a photo of our wind-speed indicator, and it read thirty-seven knots relative wind off the port bow, some damn rough conditions. We'd been under way for two days already when I reluctantly projected that it would take another two days to get to the Tortugas, and from there the wind would be on our nose for the entire last leg to Key West. That night, I decided I needed to abort the trip, as I would be running out of leave anyway. I woke up my crew and told them we were changing course to St. Petersburg, and, in unison, they yelled, "Oh, thank God!" It appeared that they'd already reached their limits for sailing that particular trip, and although they wanted to say something to me earlier, I was the salty old CO of that boat, so they toughed it out in silence.

When I turned to an easterly heading, we were on a broad reach; the wind was off our starboard side and toward the stern. When we arrived at St. Petersburg and jumped on to the dock, none of us could stand up straight because the rough ride had done a number on our balance. Next, we boarded for our trip back to Pensacola, and it was stupendous! We headed toward Cape San Blas and had an impromptu swim call. We dove into the water and splashed around a bit, then reboarded and prepared to get under way when we saw a large bull shark slowly swimming by the boat. Good timing for us, again. One more night at sea, and we were again back home in our slip but not so ready to get back to work. I began to realize I was ready to put the wheels in motion to wrap up my career.

I retired from the US Navy on September 30, 1979, after thirty-two years and four months of service. I was falling even more in love with sailing by that time, so I decided I needed to buy a bigger boat. I chose a Vagabond Voyager forty-seven-foot double headsail ketch. All of my previous boats displaced less than twenty-five thousand pounds, but this behemoth clocked in at forty thousand pounds, with thirteen thousand pounds in the keel. It had a Lehman Ford 85-horsepower diesel, hydraulic steering, a teak deck, a forward cabin for two, midship over-and-under bunks, and a large aft cabin with a built-in queen-size bunk. There were two heads, and the head in the aft cabin even had a bathtub! That boat was very simple to sail, even singlehanded, and on autopilot it was effortless to furl the main sail when the wind picked up. In the three years I lived on the Vagabond, I never reefed the main (reduced the size of the main sail) once.

This beautiful boat, built in Taiwan, was designed by William Garden. (There are many copycats of William Garden's designs, so a buyer needs to be careful not to purchase an imposter.) The boatyard where it was built was originally established by a British gentleman named Ernest Chamberlain. After World War II, Ernest and a friend of his, Bill Crealock, sailed around the world, and Bill wrote a book about their adventures: *Vagabonding under Sail* (New York: Hastings House, 1951). Later, Crealock and Garden became naval architects and shipbuilders in Formosa, what we now call Taiwan (remember when I helped liberate Taiwan?). Ernest Chamberlain started building in the northern part of Taiwan and renamed the Garden design *Porpoise* and the Vagabond 47 *Voyager*.

I bought my Vagabond in 1979, a month after I retired, and it was delivered by container ship to the Port of New Orleans. That boat always seemed so big to me, but when I first saw it on the deck of that huge ship, it looked like a lifeboat. I bought it almost totally stripped, purchasing it through an architect in Philadelphia who represented the Bluewater Yacht Builders in Taiwan. (When I bought this boat, I also became an associate of Bluewater Yacht Builders.) There were no marine toilets, winches, sails, instruments, generators, anchors and ropes, or dock lines, et cetera. Since I'd basically become a contractor and used the Bluewater Yacht Builders name, I was able to get a sales tax exemption and bought most of my missing equipment at original equipment manufacturer prices. This saved me tons of money! I also hired a CPA and obtained an investment tax credit, which really helped me out as well.

I had always intended to put my boat in boat shows in Miami, Ft. Lauderdale, and St. Petersburg, and peddling these beautiful vessels for profit seemed easy enough. I loved my sailing lifestyle at the time but also had to remind myself that as I adapted to my post-Navy future I still had to make a living for the next few years. After fully commissioning the Vagabond, I headed out in January. I spent the night in Destin Harbor, which has a large breakwater on the east side of the channel. As I motored out, the boat was pitching and rolling wildly, as the incoming waves were pretty big. When I got outside of the channel, it got a little better, so I put up my cruising spinnaker, but it somehow got jammed. At about that time, even though I had it on autopilot, the boat started to lose its heading and actually started for the beach. I rushed back into the cockpit and saw that the wheel had separated from the rudder. I rushed below, folded back the mattress, and opened a hatch underneath it, exposing the rudder post. It had hydraulic steering, and, the hydraulic ram had become disconnected from the fitting on the rudder post. A clevis pin had flipped out, and there was no cotter pin. Fortunately, the missing pin was easily within reach, and I happened to have some spare cotter pins. I had another problem in that the rudder post was swinging back and forth and I could not hold it, so I had to carefully drop the pin at the exact moment the holes were lined up. It was hectic, to be sure.

I hoped this wasn't a bad omen for the rest of the trip. I made it to Apalachicola and anchored near the main pass. The next day, I sailed overnight to Tarpon Springs, which is somewhat inland up the Apalachicola River. I decided to hole up for a while, when a strong cold front started coming in. It was bitter cold, in the teens! The Vagabond had a small wood fireplace, but, of course, I didn't have any wood. The marina operator told me that up the road a couple of miles there was a boatyard that built wooden boats and they probably had scraps to offer up, so I headed out, hitchhiking. Luck was with me, and I got a ride to the boatyard. The owner cut up a bunch of small pieces of white oak for me and even gave me a lift back to my boat. One of the great things about cruising is the friendliness of the other boaters and marina operators. Everyone is always ready to give a helping hand to a boating brother.

After a few more days, the weather warmed and I headed out through the Swing Bridge at Marathon Key and into Boot Key Harbor to rest up. After a night at Boot Key, the wind really kicked up, out of the east of course, but I couldn't delay any longer and I didn't want to miss the Miami show. I had to motor into a forty-knot headwind all the way to Miami through the Hawk Channel then up the Miami River a short distance to a slip owned by a friend of mine, Bill Stewart. When I arrived, there was room enough for six boats, and it was very well protected. With some help, I prepared a slideshow displaying the features of the Vagabond, plus I prepared a number of pamphlets to hand out to prospective buyers. I even took a few interested parties for an inspection, but only folks with a contract and a 10 percent deposit got a day sail!

By the end of the Ft. Lauderdale and St. Petersburg shows, which followed the one in Miami, I was more than ready to head back to Pensacola. Still, before too long in home port, I would get the itch to head south again. I stopped once on the way back down at the South Seas Plantation on Captiva Island, which has a great marina and was pretty affordable as well. I was offered a boat trip to Useppa Island that included lunch, so I gladly agreed to it. I really enjoyed their club there, and so I joined, for a $5,000 membership fee. It was during my time at the Useppa Club that I found a buyer for one of my boats. He was a very nice Canadian guy, and after I answered all of his questions, we closed the deal.

Leaving Miami once again, I sailed to Ft. Lauderdale for a show, and after a little difficulty, I found a slip and tied up. Coming in, I wanted to gain some steam first, but I had a twenty-knot crosswind so it was not to be. The problem going in bow-first was that part of the bowsprit overhung the dock, which could've caused someone to get a nasty knock on the head.

My son got lucky and had some time off from work and so he joined me in Ft. Lauderdale, which was great, since he was able to help me sail to St. Petersburg for the show. By then, he'd sailed with me so many times that no training was even necessary. One thing I found strange to adjust to with these kinds of shows was that the boat crews usually stayed on their boats, not only for security but also to save money. Everyone went only by their first names, which was weird for me after a lifetime of Navy greetings. For example, it was funny when the girl on the boat across from me would say, "Good morning, Allen," to which I would respond "Good morning, Jane!" (or whatever her name was). After being a stodgy old Navy guy for so long, it was actually refreshing to chuck the rank and just be a civilian.

The displays of a great many magnificent boats at the show impressed me, and there was a great deal of camaraderie among all of us in the boating culture. When the show was over, we learned that our entry fee included a fantastic after-party. It was held at the marina on the second floor of the main building, but when you arrived, you were led to a chute that you had to slide down in order to get into the party room. When you hit the bottom, someone helped you up and handed you a beer. The room was very spacious and had a band and a decent number of kiosks serving all kinds of different food plus a significant number of open bars. All I could say to myself was, "Why in the world didn't I do this when I was younger?"—although at fifty-one and fit, I still fit right in. I told myself that anyway! Richard, however, was only twenty-four, and he was cruising around the party like a pro. After a bit of networking, I started thinking about getting under way early the next morning, since the normal occupants of the slip wanted to get back in anyway. Richard concurred, but we both still squeezed in a raucous good time before turning in. Although he didn't outlast me, he certainly recovered more quickly than I did the next day. In any case, we were up early and headed for Miami. We had to go outside, out into the Atlantic, because there was a fixed bridge at fifty feet and our main mast was above that. We sailed outside until we cut into Marathon and anchored in Boot Key Harbor. The next morning, we fueled up and passed through the Seven Mile Bridge and made a course to Useppa Island via Boca Grande Pass. A little rest, and we were under way again to Terra Verde at Tampa–St. Pete. The show there seemed a lot smaller than the one in Ft. Lauderdale. It went from December 1 through December 9, and we headed back to the Useppa slip on December 10. We did a little day sailing with some friends, then the weather turned cold, so we hunkered down until March. When it warmed up outside that spring, I resigned my membership from the Useppa Island Club and headed on to Key West, which I decided would be my next home.

I've gone into some detail about my time cruising after commissioning the Vagabond because I certainly loved that life, and I hope there are some prospective or veteran sailors who have enjoyed that part of my story. I sure enjoyed reliving those years as I wrote about them! I always stayed pretty busy and was fortunate enough to stop in a number of great anchorages, not to mention that it kept me in great shape. I write these accounts for anyone who might harbor any thoughts or dreams of doing the same. Do it! I can say beyond a doubt that I truly enjoyed my experiences in the years I lived on my boats. Some moments did test my resolve; I had to make some tough weather decisions and I scared myself pretty badly a few times, but those years were still the highlight of my entire life. Six years as a POW was way too long, but six years of living aboard a sailboat, cruising all over the place, and enjoying that kind of freedom was not nearly enough.

Chapter 31

The Mariel Boatlift

Back in the Communist Countryside

On April 1, 1980, a man named Hector boarded a bus in Cuba with three friends. The bus driver was also a friend of Hector's, and he announced to everyone on board that the bus had broken down, then emptied it of all of its passengers, aside from Hector and his three friends. Hector then took control of the bus and drove it right through the front gates of the Peruvian embassy in Havana, the capital of Cuba. Armed Cuban guards opened fire on the bus, and during the shootout a Cuban guard was shot and killed. Once inside, Hector and his friends asked for permission to obtain political asylum inside the Peruvian embassy, and the top Peruvian diplomat present quickly granted it. The Cuban government immediately demanded that the Peruvian government turn over the five individuals so they could be tried for the death of the guard. The Peruvian government refused, and Cuban President Fidel Castro threatened to remove the Cuban guards who were assigned to protect the Peruvian embassy. On Good Friday, April 4, 1980, he proceeded to do so.

On April 5, about 750 Cubans assembled outside the Peruvian embassy and also asked for diplomatic asylum. By Easter Sunday there were over 10,000 people crammed into the small embassy grounds, so Castro ordered a large number of his guards back in place and blocked all access to the area outside of the embassy. In addition, motor vehicle travel was stopped within the small Havana suburb of Miramar, where most of the foreign embassies in Cuba were located.

Inside the embassy grounds, people were scattered everywhere, and most refused to leave even though it quickly became apparent that there was inadequate infrastructure to accommodate such a large crowd. The situation looked dire, then some of the other embassies, including Spain's and Costa Rica's, agreed to take on some of the refugees. Castro recognized that he was falling farther behind the situation, so ultimately he declared that the Port of Mariel, located to the west of Havana, would be available to anyone wishing to leave Cuba. While news of this decision was not widely broadcast in Cuba, Cuban exiles living in Miami somehow got word of it and quickly began making plans to sail to Mariel to pick up their family members.

Clearly, Castro was trying to look like a good guy, but in reality, he knew he had a huge political as well as a humanitarian crisis on his hands if he didn't make that move. When Costa Rica's embassy agreed to take on some of the fleeing Cubans, Castro told their ambassador that if he allowed them to go, the Cuban exiles must remain in those countries. The Costa Rican president replied, "Since Costa Rica is a free country, once your Cubans are settled, they are free to go anywhere they please," a definite slap in the face to Fidel Castro.

On April 23, 1980, I was parked in a slip at Oceanside Marina in Key West, on Stock Island, where I was living on my boat. I mounted my bike that morning like I always did and pedaled over to the marina store to get my copy of the *Miami Herald*. There seemed to be a buzz of activity on that particular morning so upon inquiring about the frenzy, I was told that the Mariel boatlift was just getting started. When I got back to my boat, an elderly Cuban woman named Ondina and her brother Angel, neither of whom I'd ever met before, walked out onto my finger pier and asked me if I would take them to Mariel to get her daughter, her daughter's husband, and their two children. Of course I was reluctant, but still sympathetic, so I called my boat insurance agent and asked him if I would be insured if I went down to Castro's paradise to pick up a few refugees. He immediately gave me a big fat "NO!" so I returned and explained my risk to Ondina and Angel, and they understood my position, with great disappointment.

At about that time, someone came down to the dock shouting that a boat carrying Cuban refugees was arriving at Truman Annex. Feeling a little pressure on my guilty conscience, I told Ondina and Angel that I wanted to drive down there and scope out the situation and then I would make my decision. Once there, I quickly spotted the boat. There was a small group of people watching dockside, and all the refugees were still being kept on the boat, all of them looking harried and exhausted. There was a TV reporter interviewing the captain of the boat, a man who appeared to be a Cuban American. I moved closer so I could hear the questions they were asking him, and the reporter inquired, "Do you realize that you could go to prison for going to Mariel and bringing these refugees back?" The captain looked at all of us and said, "I believe that these people have been in prison all of their lives, and if I have to go to prison in order to bring them to freedom, then I consider it worthwhile."

The *Vagabond,* 1981.

And I thought, *Why did he have to say it like that?* I knew I would help, having spent over six years under Communism myself. I was determined to go get those people and bring them to America.

I went back to the boat and told Ondina and Angel that I would make the trip. I contacted a good friend of mine, named Joe, who was living in Key West at the time, and he immediately agreed to go with me. I told Ondina we would probably be gone for a month or so and would most likely be made to bring back more people than we wanted. I emphasized that we needed a replenished supply of extra Type I life preservers, plus food and drinks. I told them to prepare to leave around sundown in two days, on April 25. They agreed to every request, jumped into their car, and sped off. I thought, *What in the world have I done?* I also recruited my nephew Russell to accompany Joe and me, and along with a cat we adopted, we had our crew.

In the early afternoon of April 25, Ondina and Angel returned with food, drinks, and life preservers. After getting everyone squared away on the boat, I briefed my passengers on how they could assist us if we needed them. A little before sunset, we headed out for the 110-nautical-mile trip across the Florida Straits. This is usually a fairly bumpy trip, as the current runs easterly and the wind normally blows toward the west. Our trip was turning out to be no exception. By the time we were out of sight of land, it was pitch-dark and getting rough. We dropped the main sail during the night and sailed under Yankee, clubfooted stay sail, and mizzen. (*Clubfooted* indicates that the stay sail is on a boom.) I went down below during the night to check on Ondina and found her on the large bunk aft with the port open to try to get some fresh air, and we were taking on water as we pounded forward. I got her a bath towel and tried to make her a little more comfortable, but she was really suffering. By morning, we still couldn't see land forward or astern, but by that afternoon we finally spotted the mainland of Cuba. We saw several smaller boats also headed for Mariel. I discovered the strong current had caused us to drift a little eastward, so we made some corrections and later that day we spotted the entrance to Mariel Harbor. When we entered the harbor, a Cuban patrol boat came close abeam and told us to anchor where we were for the night. I didn't speak Spanish, but Ondina and Angel were happy to interpret, and I was thankful they were there. When I dropped my anchor, I thought it would never hit bottom. It was about sixty feet deep where we were!

The next morning, a couple of patrol boats arrived and directed all of us to form a line and follow them. As we moved along, we saw several inlets and learned that there were about three thousand boats involved in the boatlift. We proceeded to the inner harbor, which was the end of the line. Once there, we were on our own to select an anchoring spot. I spotted a wooden sailboat named the *Andrea Lisa* and recognized it from our marina in Key West. Its crew members signaled for us to come moor alongside them, which we did. We were riding on their anchor, looking forward to a nice evening of drinks and swapping stories, but soon, the sky started to look dark and then turned black as an ominous thunderstorm began to press down on us. There was a large power boat anchored just in front us, and its captain cranked his engines to ease the strain on his ground tackle just as the storm hit! It was one of the worst storms I've ever been in. The wind howled, and the wind indicator pegged at sixty knots. I'm not sure how much above that it blew, but it was significant. The rain came down in sheets, and we couldn't see fifty feet in front of us. Then, to make things a great deal worse, we noticed that the power boat was slowly bearing down on us. Its captain roared as much power as he could to keep from drifting into us, and it surged forward, but then its props inadvertently grabbed the anchor line of the *Andrea Lisa* and started dragging it. The *Andrea Lisa* shifted sideways and then started dragging *us,* since we were tied alongside of her. Joe immediately grabbed his knife and cut the three-quarter-inch line, which was by then pulled taut, and it snapped with a bang. The power boat moved off and out of sight in the pouring rain, and we never saw it or the *Andrea Lisa* again, as she was dragged away. We idled in place until the storm passed, then dropped our anchor and settled in for what was turning out to be a long haul.

A few hours after the storm cleared, we began to hear loud, deep whistles blowing. Soon, a large white Cuban cruise ship came into view and anchored right in the middle of all the boats. Its crew rigged a floating dock alongside the vessel and lowered an accommodation ladder down to the dock so that the boaters could board. We dropped our dinghy in the water, cranked the outboard, and motored over to investigate. The top deck of the boat was covered with an awning, it had a large number of tables and chairs, and, miraculously, it had a bar! The ship also had an air-conditioned restaurant where you could get a steak dinner. There was a mariachi band that played every day and long into the night. We were amazed and invigorated, to say the least. There were also some boats we called "bum boats," which cruised around selling water, beer, soft drinks, and various food options. I was thankful for this, because I'd started to worry that we were going to run out of food on my boat.

Each day, a patrol boat cruised around among the many boats in all the anchorages, and via a loud speaker, its crew called individual vessels to report to the immigration dock in turn. I don't know what we would have done without Ondina and Angel, because we did not speak or understand a lick of Spanish. If not for them, we might still be anchored out there, wondering where everyone was going. We also learned that anyone who wished to could go ashore and call their relatives in Cuba. Usually Ondina would go and Russell went with her. I, of course, did not want to leave my boat. After several days of this routine, Ondina and Russell returned with a guest. Jorge Espinosa had arrived at Mariel on a shrimp boat (which is a pretty large boat), and when the folks on the shrimp boat told him they had to depart from Cuba and head home to Miami, Jorge decided to stay on with us for a bit and then hitch a ride back with another boat once he was able to retrieve his family.

Jorge was interesting. He'd left Cuba as a young man and had worked his way all the way to Spain and then to the United States. He had driven a taxi in Washington, DC, and ultimately made his way to Miami, where he established an import-export company. It never ceased to amaze me how entrepreneurial the Cuban people were when they weren't suffering under a Communist regime. The Castro brothers did much to stifle ingenuity and growth among their population. By now, you may have observed that I am not a fan of Communism. Jorge told me that he remained in contact with an uncle who was in the Cuban army. His uncle told Jorge to go to the immigration dock every day and call home. He was told that if his family didn't answer, it would mean they were on their way to the departure dock. Jorge went to the immigration dock every day until no one answered his call.

The days continued to pass. We would occasionally stop by the cruise ship and listen to its band and sip on a Hatuey, the one-eyed Indian beer. From time to time we got to go into the air-conditioned restaurant for a good meal, a cool-down, or a "personal urgency." For example, one day, Joe clogged the forward head on my boat, and while he was attempting to fix it, he first transferred the crap into a bucket to dump over the side, but unfortunately, some parts of the toilet also went inside the bucket, so of course all those pieces were gone forever, which left us with but one operating head. Thank Heaven we'd started out with two. Moving forward, some obvious instructions were promulgated—such as poop, pump, poop, pump, et cetera—but after that there were no more accidents, until our passenger capacity increased substantially. More on that later.

There was a Cuban air force base nearby, which caused me a little bit of anxiety. We could see their planes flying constantly to and from the airfield, so I climbed to the top of our fifty-seven-foot mast with a camera and snapped a few pictures of that intrepid air force, the same one I'd briefly engaged during the Bay of Pigs Invasion. When I got back home to the States, I couldn't believe that no one was interested in my pictures. But anyway, one day a Cuban patrol boat came by calling for us to report to the immigration dock. Up came the anchor, and we motored to the dock and moored. We were told we would be waiting another day or two before the family arrived. One perk of mooring at the immigration dock was the presence of more food, especially ice cream sandwiches. While we were tied up, a couple of Cuban journalists asked to come aboard and talk to us. They were from *La Prensa*, the Cuban national newspaper. They were curious about our cat, Ketch. I explained that he was a *gato capitalista,* whereupon they nodded and laughed. They asked us a few more questions about our involvement in the boatlift, and then they moved on. For all I know, Ketch ended up on the front page of *La Prensa*, silently advocating for freedom and liberty!

The next day, all of Ondina's and Angel's family members arrived by bus. It all seemed to be going so easily, then suddenly we had a real problem on our hands. I was confronted by several Cuban army types who were insisting that I take twenty-two additional refugees with me. As I looked down the barrels of their Communist AK-47s, I considered the likelihood that these new passengers came from Cuban prisons or mental institutions or were Communist infiltrators trying to gain easy entry into America. I refused, and our standoff began. Both Ondina and Jorge grew very upset and somewhat fearful. Jorge whispered to me that if I didn't take those people, I would be forbidden to take Ondina's and Angel's family members too. Furthermore, he told me that after a person's family members left their homes, they would never be allowed to return *and* they'd already given up all of their personal possessions. I held out for a while, indignant about my options, but eventually I caved when I realized I really had no other choice. More Communist ultimatums!

So, we all loaded aboard my boat and all the seasick pills we had on hand were dispensed. I put the refugees up front on the forward deck, where, with the help of one of our interpreters, I gave them a short lecture. I tried to describe what lay ahead, the difficulty of the trip mostly, and I encouraged them to behave and to keep straight. I told them that there simply wasn't enough room below for all of them to stay inside but that I would rotate them all during the night so no one got too cold. I promised I would check them out on the marine toilet, should they need to use it, but if they preferred to "go" over the side, I would be fine with that, too, and I showed them which side would be downwind.

When we headed out of the harbor, a patrol boat intercepted us and told us to anchor, as the Florida Strait was too rough to cross. So there we sat, over thirty of us on one sailboat, rocking and rolling all night long in cramped and awkward conditions. After an uneasy night at anchor, we headed out early the next morning under power, as there was no room on deck to raise the sails safely. During the passage, we observed several US Coast Guard planes circling overhead from time to time to identify and keep track of us. I had no behavioral problems at all with any of my refugees on the trip back to America, and they appeared quite happy to be leaving Cuba, whatever their situations might have been. I allowed myself to believe that they were genuinely looking forward to a much better life in the United States. I certainly knew the feeling.

We finally approached Truman Annex at about 0430. With all the red and blue lights flashing, it was easy to find. We identified ourselves to an approaching vessel, whose officer in charge requested us to anchor until further notice. Shortly thereafter, we were led to an immigration dock. We'd been gone since April 25, and it was May 14 when we returned, a total of nineteen days. At the immigration dock, the Coast Guard officer determined which of my passengers were Ondina's people, and they were released into the custody of their family, all residents of the Miami area. They then took custody of the twenty-two refugees and left my boat with them. I never learned of their fate, but I hope they made the most of living in a free country.

Next, they inspected my boat and then left, telling us to stand fast. A while later I was summoned to see the Coast Guard officer in charge who looked over the findings of the inspection. I had my documentation papers all in order, and as far as safety equipment, I had two Type 4 horseshoe flotation devices, 33 Type I life jackets, and one Avon life raft, which held six people. Plus, we had the dinghy. The Coast Guard officer complimented me on my gear and proper documentation and told me I was free to go. As tired as we were, we got back under way and headed to our slip at the Key West Oceanside Marina.

About a week later, word spread around the marina that the most recent incoming boats were being given a red sticker, which required the boat captain to move his boat to another port in Florida to be inspected, after which it was to remain until a fine of $1,000 per refugee was paid. I immediately zipped down to immigration and asked about the situation. The immigration officer asked me when I had returned from Cuba, and when I told him, he said I was OK, as they had started stickering boats sometime after my return. Imagine my surprise when, a few weeks later, I received a bill from the US Immigration Service fining me $32,000.

It was time to head north, and shortly we got under way for Pensacola, where we had a slip waiting for us. After our arrival, I got in touch with an attorney friend of mine and relayed our story to him, asking for advice. He told me he knew of a maritime lawyer in Miami who was representing several shrimp-boat captains facing similar circumstances. These shrimpers had very large boats that could easily carry between one hundred and two hundred passengers, so you get the idea of the size of those fines. The shrimp boats were *all* red-stickered, so under the current regulations, the shrimpers weren't even allowed to leave port to go earn the money to pay their fines. Your brilliant federal government at work again!

Anyhow, this lawyer wanted us to return to Miami as soon as possible, so we again headed south some eight hundred miles and in a week or so moored at Miamarina in Miami. We called this lawyer, and he came to the boat, took us to lunch, and invited us to dinner that night. When our trial date approached, he asked me to be his star witness. Apparently, having an ex-POW risk his life and fortune to help save Cuban families from the oppression of Communism was great theater in front of a jury. Our lawyer went to the opposing counsel's office to notify him of my testimony, and since all lawyers want just one thing—to win—they were somewhat depressed at his news. I would like to be able to say I saved the day, but the truth is, eventually the government dropped its cases against the red-stickered boats altogether, and I was off the hook anyway.

I also received a letter from the US Coast Guard fining me another $2,500 for "carrying passengers for hire without a captain's license" and having insufficient safety equipment on board for the number of passengers I carried. Our lawyer was again very upset, and he said he would represent us before the Coast Guard pro bono. We visited the proper US Coast Guard Office in Miami for a hearing. Our hearing officiant was a Coast Guard reserve officer recalled to active duty. In stating our case, I asked him, "What would *you* have done if Cuban army types were pointing AK-47s at you while you were in their country illegally?" He acknowledged that he would've done the same thing I did. I then said, "What evidence do you have that our dirt-poor passengers were paying me to transport them?" He also acknowledged that no such evidence existed. I reminded him that the Coast Guard officer in Key West actually complimented us on our safety equipment, as we had one flotation device for each passenger. I then said, "If I am sailing in the bay with four on board and I have four life jackets, then I see someone treading water and frantically waving at our boat for help, when I bring him on board and don't have a life jacket for him, am I in violation of the law?" He said, "But that is a case of a lifesaving measure." I replied, "When they pointed their AK-47s at me it was also a lifesaving measure, and that life was mine." He said to me, "I would like to dismiss this now, but someone up the line may kick it back, so would you be willing to take a warning?" I looked at my lawyer who nodded yes. So I replied, "I will." We shook hands and I left. We went out to dinner that night and lived it up after a successful day, but then sometime later, I read an article in the paper that said a large number of people simply abandoned their boats in Key West and never claimed them again after the red-sticker debacle. Then Key West billed the United States for millions of dollars for storing the boats and then disposing of them! That's some bureaucratic red tape for you.

In hindsight, the whole episode turned out to be somewhat of a disaster. Aside from all the fines everybody received, the United States also had to accept a great many other-than-family members, and that, not the rescue, is what made it a nightmare. Furthermore, the simple solution of how to address all those undesirables was so obvious to me: Guantanamo. I've been there so many times. Each day, the Cubans who worked on that base simply walked through the gate to work and then went home each night through the same gate. All we had to do was transport the unwanted refugees, the crazies and the criminals, back to Gitmo and walk them through the gate back to Castroland, where they belonged. Simple, right?

But nobody asked me.

The whole episode of the Mariel boatlift started when Hector executed his plan to find freedom, long in planning. As a result of his actions, and as a consequence of the boatlift, the following data was compiled:

Cuban arrivals during the Mariel boatlift episode

Month	Arrivals	Percent
April 21–April 30	7,665	6
May	86,488	69
June	20,800	17
July	2,629	2
August	3939	3
September	3258	3
TOTAL	124,779	100

Source: Council for Inter-American Security.

The Cuban government eventually closed Mariel Harbor to all boats, and the mass exodus ended, trapping the Cuban people inside a dictatorship that remains in power today. As for the Cuban exiles who made it here safely, with the passage of the Refugee Education Assistance Act of 1980, the US Congress and President Jimmy Carter provided $100,000 in cash and medical and social services for exiled Cubans and authorized $5 million annually to help that group of people in their transition to American life.

One last thing. All of the Cuban family members who came to the United States during the Mariel boatlift were legal. All the rest, the ones pushed onto us by the Cuban army, were illegal, but under the circumstances, they were still allowed to stay. Criminals and mental patients should've been returned, and there wouldn't have been many anyway. In contrast, the vast majority of the people who came to live here back then, including the ones I rescued, have become productive residents, citizens, and taxpayers, and it was my honor to play a small part in bringing them to a land where freedom and opportunity have always existed.

Chapter 32

When Retirement Fails

The Stock Market to the Ski Slopes

Following the Mariel escapade, I decided that I needed to increase my income by selling my boat and going back to work somewhat full time. I left Key West and sailed to Ft. Lauderdale, where I found a slip on Hendrix Isle, which is one of several spits of land with boat slips on each side. Those spits of land run perpendicular to Las Olas Boulevard, the main road heading to the beach. From where we were, you could walk straight to the beach.

First, I applied for a job as a substitute schoolteacher. Then I applied to work at a country club in its pro shop, you know, so I could work on my golf game, since my other goal was to attain my club professional golf instructor rating! Finally, I successfully applied to several stock brokerages to become a registered trade representative. This was definitely not as easy as I thought it would be, and it took quite a bit longer than I anticipated. I applied at Dean Witter, Merrill Lynch, Kitter Peabody, and E. F. Hutton, and in each case I had to interview with the company and take a written test, and one company even had me call a representative in New York and try to sell him a stock. I was scheduled to interview with the E. F. Hutton regional manager, who, as it turned out, was a former naval officer, too, which led to a very friendly interview, and I was hired. It wasn't my first experience with E. F. Hutton, however.

Right after my release from prison, back when I was invited to attend the Mets game in New York in 1973, a very good friend and former squadron-mate of mine worked on Wall Street as a lawyer. Since I was in town, he invited me to come up and stay with him for a couple days, and during that visit he arranged for me to meet with Bob Foman, the CEO of E. F. Hutton, in his corner office at 1 Battery Park Plaza. He was quite candid with me when he acknowledged that his firm's modus operandi was to produce income through commissions on trades. He also said I should consider getting my own professional money manager, but most of the people he knew probably wouldn't accept a portfolio of my size. In other words, my portfolio was too small! Then he chuckled and said not to worry, under the circumstances (me being an ex-POW), he had a great guy in mind who would probably take me on. He hooked me up with the firm of Ruane Cuniff, and with Bill Ruane specifically. I've had an incredible relationship with that firm ever since, and at this writing, it has been over forty-five years.

Anyway, after being hired to work for them in 1982, I was assigned to E. F. Hutton's Palm Beach office to begin my training. I received a huge box, which contained at least a dozen spiral notebooks filled with regulations, bonds, stocks, options, et cetera. After two months of studying, I took the National Association of Securities Dealers Series 7 examination, held at the University of Miami Law School. I passed, thankfully, and was sent to New York City for three weeks of classroom instruction. During this time, I lived high on the hog, staying at the Omni Hotel in the World Trade Center.

I went on to work in Palm Beach for two years thereafter but discovered that although it was a fine job in a lovely place, it was just not my cup of tea. I found it more of a sales job, which seemed to be one that rarely had the best interest of the client in mind. As luck would have it, while delivering a presentation for E. F. Hutton, I learned of the Burney Company, which was established by a host of former military sorts, my people! I called Jack Burney and talked to him about my future, and for the next nine years, I worked for this wonderful company.

Although I could live wherever I wanted, I moved back to Pensacola. I was making a really good living managing financial portfolios by then, mostly dependent on how much time I was willing to work, of course. After I had worked by myself for a year, my son, Richard, having completed college, came to join me. Rich and I set up our Burney Company offices in the lowest floor of his beach house, right on Pensacola Beach, where I also bought a beautiful condominium overlooking the sugary white sands and the turquoise waters of the breathtaking Gulf of Mexico. For the next decade, I lived simply, enjoying the island life, my son and me finding happiness as resolved bachelors. Riding bicycles on a hot day and determining how many hot wings I could eat was about as much stress as I had to endure. It was good, easy living for a time, but in 1994 we both grew somewhat burned out with that line of work so we sold our clients to another portfolio manager in the company and moved on to our next adventures, Richard in the North Atlantic and me on the ski slopes of the Pacific Northwest.

Chapter 33

Reunion

A Brotherhood

At age sixty-three, I remained single, and although I was enjoying my life on Pensacola Beach, it did get lonely. Richard's new job as a navigator on a Norwegian drilling ship kept him away, and ultimately he settled permanently in the country of Panama, where he retired and married a delightful local girl. He now owns a home right on the Pacific Ocean, and the locals have welcomed him in as if he'd lived there his whole life. Almost in his sixties now, Richard still enjoys a good surf break and a long bike ride. He and his wife are raising two precious daughters, both of whom also surf like pros. My daughter, Lisa, had already married by the time Richard left Pensacola, and she settled in Atlanta, starting her own family of world travelers and beginning her career as a physician's assistant, specializing in anesthesiology. I must say, my children are both success stories, and I still give full credit to Louise, who by the early nineties was remarried to a family friend, a man I always greatly admired.

That left just me. For about six months, a friend of mine kept insisting on introducing me to a woman who lived near me, who conveniently clocked in at twenty years younger. I felt like the luckiest guy in the world! When I finally met her, I also discovered that she enjoyed sailing, a definite plus. Dianne was a registered nurse who was also very pretty, another plus. We dated for six months then decided we wanted to get married. That was twenty-five wonderful years ago, solid proof that you never know what surprises life holds in store. I can't imagine what my life would be like now if I hadn't met her. It seems that sometimes your best years *do* come at the end.

In 1999, on a plane ride to Wenatchee, Washington, to visit Dianne's youngest daughter, I met a man named Gene Sharratt. He happened to be the Superintendent of Schools for Eastmont County and was also, hands down, one of the most impressive men I'd ever met. We arrived in Wenatchee and discovered, to our added surprise, that its pristine beauty was matched only by the nice people like Gene and his wife, Carol, who lived there. Wenatchee is a beautiful small town on the Columbia River, and between seeing this amazing new part of the country and meeting the Sharratts, Dianne and I fell completely in love with everything about the idea of moving to the Pacific Northwest. So, with my beautiful wife, my next phase in life involved buying a mountain home in 2000. Near where we settled, there was a ski area with four lifts and quite a few runs. There was only one green run, which is the easiest, and all the rest were blue, black, and black diamond. I was invigorated with the climate and dedicated myself to perfecting my snow-skiing skills. Then, at age seventy-two, I actually became a ski instructor, if you can believe that, and it first started because I just so happened to need something to do during the day while Dianne worked at the local hospital. My new job didn't pay very much, but, on the upside, I got to ski all I wanted. We spent our winters skiing and our summers golfing, and, on occasion, we could still take an easy flight back to Pensacola for the spring and the fall, hands down the best times of the year here.

It was at the time Dianne and I were living in Wenatchee that I last saw many of my cellmates and brothers from Vietnam. Over the years, there were numerous 'Nam POW organizations that often held big celebrations for us, and I've been to several of them, so many I can't even count. I went to one in Los Angeles well before I ever met Dianne; I went to one in Dallas once; and I attended another one at Yorba Linda, California, at Richard Nixon's library.

Dianne and I threw one last party, in 2002, one of the very last, with Gene Sharratt's encouragement. Gene was the patient listener to many of my war stories, and he was electrified at the idea of getting to meet all of the old dudes. Plus, it made sense to think about the significance and the momentousness of what he was promoting because, I had to admit it, I missed them very much.

As I've mentioned, being one of the senior officers while in prison in Vietnam, I was almost always kept away from the junior officers, so when we went to any of the big POW reunions, I would be in a room with hundreds of these men and not know but perhaps twenty of them. Interestingly, I still knew all their names (ABR, ABRU, et cetera), but I didn't know them personally, and I certainly had no idea what they looked like. So that's sort of how we came up with the idea to have a mini reunion at my house in Wenatchee and to invite all the POWs I actually knew, the ones I lived with, the guys from Rawhide Theater, the guys from Building 7, and so on. Gene Sharratt launched into action,

POW reunion, Dallas, Texas, 1995: Carl Crumpler, Byron Fuller, Tom Kirk, Fred Crow, and me.

networking locally around the Wenatchee area, rounding up several companies that graciously donated the money to host this reunion. Hotels and meals were completely furnished, there was a huge parade organized for us, and we were treated to riverboat rafting and several other fun local activities.

We also tried to incorporate this special get-together into a history-based program called "Honor by Listening," a curriculum already being taught in the local high schools, whereby honors-level English students interviewed old World War II veterans. Gene and his network of friends in the school system changed this just a bit, and, instead, he had the students each choose one of us to interview. At the conclusion of their research, which included personal interviews, their school printed a commemorative book complete with biographies, pictures, and a comprehensive oral history of our time in captivity. It was so well-planned and extremely touching from start to finish, a top-notch undertaking. Additionally, and most importantly, all of the POWs in my closest inner circle were given the opportunity to come up and visit each other. Plus, the local community of Wenatchee, Washington, had the chance to host a rather rare gathering that was captured for posterity for an eager and enthusiastic group of young people. We had a ball!

During one of the greatest weekends of my life, over those three days I gathered with Fred Crow, Byron Fuller, Tom Kirk, Leo Profilet, Robbie Risner, Mike McGrath, Al Stafford, Ken Coskey, Carl Crumpler, Bob Flynn, Ralph Gaither, Swede Larson, Doc Mitchell, Bob Schurman, and Nguyen Quoc Dat.

Left: Mary and Fred Crow at the POW reunion in Dallas, Texas, 1995.

Below: Jim Stockdale and me, Dallas, Texas, 1995.

Me (*standing*) with Colonel
Bud Day, 2008.

Jim Stockdale was also scheduled to attend, and then the strangest thing happened. His wife called me to discuss the plans, and when I spoke to Jim about the
details he said suddenly, "We can't do this, Allen, people are using us! People are
always after us, and then they will use us to see what I say and then sell it!" I said,
"Jim, it's not like that; these interviews are for high school kids." But I couldn't
make him understand the wholesomeness of what we were doing. He opted not
to come after all, and it was unfortunate. I do believe something was terribly
wrong with him by then; my guess was the early stages of dementia. After all he'd
been through, it seemed odd to me that this event was something he just couldn't
deal with. And now he's gone. He was our guy, one of the most important men
I've ever known, and an invaluable source of leadership to me and all the men
who were with us in that prison. Everyone so highly respected him; I know I did.
He was a great leader, and I sure wanted to see him one more time.

I made a number of calls to John McCain, but he never called me back. It
pissed me off, to be honest, but I tended to forget that serving in the US Sen-
ate made for a rather demanding schedule, even at our age. Bud Day was also
invited, but he wasn't well enough to come, although fortunately he and I saw

Senator John McCain (*at left*) with me and grandson Ben, during a 2008 campaign stop in Pensacola, Florida.

each other often in the years before he died. He lived just forty-five minutes away from me in Ft. Walton Beach, Florida.

The last time I saw Bud was when John was campaigning for president in 2008 and his bus made a stop in Pensacola. Bud drove over for the day and accompanied me to the rally, where we got to visit with John very briefly. When I heard of Bud's passing in 2013, it really got to me. He was a truly great man, the toughest man I ever knew. Finally, Rear Adm. Jerry Denton was not there either, but, to be honest, he wouldn't have come even if I'd invited him. In spite of the high regard I hold for him because of his conduct during the war and the leadership he provided for all of the men in our group, Jerry and I fell out of favor with one another in the years just after we returned home, and I was never sure exactly why. I have some suspicions that it was related to his rigid beliefs about religion and divorce, but I'll never know for sure. Still, he represented all of us with class and dignity, and when I heard of his passing in 2014, I certainly believed America lost a hero and a true public servant.

All told, the reunion was still a smashing success, and the camaraderie we all enjoyed was unmatched. Dianne and I continued to live bicoastally for the next three years, then we sold the house in Wenatchee and moved back to Pensacola permanently, where we remain. We endured the catastrophic Hurricane Ivan together in 2004, a storm so severe that it caused us to sell our home and move further inland. The storm surge from Ivan was twenty-one feet high in some places, namely the residences near the water, like ours, and Dianne and I rode out the storm sitting atop a refrigerator in our kitchen. I have to admit, it was far worse than my memories of the Mystic hurricane in 1938, and it rivaled the most afraid I ever remember being in Hanoi.

Dianne was still an active critical care nurse at that time, so in the middle of this upheaval, we managed to do some traveling, when she accepted travel nursing assignments. We had a bad habit of choosing assignments located near ski areas so that I could continue to teach while she worked. We lived briefly at Mammoth Lake, California, in 2005 at a relatively large ski resort, and I was able to get a few more years of skiing in, before I decided to hang up my poles for good, in 2015.

I turned eighty years old in 2009, and that same year, Dianne surprised me by hosting the very last of our POW gatherings, in honor of my big birthday. The group was significantly smaller this time, even smaller than in Wenatchee, because by then we were beginning to lose many in our group. A generation, slowly passing on. Still, Fred, Byron, Tom, and Carl joined me one last time here in Pensacola, and we spent the evening laughing about the good old days *and* the bad old days. It was the last time I saw all of them.

Dianne retired in 2015, and our traveling ended. Since then, it's been a life of quiet reflection and relatively little stress, aside from squeaky hip joints and irksome home repairs. I have no complaints. Dianne is by my side, and as we enjoy our golden years with our friends, our children, and our grandchildren, we are often still amazed at the blessings life continues to bestow upon us.

Chapter 34

Where Do We Get Such Men?

A Life Well Lived, a Story Finally Told

Being a prisoner of war has certainly defined my life. It is a rare instance when meeting someone new, and my time in Vietnam gets brought up, that I don't end up telling a story or two about my years in the Navy. It has never bothered me to share my experiences, and more than once I've been accused of being somewhat long-winded in that regard. I am so proud of the experiences of my life and honored to have had the opportunity to serve my country and to be from a family that did the same. I am thankful to be one of the many who came home without too much permanent damage. Just a bad back, thankfully.

My friend Dat often attended the events with our group as part of our 4th Allied POW Wing, the 'Nam POWs, and I was always happy to see him at any of our functions. It was Ross Perot who found him and brought him over to the United States to live after he was sent back to South Vietnam when the war was over. Today, I think he lives with his wife in California. Rear Adm. Byron Fuller, Col. Tom Kirk, and Lt. Col Carl Crumpler continue to be available to me anytime I need to call someone up and have them make a joke at my expense, or if I want to share a memory from the days when I got excited simply seeing their eyeballs under the doors of our cells. The cliché is true: the best kinds of friends are the ones who reunite as if no time at all has passed. They are a gen-eration of men unmatched in their bravery and their honor, unrivaled in their service to our country. They have my highest respect, and I sure miss them.

Col. Fred Crow and his wife Mary ("Aunt Mary") made their home in An-napolis, Maryland. I haven't seen him since my eightieth birthday gathering, but more than once I've had to call him up to ask him questions about the stories I've told in this book. What can I say about this man that you haven't already ascer-tained for yourself? He is my best friend. I can't qualitatively describe the bond I

Dianne and me at home in Pensacola, Florida, 2017. (Photo courtesy of Heather Johnson Photography)

have with him except to say that I believe my experience in prison would've been much worse had he not been the one who was chosen to share it with me. For many years, Fred and Mary came to visit us, when their minds and bodies were much younger and when ours were as well. As I trudged through the writing of this memoir, there were so many times when I needed to ask Fred to help me remember something, and when I *was* able to get him on the phone I was sad to learn that sometimes his memory fails him in much the same way mine does. That's the gift of this book. I wish so badly that I could share the conclusion of this project with him, and I wish he could join me in the celebration of its release. If I get to see him once more, I will give a toast to him and to the tens of thousands of hours he and I spent talking about our stories herein when we were locked in those cells together. I finally got it all written down, Fred, for you and your family as much as for me and mine. He was so much a part of those chapters.

Louise and her late husband Rush stayed in Virginia, and Louise still calls Virginia her home. She remains a devoted mother to our children, Richard and Lisa, and a devoted grandmother to our grandchildren, Drew, Claire, Layla, and Coral. As is her nature, Louise has continued to be a friend to me as well, and

I have often consulted her throughout the writing of this book. She never fails to assist me, whether it be in providing some of my old letters and pictures or simply remembering a name that won't come to me. Dianne and I are immensely grateful to her for all she has done for us. Richard and Lisa and I continue to be very close. My children are a result of extraordinary mothering, and I am very proud of the people they grew up to be, in spite of the many years I was absent from their lives and was unable to be there for them.

Hỏa Lò prison was demolished in stages throughout the 1990s. Two high-rise buildings sit in its original location, but one remaining building of the original construction now serves as a museum to the prison's uses throughout its French colonial period and the Vietnam War. Interestingly, the Vietnamese still incorporate extraordinary methods to promulgate their propaganda, including pictures in the museum of American POWs playing pool and growing vegetable gardens. I don't know who did those things, perhaps Bob and Ed, but the image they wish to promote to their visitors remains comical. *I want to make for you happy,* right? Some things never change. I am also always reminded of the unfinished business that seems to linger around the Vietnam War as we mend fences with Cuba under modern presidential administrations. Generations of new Americans, as well as the modern presidents they elect, do tend to forgive and forget, but it's a little harder for me. We never learned the identity of Fidel and Chico, and because of that, I will resist the urge to ever consider Cuba an ally.

Since I broke my L4 spine segment on ejection over Vietnam with no subsequent medical attention while in prison (but I'm not complaining!), I've lived with the lasting physical consequences. Sleeping on wooden boards or concrete beds for over six years with those unhealed injuries definitely took a toll on my spine and joints. Still, I'm in good shape, all things considered, and I believe that most of the POWs came through our ordeal relatively well, both physically and emotionally. My group was pretty small, mostly military college graduate officers who endured many psychological tests that determined our suitability to fly, plus we had an incredible amount of training, including survival school and escape, evasion, and resistance training. If *we* weren't prepared for capture and detention, someone sure wasted a lot of taxpayer money on us. Even though no one ever successfully escaped from captivity in North Vietnam, we still kept ourselves busy thwarting our captors by communicating and by defying and resisting them every chance we got, a testament to our dedication to serve honorably in the American military and to the commitment we made to protect the Constitution of the United States of America.

I've used the phrase "Where do we get such men?" for a great many years. I can't begin to tell you how many amazing people I've met in the service, men and women both, who are worthy of such accolades, in addition to those I've discussed in these stories. Many people who dedicate their lives to serving our country have the ability and the opportunities to do other great things in the private sector, careers in which they could earn lucrative salaries. Still, they have chosen to spend their lives in service to the United States of America. Believe me, it's not money that motivates people like that.

Author James Michener also used the phrase "Where do we get such men?" in his book *The Bridges at Toko Ri* (New York: Random House, 1953). Michener was visiting an aircraft carrier during the Korean War and found it absolutely mesmerizing to watch the pilots launch and then recover their aircraft before and after a combat mission, flying over a freezing sea to carry out an attack while under heavy antiaircraft fire. The red, white, and blue of our stars and stripes caught his eye. They were emblazoned on the sides of the planes and they flew from the mast above the carrier as it barreled through the Sea of Japan, carving a path into a part of the world where freedom and liberty needed desperately to find a safe place to exist. In response to Michener's expressions of awe, the pilots would simply shrug and say to him, "Eh, it's all in a day's work," but we know better.

Epilogue

As I write this, we have so many who have made multiple deployments to the Middle East to fight terror and radical Islam. When you keep going back again and again, one can't help but feel that your odds are changing for the worse each time. Members of our present all-volunteer force understand this risk. However, during the Vietnam War millions of draftees were sent to a war that they, perhaps, disagreed with. Some say the all-volunteer force is too expensive to maintain, but that may not be the case. Under the draft, there were large turnovers in personnel, which reduced the effectiveness of the entire force. Additionally, one administration might cut the military, which would then require subsequent administrations to restore funding. Certainly, emerging technology, such as drones, helps somewhat reduce boots on the ground, but in the long run it still takes real soldiers driving real tanks and pilots flying real planes to hold any ground taken. This will never change. We will always need people who are willing to serve their country, people who are willing to give their lives defending her.

These issues are important to me, and I hope our citizens choose to stay informed and enlightened so that when they disagree with or disapprove of our government's actions, they can voice or vote their wishes. Having lived through fourteen presidencies, I have seen the political tide ebb and flow many, many times in my lifetime, plus I had a father and a brother who, like me, were career naval officers who fought in multiple wars. I hope that future generations of Americans won't render our service and our fight to protect liberty a waste of time by simply waiting around for others to step up and do the right thing, whatever the right thing might be.

One thing seems lacking in America today, and that is honor. While we were in prison, our motto was "Return with Honor." It was important to us, something we tried to exhibit in our actions as much as in our words. When I was a child, people could shake hands on an agreement, and a man's word was his bond. At the Naval Academy, honor was essential to your success and to your future. I'm not sure why this has changed, but as a nation we need to go back to our roots, when liberty, service, honesty, and integrity were placed above everything else. Most importantly, if we do not include honor as a basic part of our human makeup, as the men and women I've known in my lifetime have done, we are in grave danger of losing our republic. I apologize for preaching, but we in the service take honor very seriously.

I hope you enjoyed my book. GBU.

Suggested Reading

For further reading on the topics discussed in this book, the author enthusiastically
  suggests the following:

Alvarez, Everett. *Chained Eagle: The Heroic Story of the First American Shot Down
  over North Vietnam.* Lincoln: Univ. of Nebraska Press, 2005.

Coram, Robert. *American Patriot: The Life and Wars of Colonel Bud Day.* New York:
  Little, Brown, 2007.

Crealock, William, and Ernest Chamberlain. *Vagabonding under Sail.* New York:
  Hastings House, 1951.

The Cuban Program: Torture of American Prisoners by Cuban Agents. Washington,
  DC: GPO, 1999.

Denton, Jeremiah A. *When Hell Was in Session.* Washington, DC: Morley Institute
  for Church & Culture, 1998.

Duiker, William J. *Ho Chi Minh: A Life.* New York: Hyperion, 2000.

Hawk, Amy Shively. *Six Years in the Hanoi Hilton: An Extraordinary Story of Courage and Survival in Vietnam.* Washington, DC: Regnery, 2017.

Johnson, Sam, and Jane Winebrenner. *Captive Warriors: A Vietnam POW's Story.*
  College Station: Texas A&M Univ. Press, 1992.

Kennedy, Robert F., and Arthur Meier Schlesinger. *Thirteen Days: A Memoir of the
  Cuban Missile Crisis.* New York: Norton, 1999.

McCain, John S., and Mark Salter. *Faiths of My Fathers: A Family Memoir.* New
  York: Random House, 1999.

Michener, James. *The Bridges at Toko Ri.* New York: Random House, 1953.

Rochester, Stuart, and Frederick Kiley. *Honor Bound: The History of Prisoners of
  War in Southeast Asia, 1961–1973.* Honolulu: Univ. Press of the Pacific, 1998.

Tamayo, Juan O. "Former U.S. POWs Detail Torture by Cubans in Vietnam." *Miami
  Herald,* August 22, 1999. Available online at *Organización Auténtica O/A: Por
  una Cuba Cubana,* http://www.autentico.org/oa09872.php.

U.S. Committee on International Relations. *The Cuban Program: Torture of American Prisoners by Cuban Agents.* November 4, 1999. Available online at https://
  archive.org/details/gov.gpo.fdsys.CHRG-106hhrg65278.

Zimmerman, Frederick. *Basic Documents about the Treatment of Detainees at
  Guantanamo and Abu Ghraib.* Ann Arbor, MI: Nimble Books, 2004.

Index

Page numbers in italics refer to illustrations.

A4s: in air strikes, 3–4; A6s compared to, 116; mechanical problems with, 92, 95–96; *Skyhawk* Replacement Air Group (VA-44 *Hornets*), 106; *Skyhawks, 81,* 82, 106; *Skyraiders,* 64, *70,* 71, 76–77; tankers for, 94–95; weapons on, 98–99, 113–14
A4 *Skyhawk* Replacement Air Group (VA-44 *Hornets*), 90–91
A6 Acquisition Program, 198–99
A6 Replacement Training Squadron, 195
A6s, 3; A6 Replacement Training Squadron, 195; Acquisition Program, 198–99; in bombing missions in North Vietnam, 3–4, 6–7, 117–18; Brady training in, 116; Brady's letter defending, 198–99; ejection from, 4–5; Es vs. As, 195; *Intruders,* 116, *118,* 118–21; troubleshooting problems with, 113, 196–97
Abrigo, Chief Petty Officer, 178
aircraft carriers, 98, 106; flying *Skyraiders* vs. jets off, 76–77; landings on, 95–96, 99–100, 198; training flights from, 92–93
air flights, Brady family's first, 44
Air Force Special Weapons Project, 79
airliner, civilian, 72
air strikes, on Vietnam, 3; effects on POWs, 172–73; prisoners' awareness of, 21, 23; targets of, 13, 147
Albuquerque, New Mexico, 90, 91
Alcatraz prison, 148, 150
Angel, on Mariel boatlift, 212–17
antiaircraft artillery, 3–4; in Cuba, 102; in North Vietnam, 117–18; POWs' awareness of, 23, 172
antiwar movement, 152–53, 179
Apollo 11 moon landing, *158*

astronaut training, Brady volunteering for, 111–12
Attack Squadron 34 (VA-34 *Blue Blasters*), 93, 98–103, 105
Attack Squadron 42 (VA-42), 116
Attack Squadron 85 (VA-85), 116
Attack Squadron 95 (VA-95), 67–68, 152
Attack Squadron 216 Black Diamonds, 73–74
Atterbury, Ed, 148
Ault, Frank, 73–74
aviation command, Brady awarded, 114

B-26s, 101
B-52s, 83, 173
Bardshar, Frederick, 168–69
Baugh, Bill, 20
Bay of Pigs Invasion, 98–103
Bean, James, 163
Beaver, Sid, 188
Bendett family, 53–54
Bikini Atoll, nuclear testing on, 79
Billard Academy, 54
Bluewater Yacht Builders, 207
"The Bob and Ed Show," 152–54
Bomar, Jack, 139–40
Brady, Allen, *55;* aboard *Yorktown, 75;* after release, *178, 182, 186–87, 190;* capture of, *7;* with family, *77, 114, 121, 183–84;* at Naval Academy, *58, 62;* at POW reunion, *226–28;* as project pilot, *80, 84;* ranks of, *67, 101, 122;* with wife, *231*
Brady, Dianne (wife), 223–24, 229, *231*
Brady, Elizabeth Burrows Colby (mother), 34–35, 38–40, *55;* at attack on Pearl Harbor, 51; in Great Hurricane, 45; insisting on reading, 49

Brady, John (brother), 33, 35, 54, *55;* at attack on Pearl Harbor, 51–52; childhood of, 37–39, 45, 48–49, 52; on family travels, 42–43

Brady, John Huston (father), *34,* 45, *55,* 78; naval career of, 33–35, 47, 53–54, 57, 66; in WWII, 51–52, 54–55

Brady, Lisa (daughter), *90, 121;* father and, *114,* 177, 232; at father's release, *183–84,* 186; marriage and family of, 223; sailing with father, 202–3

Brady, Louise (wife), 116, *121, 153, 196–97;* after husband's release, 177, *183, 186–87, 190,* 191; husband's letters to, 143–44, *144–45;* as mother, 90, 223, 231–32; ongoing friendship with, 231–32

Brady, Richard (son), *77, 90,* 106, *121;* after father's release, *183–84,* 186; father and, *114,* 177, 222, 232; marriage and family of, 223; sailing with father, 199–200, 202–3, 208–9

Brady parents, 36, *36,* 49–50; appearance of, 33, 35; family travels with, 42–43; and son as POW, *119, 174,* 196; visiting son, 78, 201–2

Brunstrom, Al, 157

the Bug, torture of POWs by, 18–19, 135–37, 164

Burney, Jack, 222

Burney Company, 222

Burns, John, 85

Busch, Sallie, 57–58

California, Brady stationed in, 67–68

Calley, William, 130

Camp Unity, 154, 162–63, 165, 168

captain, Brady's promotion to, 146

Carpenter, Allen, 139

Carrier Control Approach Unit, 198

Carrier Division 6, 105, 110–11

carrier qualifications, 63–64

Carter, Jimmy, 220

Castro, Fidel, 90, 92, 139, 141, 211, 216; in Cuban Missile Crisis, 109–11; efforts to oust, 100–103

Castro, Raul, 141, 216

Centaur, 200

Chamberlain, Ernest, 206

Chapman, Deac, 58

chemical bombs, on North Vietnam, 118–20

Chico, torture of POWs by, 138–41

Chief of Education and Training Support, 203–5

Chiles, Lawton, *190*

China, 72; family deploying to, 40–41; supporting North Vietnam, 117, 134; Taiwan vs., 74–76

Christian, Mike, *182, 187, 189*

CIA, and Bay of Pigs Invasion, 100–103

civilians: Japanese, 79; Vietnamese, 6, 8–9, 13, 118–20, 126–27

Coast Guard, and Mariel boatlift boats, 217–19

Cobeil, Earl, 139–41

Code of Conduct, for POWs, 154–55

Coker, George, 147

Colby, Alfred (grandfather), 44–46

Colby, Edna (grandmother), 44, 54

Cold War, 79, 132–33

Columbian Prep, 56–57

communication, among POWs, 25, 149–50; code for, 17–18, *18,* 20–22; information passed by, 157–58; methods of, 151, 157, 160, 162–63, 171, 191

Communism, 216; Mariel boatlift as resistance to, 213, 218–19; movie showcasing, 160–61; US concern about, 132, 134; in Vietnam, 133–34

Compton, Brian, 198

Congressional Medals of Honor, 149–50

Corry Field (Corry Station), 63

Coskey, Ken, *160,* 161

Costa Rican embassy, Cuban refugees at, 212

court-martial, proposed for cooperative POWs, 155

Crealock, Bill, 206

Crockett, "Davy," 178

Crow, Fred, 23–24, *24;* background of, 29–30; as Brady's cellmate, 25–29, 97, 112, 135–36, 143; kept in Heartbreak Hotel, 162–63; ongoing friendship with, 230–31; as POW, 150–53, 159, 161–62, 166; at POW reunions, *225–26,* 229

Crow, Mary, 143, *226,* 231

Crumpler, Carl, *160,* 161, *225,* 229, 230

Cuba, 141, 210, 232; Bay of Pigs Invasion of, 98–103; fine for bringing refugees from, 218–19; Mariel boatlift from, 212–20; undesirable refugees from, 219–20

Cuban Missile Crisis, 109–11

Cuban Program, 138–41

D'Aquino, Iva Toguri ("Tokyo Rose"), 131

Daughtry, Robert, 139

Day, Bud, 148–49, 165, *227,* 227–28

death notifications, 195–96

Denton, Jerry, 22, 128, 150, 166–67, 179–80, *187,* 228

Diaz-Canel, Miguel, 141

Dirty Bird Annex, 147
dishwashing duty, for POWs, 150–51
Douglas A4 (A4D) *Skyhawk.* See under A4s
Dramesi, John, 148
duty officer, at Naval Air Special Weapons
    Facility, 89

E. F. Hutton, 221–22
economy, 35–36
education, 49; Brady's, 56–59, 112; at Iolani
    Episcopal Day School, 48–49, 52; moth-
    er's, 34–35; at Mrs. Howe's Academy, 40;
    at Mystic Academy, 45, 54
Eisenhower, Dwight, 90
English, Captain, 105
Eniwetok Atoll: life for project pilots on,
    82–83; nuclear testing on, 79–81, 88–89;
    scuba diving at, 87–88
escape attempts, by POWs, 147–50
Espinosa, Jorge, 215–17
Essex, USS, 98–103

F2H-3 *Banshee*, 76–77
F4s, in air strikes, 3–4
F9F-6 *Cougar*, 73
families, giving death notifications to, 195–96
families, POWs': after release, *183–84*, 184,
    186–87, 197; letters to, 126, 129, 142–46,
    144–45; notified of release, *174*; packages
    from, 127, 136, 159; visiting prisons, 154
FD Roosevelt, USS, 200–201
Fellowes, Jack, 178–79, *181–82*, 185, *187*, *189*
Field Command of the Armed Forces Spe-
    cial Weapons Project, 78–79
Finley, Jack, 163
First Taiwan Strait Crisis, 74–75
flight training, Brady's, 56, 72, 195; compo-
    nents of, 62–64; in "level readiness" for
    Navy Air Groups, 97–98; at Pensacola,
    Florida, 62–63; on Saratoga's European
    cruise, 93–94
Flynn, Bob, 134
Flynn, John, 163
Foman, Bob, 221–22
Fonda, Jane, 130–31, 154
Fontaine, Rich, 58
Ford, Gerald, 131
Fowler, Hank, 21
France, Indochina under occupation by,
    9–10, 132–33
Franks family, 51–52
Ft. Lauderdale, sailing to boat show in, 208
Fuller, Byron, *160*, 161, *190*, *225*, 229, 230

Gaddis, Norm, 163
Galle Face Hotel, 43
Garden, William, 206
Gemini astronaut program, 111–12
Geneva Accords, Vietnam split in, 133–34
Germany, Brady family passing through,
    43–44
Glenn, John, 89–90
Great Depression, 35–37
Great Hurricane, in Mystic, Connecticut,
    45–46
Greece, bombing competition with, 107–8
Green Berets, 97, 169
Guantanamo Bay, Cuba, 91–92, 219–20
guards, Vietnamese: Brady challenging
    Communism of, 158–59; in Hỏa Lò
    prison, *136*; managing prisoners' interac-
    tions, 154–55, 161; in manipulation and
    propaganda, 142–44, 159, 160; prisoners'
    communications and, 149–51; prisoners'
    defiance of, 149, 165–66, 232; prisoners'
    relations with, 25, 128, 151, 165
Guarino, Larry, 155
Guy, Ted, 155

Hai Phong harbor, 117
Hanoi March, of POWs
Harvey, Bill, 105
Hatch, Glen, 203–4
Hawaii, 29–30; Brady family in, 47–49,
    52–53
Heartbreak Hotel, in Hỏa Lò prison, 13,
    162–63
Hector, 211, 220
Hiroshima and Nagasaki, 78–79
Hitler, Adolf, 43–44
Ho Chi Minh, 133–35
Hỏa Lò prison (Hanoi Hilton), *10*, 171;
    American delegations visiting, 154–55;
    Brady's arrival at, 9–10; cells in, 15–16,
    23–25, 135, 165; conditions in, 15–16, 27–
    29; demolition of, 232; Heartbreak Hotel
    in, 13, 162–63; interrogation in, 11, 13, 19;
    Little Vegas in, 15, 19, 24–25; New Guy
    Village in, 11; regulations in, 15–16; subdi-
    visions of, 13–14, 16–17; Thunderbird in,
    20–21, 159. *See also* guards, Vietnamese;
    prisoners of war (POWs)
homes, Brady families': boat as, 206, 210,
    212; in China, 40; in Hawaii, 48–49;
    in Manila, 38; in Mystic, 44–46, 54; in
    Pensacola, 229; in South Carolina, 66; in
    Wenatchee, 224, 229

"Honor by Listening" program, 225
Hornet, USS, 71–73, *73*
Hubbard, Ed, 139
hunger strike, POWs', 166–67
hurricanes, 45–46, 229

Independence, USS: in PORTREX exercise, 109–11; training flights from, 92–93
Indochina, concern about Communism in, 132
injuries, Brady's, 126, 232
instrument flight training, 63, 91
interrogations: on communication methods, 149–50; in Hỏa Lò prison, 11, 13, 19; POWs seeking information through, 157–58
Iolani Episcopal Day School, 48–49, 52
Italy, US missiles in, 109, 111

Jacksonville, Florida, 90
Japan, 41, 50–51
jet fuel, switch of, 96
jets, *Skyraiders* vs., 76–77
jobs, Brady's postretirement, 221–22, 224, 229
Joe, on Mariel boatlift, 213, 215–16
Johnson, Louise, 66–67, *67*
Johnson, Sam, 166

Kasler, Jim, 139–40
Kennedy, John F., 112; Bay of Pigs Invasion under, 100–103; changes to military operations, 97–98; Cuban Missile Crisis and, 109–11
Kerry, John, 130
Key West, Florida, 205–6, 209
Khrushchev, Nikita, 109
Kidd, Isaac, Jr., 199
Kiley, Frederick, 138
Kirk, Tom, *225,* 229, 230
Kirkland Air Force Base, Naval Air Special Weapons Facility on, 77–78
Kitty Hawk, USS, 3, 117, *118,* 122
Korean War, 66–67

LA-11 fighters, Chinese, 72
Larson, Swede, *178*
"level readiness," 97–98
Little Vegas section, of Hỏa Lò prison, 15, 19, 24–25

Madison, Tom, 21
Manila, Philippines, 177
Manor, LeRoy, 168
Mao Zedong, 134
Mariel boatlift, 212–20

Maringello, Danny, 87
marriages, Brady's, 67, 197, 223
Matwing (Medium Attack Wing), 195–98
Mayo section, 171
Mayport, Florida, 200–202
McCain, John, 143, 227–28, *228*
McDaniels, Red, *182*
McGrath, Mike, drawings by, *12, 136*
McKnight, George, 147
medical care, for POWs, 125–26, 232
Miami, sailing to boat show in, 207–8
MIA telegram, sent to Brady parents, *119*
Michelson, Albert Abraham, 112
Michelson Laboratory, 112
Michener, James, 233
military, US, 35; accusations against, 130–31; dangers of, 95–96; Kennedy's changes to, 97–98; postings in Manila, 38–39
Miller, Ed, 153–56, 173
Mint (section of prison), 159
Mrs. Howe's Academy, 40
Mulligan, Jim, *187*
My Lai Massacre, 130
Mystic, Connecticut, Brady family in, 44–46, 53
Mystic Academy, 45, 54

NAS Oceana, POWs' arrival at, *180–83*
Naval Academy, US: Brady at, 56–59, *60–61;* Honorary Parade at, *189*
Naval Air Special Weapons Facility, on Kirkland Air Force Base, 77–78
Naval Air Special Weapons Project, Brady as project pilot for, 79–82
Naval Aviation Safety School, 90
naval aviators, 176; Brady earning certification as, 64–66, *65;* dangers of, 195–97. *See also* pilots
Naval Education Training and Support, 199
Naval Ordnance Test Station (Naval Weapons Evaluation Facility), 112–15
Naval Weapons Evaluation Facility, on Kirkland Air Force Base, 78
Navy: Brady's decision to fly for, 44, 56; Brady's father's career in, 33–35, 47, 66; Brady's promotions in, 114, 145–46, 195; Brady's retirement from, 205–6; effects of switch of jet fuel, 96; POWs staying in, 191
Navy Air Groups (Air Wings), "level readiness" for, 97–98
New Guy Village, of Hỏa Lò prison, 11
New York Mets, honoring POWs, 191
Nguyen Quoc Dat ("Max" or "Dat"), 172, 230

night flying training, 63
Nixon, Richard, 131, 176
North Vietnam, 133–34; targets in, 117–20; treatment of prisoners, 125–29
nuclear testing, 79–82; effects of, 87–89; monitoring pilot radiation exposure during, 82–87; video footage of, 86–87
nuclear weapons, 74–75, 78

Oahu Country Club, caddying at, 49
Obama, Barack, 141
officers, in Hỏa Lò prison, 163, 165–66; separation of, 125, 224; treatment of, 150, 155
Ondina, on Mariel boatlift, 212–17
Operation Hardtack, 79–88
Operation Homecoming, 179
Operation Ivory Coast, attempt to free POWs as, 168–70
Operational Readiness Inspection (ORI), 59–62
"other Fidel," torture of POWs by, 138–41
"Outer Seven," 152–56, 173

Page, Airman, 84
Palau, USS, 59–62
Paris peace agreement, 173, 175
patriotism, 35; POWs', 158–59, 164–65
peace organizations, 129
Pearl Harbor, Hawaii: father posted to, 47–49; Japanese attack on, 50–51
Pearson, Drew, 103
Pensacola, Florida, 59; Brady sailing to, 199–204; Brady's return to, 222, 229; flight training at, 62–63
Peruvian embassy, Cubans gathering at, 211
Pfeiff, Bob, 106
Philippine Sea, USS, 72
Philippines, 177; father's posting to, 37–39, 42–43
pilots, 94; for A4 tankers, 94–95; accusations against, 129, 131; "level-readiness" training for, 97–98; training for, 93, 105, 116. See also naval aviators
PORTREX (Puerto Rico Exercises), 109–11
Portsmouth Naval Hospital, returned POWs in, 184–91
post-traumatic stress disorder (PTSD), POWs', 197
Potzo, Ensign, 102
POW bracelets, 178, 179
prisoner reunification, after Son Tay Raid, 127
prisoners of war (POWs): accusations against, 130–31; attempt to free, 168–70; church

services of, 165, 171; Code of Conduct for, 154–55; coerced into making propaganda, 140, 150; conditions for, 25–26, 171; defiance of guards by, 165–66, 232; effects of Ho Chi Minh's death on, 134–35; effects of imprisonment on, 167, 197, 230, 232; entertainment methods of, 26–29, 112, 163, 167, 172; escapes by, 147–50; hunger strike by, 166–67; letters from, 126, 129, 142–46, 144–45; propaganda and, 152–54, 232; proposed court-martial of, 155; relations among, 16–20, 25, 129, 161, 163–65; reunions of, 224–29, 225, 229; rules governing treatment of, 125–28, 165; separation of officers, 125, 224; shuffled around within prison, 162, 171; South Vietnam allowing inspection of camps for, 129; torture of, 135–41, 167; treatment of, 125–28, 147, 232. See also communication, among POWs
prisoners of war (POWs), release of: arrival at NAS Oceana, 180–83; beginning of, 173–74; Brady's, 175–76; expectation of, 128, 176; on flight home, 175–80, 178; honors after, 185, 189, 191; life after, 191, 197; welcome home, 179–80, 184–85, 190
prisons, Vietnamese: American delegations visiting, 154–55, 157; number of, 13–14. See also specific prisons
Profilet, Leo, 127
Project Bullet, 89–90
project pilots, for Air Force Special Weapons Project, 79–88
propaganda: antiwar, 130–31, 154, 179; in Hỏa Lò prison, 19–20, 160; POWs coerced into, 140, 150, 152–54, 159; prisoners used for, 8–9, 126–28, 142, 232

Rabbit, 159
rationing: in Great Depression, 35–36; during WWII, 53, 54–55
Rawhide section, in Hỏa Lò prison, 162, 165
Red Cross, and POWs, 128
religion, prisoners', 127, 165, 171
Replacement Air Group training, 115
retirement, Brady's, 205–6
Rice Hope Plantation, 66, 66
Richardson, Elliott, 185
Rochester, Stuart, 138
Ruane, Bill, 222
Ruane Cuniff, 222
Russell, Bertrand, 129
Russell, on Mariel boatlift, 213, 215
Rutledge, Howie, 162–63

sailing, Brady's, 199–206
Saratoga, USS, 98, 105; accidents on, 95–96; bombing competition flown from, 107–8; European cruise by, 93–94
Sayers, Sam, 195
Schweitzer, Bob, 152–56, *153*
Schweitzer, Mrs. Bob, 156
scuba diving, at Eniwetok Atoll, 87–88
Seifert, Bill, 199
SERE (survival, evasion, resistance, and escape) training, 98, 116, 232
Shangri-La, USS, 107–8
Sharratt, Gene and Carol, 223–25
Sikes, Bob, *190*
Simons, Arthur "Bull," 168–69
ski instructor, Brady as, 224, 229
Skyraiders. See under A4s
Son Tay POW Camp, raid on, 14, 127, 168–70
South Vietnam, 129, 133
squadrons, officers for, 115
Stalin, Joseph, 134
Stanley, Dick, 73–74
Stardust section, of Hỏa Lò prison, 162
Stockdale, Jim, 20, 150, 163, *226,* 227
Students for a Democratic Society (SDS), 153, 156
submarines, 51; father's career in, 37, 39–40
surface-to-air missiles, 4, 21, 117–18

Taiwan, vs. China, 74–76
Tanner, Nels, 129
Tartan, 201
Thach Weave, 71
Third Geneva Convention, on treatment of POWs, 125–28, 165
Thunderbird section, of Hỏa Lò prison, 20–21, 159
Top Gun, 74
torture, in Hỏa Lò prison, 19, 167; perpetrators of, 18, 138–41; reasons for, 148–50; "the ropes," 11, *12*
training/safety officer, Brady as, 93
Trump, Donald, 75–76
Tsai Ing-wen, 75–76
Turk, Herm, 195
Turkey, US missiles in, 109, 111
TV-2 (T-33) *Shooting Star,* 77, 89

United States: concern about spread of Communism, 132, 134; involvement in Vietnam War, 134, 232
US Naval Post-Graduate School, 111–12
Useppa Club, 208–9
USSR: Cuban Missile Crisis and, 109–10; spread of Communism under, 132–33; supporting North Vietnam, 117, 134

Vagabonds, 207–9
Vagabond *Voyager,* 206–7, *213,* 216
Valentine, Bob, *75,* 152
Valentine, Mrs. Bob, *153*
Viet Minh, 133–34
Vietnam: Brady's bombing runs over, 118–22; French occupation of, 9–10; split in Geneva Accords, 133–34
Vietnam Veterans Against the War (VVAW), 130
Vietnam War: casualties in, 115–16; end of, 173, 175; opposition to, 129–31, 152–53, 156, 179; rules of engagement in, 117; training prior to deployment to, 116; US involvement in, 134, 232
Vietnamese, 6–9, 132

Waterhouse brothers, 49
Waters, Ron, 5
weapons engineering, Brady in, 112–14
Weekly Raider (brothers' newspaper), 52
Wenatchee, Washington, 223–26
Wilber, Gene, 154, 155, 173
Williams, Royce, 178
Wilson, "Willy," *75*
Winn, David, 163
World War II, 49–50, 52–55, 131

Yamnicki, John, 103–4
Yankee Station (Gulf of Tonkin), 116–17
Yarborough, Bill, 4–5
Yen Phu power plant, as air strike target, 147
Yorktown, USS, 74

the Zoo, 138–39, 148